Take a group of men.
Speak of culture, class, language,
nationality, or religion.
And you are likely to be left
with groups of men.

DIVIDED & CONQUERED

An Analysis of Man-made
Weapons of Mass Separation

MOKOKOMA MOKHONOANA

sekoala
PUBLISHING COMPANY (PTY) LTD

sekoala
PUBLISHING COMPANY (PTY) LTD

ISBN: 978-0-620-57555-3 (paperback)
ISBN: 978-0-620-60048-4 (e-book)

Cover design: Mokokoma Mokhonoana
Book design: Mokokoma Mokhonoana

Sekoala Publishing Company (Pty) Ltd

www.sekoala.com

"Books can be dangerous. The best
ones should be labeled:
This Could Change Your Life."

— **Helen Exley**

PROLOGUE

The Tower of Babel

Once upon a time, gazillions of men grouped themselves in pursuit of a common goal; namely, to go to heaven. They attempted to do so by erecting a tower as tall as necessary.

As "unrealistic" as their ambition was, they were not all talk and no action; they did manage to get their endeavour off the ground.

After some months (possibly years) of working their fingers to the bone, their dream seemed, I presume, attainable. For it is said that God then devised a plan to obstruct their endeavour to set foot in His neighbourhood. Apparently, God was intimidated by humanity's unity—the power and the possibilities that were made possible by a united human race, to be precise. ("And the Lord said, 'Behold, they are one people, and they have all one language, and this is only the beginning of what they will do. And nothing that they propose to do will now be impossible for them.'" — Genesis 11:6, ESV.)

It goes without saying that the simplest way for God to stop them was to either kill all those involved or, less bloody, make the tower collapse. However, God opted for arguably the most ingenious tactic: he used language. And all of a sudden, the men toiling to set foot in heaven whilst they were still alive spoke different languages (remember, they had only one language before that); languages that were, of course, alien to most men whom they spoke with and whose tongue they understood not so long ago. ("Come, let us go down and there confuse their language, so that they may not understand one another's speech." — Genesis 11:7, ESV.)

Out of the clear blue sky, it was then impossible for the men to communicate with each other—effectively, that is. It is said that because of nothing but the then recent division of the physically united men, by a mental fence called language, when one man asked for, say, a spade, the other gave him a wheelbarrow.

Believe it or not, the men remained adamant in spite of that; they all tried their level best to overcome the hurdle that suddenly speaking completely different languages brought about. But after some time, all men gave up. And to this day, there isn't, I presume, a single human being with a heartbeat in heaven.

Weapons of Mass Separation

Because of nothing but a social construct, which is, of course, reinforced with a fence called a border, a man in Musina (the northernmost town in the Limpopo province, South Africa) readily calls a man in Zimbabwe an "alien," whereas he calls the one in Cape Agulhas (the southernmost point of South Africa) a "brother." Yet the man in Zimbabwe is way closer to him, with regard to distance, than the one in Cape Agulhas!

It goes without saying that while the erection of borders sure provides us with some benefits, there are gazillions of men who have lost and countless who continue to lose their lives because of nothing but the mental division that was brought about by the invention of countries.

I will, with this book, attempt to explore things that have in a way divided the human race. Having said that, my interest is not in all kinds of things that do so. I am only interested in man-made things (particularly those that only "exist" in our minds). For example, while the division of the human race by means of continents can undoubtedly be labeled as natural, the division of human beings by means of countries is man-made.

Though there exist gazillions of such *social constructs*

(i.e., a perception of an individual, group, or idea that is "constructed" through cultural or social practice—in other words, things whose "existence" is dependent on the human mind), this book is only made up of five social constructs; namely, *language, culture, the monetary system, countries,* and *religion*. Having said that, I will, in the course of exploring the aforementioned social constructs, necessarily touch upon gazillions of other social constructs.

Social Criticism ≠ Pessimism

At the risk of coming across as a pessimist, i.e., a creature with a tendency to see only the worst aspect of things, I will exclusively focus on the undesirable, detrimental, and at times deadly, aspect of the social constructs that I am about to attempt to explore, even though I, like most people, am aware of their usefulness.

So, while many a man blindly praise, say, technology, for what it gives, I, as a social critic, am one of those Jeremiahs who will bring, to their praise, what technology takes. And while most people are mindlessly praising, say, a penis, for the pleasure that it affords some women and all men, I, as a social critic, am one of those party poopers who will bring rape to their excitement, even though I am well-aware that, apart from occasionally affording me the opportunity to experience an orgasm or two, like most human beings, a penis played an essential role in my being.

Allow me to justify such a seemingly pessimistic approach. There really is no value, unless for their ego or for perseverance's purposes, in telling someone who is doing something right that they are doing something right. Your observation is more likely to be of significant value in instances where you tell someone about something that they are doing wrong, or that what they are doing is wrong, as opposed to telling them about what they are doing right, or that what they are doing is right. Owing to the fact that the former increases the chances of them: (1) attempting to do right whatever that they are doing wrong; or (2) abandoning whatever that they are doing, if it is indeed wrong.

To wit, to help a good-looking woman with a bad breath: talk about her breath, not her looks. Granted, telling the poor woman about her good looks will make her feel like a million dollars. However, choosing that over telling her about her bad breath will impoverish her relationship with those who she frequently converse with and, perhaps more unfortunate, he or she or they whom she will kiss.

Anyway, in many a case, *pessimist* is nothing but a label given to someone who calls a spade a spade. While in some cases, a "pessimist" is merely someone who has "carelessly" phrased an observation differently. For example, though the two would have technically said the very same thing, he who says that "one man's trash is another man's treasure" is likely to come across as an optimist, whereas he who says that "one man's treasure is another man's trash" is likely to come across as a pessimist.

Speaking of calling a spade a spade, I would like to cite, in defense of the hard to find men who call a spade a spade, what Walpola Rahula is said to have said about Buddhism. "First of all, Buddhism is neither pessimistic nor optimistic. If anything at all, it is realistic, for it takes a realistic view of life and of the world. It looks at things objectively (*yathābhūtam*). It does not falsely lull you into living in a fool's paradise, nor does it frighten and agonize you with all kinds of imaginary fears and sins. It tells you exactly and objectively what you are and what the world around you is, and shows you the way to perfect freedom, peace, tranquility and happiness.

"One physician may gravely exaggerate an illness and give up hope altogether. Another may ignorantly declare that there is no illness and that no treatment is necessary, thus deceiving the patient with a false consolation. You may call the first one pessimistic and the second optimistic. Both are equally dangerous. But a third physician diagnoses the symptoms correctly, understands the cause and the nature of the illness, sees clearly that it can be cured, and courageously administers a course of treatment, thus saving his patient."[1]

In other words, as Aldous Huxley is said to have said, "Facts do not cease to exist because they are ignored."

"In a decaying society, art, if it is truthful, must also reflect decay. And unless it wants to break faith with its social function, art must show the world as changeable. And help to change it."

— **Ernst Fischer**

CONTENTS

"The point of philosophy is to start with something so simple as not to seem worth stating, and to end with something so paradoxical that no one will believe it."

— **Bertrand Russell**

LANGUAGE

What Is Language?

Take a group of men, ask each to define *language*, and you are likely to get as many different definitions as the number of men who have responded.

When people communicate, language functions as an attempt to move, or rather duplicate, a thought, a question, or an order, from the speaker's mind to that of the listener, or from the writer's mind to that of the reader. The same can, of course, be said about the deaf, who rely on visual gestures and signs to achieve the very same thing.

I moved from *move* to *duplicate*. But as fitting as *duplicate* might be, it is misleading, in every single instance of a misunderstanding, to refer to the process of human communication as the duplication of a thought or thoughts. More on that later. Anyway, I opted for *duplicate* simply because, in instances where communication is without a misunderstanding, after a speaker speaks, though the listener will then be thinking about whatever it is that the speaker said, whatever the speaker said will by no means be lost (by the speaker's mind); it will merely be duplicated (by the listener's mind).

For a simple analogy, think of the process of combustion. When a burning candle, candle$_1$, is used to light another, candle$_2$, it is not at the expense of candle$_1$'s flame. Even though candle$_2$ will, at some point, have the "same" flame as candle$_1$.

Perhaps the word *attempt* is the most important part of what I said as to what the function of language is. I regard the process of communication as an attempt simply because communication isn't always a successful exchange of information: it is merely an attempt to do so (in other words, a misunderstanding is nothing but such an attempt's lack of success). And, equally important, by seeing something as an attempt, we become less defensive whenever someone directs our attention to the thing's defects. For once we have agreed on what the function of a thing is, it then becomes possible for us to objectively examine the thing in question (i.e., look at the thing through eyes that are not contaminated by our worldview, our beliefs, our affection for the thing, etc.) and, more important than the thing itself, the thing's effectiveness. For you cannot sensibly call a man lost, unless you know where he is and, more importantly, where he intended to be.

Having said that, this book isn't merely an attempt to tell the reader what a particular social construct is, and then comment as to whether or not the social construct achieves its purpose. Every single social construct that I will explore in this book achieves, as I am about to attempt to illustrate, what I believe it was made to achieve. My interest is in why and how these social constructs divide the human race, not in whether or not they fail to achieve what they were supposedly invented to achieve.

Lastly, let us return to the question that this writing's title is made up of.

Perhaps the most insightful answer to that question is that that depends on who is using the word *language*. That is to say, the answer to "What is language?" depends on what the person answering means by *language*, whenever he or she uses the word *language*. In addition to that, an observant person is likely to include, in their answer, the illusion (and thus the confusion) that the word "is" usually bring about. Thanks to such an illusion, we inevitably end up believing that things and people are their attributes or characteristics.

In any case, we cannot really say what a thing (e.g., an apple) *is*. We can only say things (e.g., red, juicy, round, nutritious, cheap, stolen, etc.) *about* the thing. What's more, it is usually impossible to perceive and therefore know, and for that reason say or write about, every single thing about a thing. And because of that, this chapter will by no means cover every single facet of its subject: language; the same applies to every single subsequent chapter and this book as a whole. Apart from it being impractical to explore every single aspect or facet of the social constructs that constitute this book, doing so is not a prerequisite to achieving what I am hoping to achieve with this book.

Words and Meanings

Words are inherently devoid of meaning. When reading about the relationship between words and meanings, we are often told that words are nothing but vessels, which we fill with meaning.

That is, to some extent, true. Having said that, such a statement is misleading because some people then end up believing that whatever meaning a word is given resides within the word. If that were true, then there would not exist things called dictionaries, since the meanings of words would be carried within the words.

Anyway, words are used to *refer to* whatever meaning or meanings that we have attached to them through usage. Words do not, in themselves, mean anything. As someone once said: "Words don't mean, people mean."

To illustrate the assertion that it is people who mean, not words, I will simply share two words that went through a *semantic change*, that is to say, a change in one of the meanings of a word. "*Awful* — originally meant 'inspiring wonder (or fear)'. Used originally as a shortening for 'full of awe', in contemporary usage the word usually has negative meaning." *Mouse* — primarily used to refer to a small rodent. Informally used to refer to a lump or a bruise. However, a new meaning was added to that word when computers were invented. Since then, *mouse* is also used to refer to a small hand-held device with which a computer user moves a cursor.

As we all know, the meaning attached to some sentences has absolutely nothing to do with (the meaning of) words that the sentence is made up of. Such a sentence is, of course, called an idiom, which is defined as, "a group of words established by usage as having a meaning not deducible from those of the individual words."

Allow me to share a few idioms (with their meanings bracketed): *add fuel to the fire* (whenever something is done to make a bad situation even worse than it is);

barking up the wrong tree (be pursuing a mistaken or misguided line of thought or course of action); *curiosity killed the cat* (being inquisitive can lead you into a dangerous situation); *hit the nail on the head* (find exactly the right answer); lastly, relevant to this book, *a doubting Thomas* ("a skeptic who refuses to believe without direct personal experience—a reference to the Apostle Thomas, who refused to believe that the resurrected Jesus had appeared to the ten other apostles, until he could see and feel the wounds received by Jesus on the cross," more on that later).

To sum up, a word is used to refer to a person, an object, a thought, an emotion, or a meaning. For example, the word *car* can be used to refer to a type of a thing (e.g., "she bought a car") or a particular thing (e.g., "she bought his car"), or to say "a road vehicle, typically with four wheels, powered by an internal combustion engine and able to carry a small number of people" with just one word.

The Name and the Named

What we call things does not really matter, provided that the word that is used to refer to a thing refers to the very same thing in the minds of those communicating.

For example, if you and I, for whatever reason, decide to call a pencil a horse, and then I ask you to pass me "that horse" (without pointing at the pencil), you would undoubtedly understand what I meant. Whether or not you will do so is beside the point. What would matter is that the word *horse* would have achieved what we would have in that case used the word to achieve, by referring, in both our minds, to the drawing instrument in question.

Finally, I would now like to introduce one of the most important words to be found in this book. The important thing is, of course, what the word means or refers to, not the word itself. In semantics, the word *referent* refers to a concrete thing to which a word refers. For example, the particular object to which one refers with the word *table* is the referent of the word *table* (in that particular case). Having said that, some referents do not have a physical or concrete existence. For a simple example, think of the "thing" to which words like happiness or love or fear refers.

Thanks to the average person's ignorance of semantics, most people end up confusing the name with the thing to which the name refers. Let us take the word *prostitute* as an example. The word *prostitute* is not the person to whom it refers. *Prostitute* is nothing but a word whose function is to refer to a person who earns a living through having sex with strangers (well, that is provided that the stranger has a dollar or six). That is to say, as any student of semantics is likely to have read or heard, "the name is not the thing" (the word *prostitute* is merely a symbol used to refer to a person who is in the business of renting their genitals) and "the map is not the territory" (a map is merely an illustration depicting a territory, not the actual territory).

Needless to say, naming people, emotions, processes, and things was made necessary by our need to communicate. And even though our ability to communicate with each other played a crucial role in our altering the environment and our invention of things, things that were not made or caused by human beings would have still existed should we have not assigned names to them. In other words, the organism to which we refer with the word *tree* led to the coining of the word *tree*, not the other way around.

Lastly, there is absolutely nothing "girlish" about the colour pink or anything "bad-luck'ish" about the colour black. In other words, there is no logical reason why trees are called trees. The word *trees* could have been used to refer to anything, and the organisms to which we refer with the word *trees* could have been named anything. (The sexual activity that precedes intercourse is testament to that, in that looking at what foreplay is, sexual intercourse is a game.) Having said that, that is, of course, with the exception of words that were formed onomatopoeically, namely, words that were formed by imitating a sound made by or associated with its referent; words like woof, meow, moo, or sizzle.

"Speed" Does Not Kill

As I have attempted to remind the reader with the previous writing, because of our ignorance of semantics, we end up confusing the name with the thing to which the name refers.

Anyway, although I find the aforesaid writing to be satisfactory, I could not resist sharing, as an anecdote, what I heard some "creative" motivational speaker feed his audience. He zestfully shouted that *impossible* simply means that "I'm possible" and that *disease* merely means that one's body is at "dis-ease." Apparently, accepting or admitting that you "have" a disease gives the word *disease* power. Either that or accepting or admitting that you "have" a disease gives the disease power.

I trust that the reader is now what one might call "semantics literate" enough to notice what is misleading about those statements. Or at least what inspires people to say such quasi-profound statements.

The Named and the Named after

According to the Book of Genesis, Seth was born after the killing of his brother, Abel, by his other brother, Cain. It is said that their mother, Eve, believed that God has granted her Seth as a replacement for Abel. ("Adam had sexual relations with his wife again, and she gave birth to another son. She named him Seth, for she said, 'God has granted me another son *in place of* Abel, whom Cain killed.'" — Genesis 4:25, New Living Translation.)

While minding my own business, both literally and figuratively, at a stall where I briefly sold the book that I penned before this one, two men came by to buy two bags of potato chips from the lady that ran the stall next to the one that I occupied. As soon as that transaction was complete, the two men carefully opened their bags, and then devoured the chips.

A few minutes later, one of them left. But the other remained to converse with us—the lady that they just bought potato chips from and I. He initiated the conversation by telling us that the man whom he was with is his younger brother; and that after his family spent a lot of money on financing his younger brother's six or so years of university, his younger brother suddenly lost his mind.

I wish not to bore the reader with every single thing that he said. So I will fast-forward to the parts that made me regard this anecdote as worthy of sharing.

"It is only recently, after I have given it some thought," he said, "that I realized that our father is to blame for my younger brother's sudden mental illness." Apparently, the man's younger brother's name is Seth and, interestingly, the two brothers have another brother named Abel. The man then said that his younger brother, Seth, is going through whatever that he is going through merely because he was named Seth (by their father) *whilst* his other brother, Abel, was still alive. (In the Book of Genesis, Seth is born *after* Abel's passing, which is why Eve believed that God granted her Seth as Abel's "replacement.")

In the course of the same conversation, the man told us of a relative of his whose toddler daughter could not stop crying, until they changed her name from Dikeledi, which means "tears" in Sepedi, SeTswana, and SeSotho.

Unfortunately, he did not share Dikeledi's new name with us. Fortunately, that is insignificant.

Lastly, he then told us about his neighbour's son who, like Judas, the biblical "character" that he was named after, ended up hanging himself.

Needless to say, the man in question, like many people, believes that words have power within themselves, and that a person's name has the power to shape their character or future. The fact that the man's younger brother could have still lost his mind, or that any Judas that ended up hanging himself could have still hanged himself should he have been named otherwise, seemed far-fetched to him.

I hope to have demonstrated how our beliefs easily shape and direct our attention.

To sum up, when a man meets someone with a personality that is similar to that of someone else that he knows, he seldom devotes his time and mental energy to their personalities' similarity. However, he seldom fails to entertain the belief that the name John is likely to have had something to do with the fact that all the three guys named John that he knows love beer.

I will, in due course, come back to that.

(Side Note: It is undeniable that what we call things and how we phrase statements have the power to influence our attitude towards things, people, and situations. For example, apparently, "I have no choice but to *let you go*" is three times easier to accept than "I have no choice but to *fire* you," when such words are said to an employee by his or her employer. Even though *let you go* and *fire* mean, *in that context*, the very same thing. Perhaps. Having said so, the phrase *let you go* isn't going to put food on such an employee's table.)

Words, Meaning, and Background

Amongst other things, I have thus far managed to say a few things about language; share what I believe is the primary function of words and language; imply that language is a means to an end; and remind the reader about the relationship between words and their referents.

From here on, I hope to shed light on some shortcomings of our everyday languages (i.e., non-technical languages), by the mere act of exploring a few facets of language. While I will not offer suggestions as to how to fix or overcome the defects that I am about to touch on, being aware of them alone should make a huge difference whenever the reader communicates with others.

At any rate, we usually forget that what we mean by

some words was shaped by our background, and what such words mean to those with whom we are communicating was shaped by their background, a background that we usually know very little or even nothing about.

As may be expected, in some cases, when $person_1$ speaks of one thing, a different thing comes to $person_2$'s mind. Let us take the word *house* as an example. When a rich man and a poor one are asked to think of their house, the two will undoubtedly have different mental images. The poor man will have a mental image of a four-room shack that is occupied by a family of twenty, whereas the rich one will have that of a twenty-room mansion that is occupied by a family of four: one word, two different referents. (Granted, there is room for the reader to argue that regardless of their differences, a shack and a mansion serve the very same purpose. But that would be a sign of having missed the point. With that example, I was merely trying to show how one word easily brings different things to the minds of those communicating.)

Needless to say, such miscommunication is generally caused by words whose referents are *relative* (like in the previous example) and words that refer to *abstract* referents ("things" that do not have a physical or concrete existence). By relative words or labels, I refer to words that do not refer to a particular individual or thing, that is, words whose referents are considered *in relation to* something else. For example, the particular person to whom the word *dad* refers depends on who is using that word. However, *Mokokoma Mokhonoana* refers to a particular person, irrespective of who says or writes that. That is, of course, provided that there exists no other person named Mokokoma Mokhonoana. What's more, anybody who knows me very well could obviously argue that by *Mokokoma Mokhonoana* the person saying that could be referring to my late great-grandfather, whom I am named after, not me. But I trust that the reader gets the point that I was trying to make.

Anyway, unless you know the person using the word *dad* (when referring to their own father), you will not know who the referent is, that is to say, the particular person to whom the word *dad* refers (in that particular case). The same can, of course, be said about words like *wife, friend, teacher, enemy, neighbour, mistress,* et cetera. Such words reveal only the relationship between the writer or speaker and the person to whom they are referring. The particular person to whom such a word is referring remains unknown to the reader or listener.

Finally, for a simple example that reminds us that one symbol or word can mean totally different things to different people, I would now like to share a passage from

Here's Something about General Semantics, a book that is said to have been written by Steve Stockdale. "Prior to Hitler's German National Socialists appropriating the swastika symbol for its own branding, the symbol had been used as an expressive symbol for good fortune, good luck, good wishes, etc., ... *for centuries*. In fact, Rudyard Kipling featured the symbol prominently on the front covers and title pages of several early editions of his books, at least through the 1920s. Was Kipling a Nazi? Even *before* there were Nazis?

"We need to remember that every symbol — every word, sign, icon, code, etc. — was created by humans. Just as there is no, to my knowledge, piece of music or art that spontaneously emanated with inherent (and in-errant) 'meaning,' there exists no symbol with *inherent and inerrant* 'meaning.' As the American pragmatist philosopher Charles Sanders Peirce put it: 'You don't get meaning; you respond with meaning.'

"While traveling in India in 2007, I learned there is a neighborhood known as 'Swastik' in the ancient city of Ahmedabad, home of Gandhi's Ashram. From a professor at a city university I heard a story that the swastika symbol, according to Indian tradition of more than three thousand years, depicted the life-sustaining image of a water wheel.

"From my standpoint, I'm not particularly interested in where or when the symbol originated. I find it important to remember that the *symbol* we recognize and call a 'swastika' can convey — or, perhaps more appropriately, can *evoke* — different meanings among different people in different contexts. The *symbol* itself carries no inherent meaning or sense of goodness or evil or luck. As George Carlin said of 'dirty words' ... *they're innocent!* It's the people who use the words — or in this case the symbols — that you have to worry about and scrutinize."

The Impact of Context on Meaning

Our experience or background is by no means the only factor that determines what we presume that those with whom we are communicating mean by a certain word. I would now like to touch on a few other factors that usually determine what we presume is meant by some words.

Let us start with *context*, with which I refer to "the circumstances that form the setting for an event, statement, or idea, and in terms of which it can be fully understood and assessed," to illustrate that, allow me to cite an example (that revolves around the different meanings of the word *beat*) from *General Semantics: An Outline Survey (3rd Edition, 2004)*, a book that is said to have been written by Kenneth G. Johnson:

> She *beat* (hit) the drum with a stick.
> He *beat* (defeated) Joe at chess.
> This reporter has the mayor on his *beat* (area to cover).
> *Beats* me (don't know), I ain't the regular crew chief.

As the attentive reader is likely to have noticed, one must first know the context in which the word *beat* is used, for one to stand a chance of figuring out which of the various meanings of the word is meant by the writer. In the same way that one needs to be aware of the context (i.e., the other eye) in order to differentiate a blink from a wink. For without sight of the other eye, a blink and a wink are indistinguishable.

Another factor that usually determines what is meant by a certain word is, of course, the period in which communication takes or took place. For example, I learned only recently that the word *know*, in the sense that is meant by the writer of Genesis 4:25 ("And Adam *knew* his wife again, and she bore a son..."), also means to have sexual intercourse (with someone). But I will, in defense of my ignorance, simply remind the reader that that particular meaning of the word *know* is classified as archaic, and as the learned reader knows, and as the learned reader knows, that simply means that that particular meaning of the word *know* is no longer in everyday use, or rather, people no longer use the word *know* to refer to the act of having sexual intercourse (with someone).

Needless to say, as an alternative to that justification of my ignorance, I could simply bring, to the reader's mind, what etymology is, namely, the study of the origin of words and the way in which *their meanings have changed throughout history*. That in itself should remind the reader that: (1) some words do not mean what they used to mean; (2) some words will someday have a new meaning added to their current meaning or meanings; and (3) some words will have a meaning removed from their current meanings.

At any rate, it helps to approach every single thing that was written a very long time ago with the understanding that some words are likely to have had a different meaning or meanings to the author and his contemporaries. That is why, to borrow Kenneth G. Johnson's words, a dictionary should be considered a book of history, not of law.

The impact of context on meaning is by no means limited to meanings of words. Sometimes context determines which of the possible meanings of a gesture is meant by that gesture. For example, not every man who sends a woman flowers does so as a gesture to say, "I'm romantically interested in you." Some men send some women flowers merely as a gesture to say, "My condolences (on the death of your husband)." What's more, there probably exist people to whom witnessing such a gesture will be puzzling, and those to whom that gesture will come across as stupid, because of nothing but their cultural conditioning.

Let us use acting as our second example. When a woman kisses another woman's husband behind closed doors, it is called "cheating." Yet, should the very same man and woman kiss in front of a cameraman, "acting" it will be called.

In closing, I would like to cite an extract that I find relevant to what we have just touched on. "No foreigner can really learn a tribal language from books," Stuart Chase is said to have written, "for it is a mixture of words and *context of situation.*' For this reason, too, no living person can get more than a fraction of the meaning out of dead languages, for he can never personally live through the experiences of the culture which fashioned them. To the modern student, Greek and Latin classics are isolated documents severed from the context of situation."[1]

Porn Shops That Sell Second-hand TVs

Even though most of us assume that every statement that is expressed through speech would have expressed the very same meaning should it have been expressed in written form, the medium with which a message is expressed, too, adds another dimension to the complexity and defects of language.

I once attempted to demonstrate that point with this aphorism: "To a blind man, *pawnshop* and *porn shop* are indistinguishable. To an uneducated one, *oversleeping* and *sleeping over* are opposites."

Needless to say, the words that the first part of that aphorism is centered around, namely, *pawnshop* and *porn shop*, are called homophones. Homophones are each of two or more words that have the same pronunciation but different meanings, origins, or spelling. For example, (1) *which* and *witch* (2) *for*, *fore*, and *four* (3) *right*, *wright*, *rite*, and *write*.

At any rate, in speech, one relies on context, that is, the word's surrounding words, in order to distinguish, say, *right* from *write*. For, without context, *four* can easily fool the ear into confusing it with *fore* or *for*.

To confuse the eye, we have homographs, which are each of two or more words spelled the same but not necessarily pronounced the same and having different meanings and origins. (One can reasonably say that homophones are homographs of speech. For, as I once quipped, spelling is the pronunciation of writing.) For example, *bark* could refer to the sharp explosive cry of a dog, the skin of a tree, or a sailing ship.

It goes without saying that to figure out which of the various meanings of that homograph is meant by the writer, one needs to know the context in which the homograph is used. (That, of course, also substantiates the seemingly ridiculous assertion that people are the ones who mean, not words.)

Words Do Not Convey Actual Emotions

Although words are capable of bringing a particular concrete referent, say, a house or a person, to the minds of those with whom one is communicating, they cannot make those with whom one is communicating feel what one is feeling or once felt.

Reason? Simple. Although words are capable of leaving readers or listeners feeling a certain way, as per the intent of the writer or speaker, they are not capable of carrying the actual feeling or emotion from the speaker or writer's mind to that of the reader or listener. (If they were, then we would emotionally be slaves to words of others, and we would unavoidably be angered by whatever swear word that is directed towards us. But, as may be expected from someone who has asserted that words are meaningless in themselves, I am of the opinion that swear words are not inherently offensive—which, of course, implies that one can simply choose not to be offended by a swear word. I will explore that in a few writings' time.)

At any rate, when it comes to subjective and abstract things such as emotions, words can at best only give readers and listeners an idea of the particular feeling or emotion that the writer or speaker is discussing or referring to.

The inability to convey an actual feeling or experience from one person to another is, of course, not limited to words. For example, making a man watch a video of his wife give birth, too, cannot, even for a millionth of a second, make him feel even a billionth of the pain that his wife felt. Even being present while his wife gives birth cannot make him feel the actual pain that his wife is experiencing. However, the reader will—in about 3 seconds time—have a mental image of a young pink elephant.

Although telling the reader about the pain that I felt when my first girlfriend told me to go to hell is incapable of leaving the reader feeling what I felt then, the last sentence is capable of leaving, and is likely to have left, the reader with a mental image of a pink elephant. Obviously, the details of the mental image will differ from reader to reader. But that is not really important. To substantiate that, I will simply remind the reader about how effective a novel can still be, despite the fact that it is impossible for it to leave all or even two readers with the very same mental image.

In a word, words are not capable of making those with whom we are communicating feel what we are feeling or once felt, they are only capable of making them "imagine" or have an idea of what we are feeling or once felt.

Putting Words into Words

We cannot really say what we mean by some words. Sadly, that includes words whose referents we are willing to die for. Let us use love as an example.

While conversing with a friend of a friend, he kept on using the word *love*, and out of curiosity, I ended up asking him what love is. That was before I was aware of the illusion that is usually brought about by the word *is*, otherwise I would have phrased that question differently. Anyway, he answered me nonetheless, and with great enthusiasm, I might add.

Having said that, he failed to give me a satisfactory definition. What he said, in his attempt to define *love*, wasn't really a definition of *love*. His answer was made up of nothing but deeds that he, like most people, regards as an indication that the doer is in love with whomever that the deeds are done for: things like calling someone every second hour, taking care of them, worrying about their well-being, cooking for them, et cetera. I don't know about the reader but, as common as his way of defining *love* is, I found his definition ridiculous. Because that is like describing how a starving homeless man turned a dustbin inside out as an answer to the question, "What is hunger?" Or describing how a sexually excited couple took their restless kids to their grandparents' house for the night, just so they could have their house to themselves, as one's answer to the question, "What is the meaning of the phrase: *make love*?"

At any rate, as I have said a few times already, we cannot really say what a thing is, we can only say something about the thing.

Anyway, if the speaker or writer cannot really say what they mean by a certain word, what are the chances of the listener or reader knowing what they mean? Bearing in mind that the poor listener or reader has only the speaker or writer's words to try to make sense of what they have said or written.

What Do You Mean By That?

As I have argued with the previous writing, we cannot really say what we mean by some words. In addition, we cannot really say to what are we referring with some words. Now the question is, what's the best that you can get from arguing with someone about something that they cannot even say what they mean by it?

I have patiently developed a habit that seems to be an effective antidote for the countless misunderstandings that are caused by the fact that we have attached different meanings to the very same words. That is, of course, usually not applicable to words whose referents have a physical or concrete existence. Anyway, when engaged in a conversation, and the other person uses a word whose referent exists nowhere except in our minds—a word that I know is likely to mean different things to us, I simply ask them, "What do you mean by X?" For example, when whomever that I am communicating with talks about, say, communism, I will politely ask, "What do you mean by *communism?*" (Note how my focus is on what *the person* means by the word, not on what *the word* means or is said to mean.)

That there is a straightforward, not to mention inoffensive, question, be that as it may, believe it or not, I am almost always misunderstood. For some reason, most people think that I'm implying that they do not have an idea what, to use the previous example as an example, communism "is." As may be expected, they get offended and naturally they get defensive. (I would, to some extent, understand their reaction if I—instead of "what do *you* mean by *communism?*"—asked them what communism is.) Such people never tell me what they mean by the word whose meaning my question revolves around. Because that could lead to what most people are terrified of: being "wrong." Even though, by asking what *they* mean by whatever word, I am implying that I am open to working with whatever they mean by such-and-such a word, not what "everybody" means by it.

In closing, when people who are mindful of the shortcomings of our everyday languages communicate, the listener or reader will concern himself with what *the speaker or writer* means by a word, not what *the word* means (to him or everybody else).

Right Word, Wrong Referent!

We are a million times more likely to steer clear of bringing the wrong thing to the minds of those with whom we are communicating, when using words to refer to concrete things, than when using them to refer to things that only exist in our minds.

As usual, I will use an example to demonstrate that. $Person_1$ and $person_2$ are engaged in a conversation behind $person_1$'s house. $Person_1$ then decides to tell $person_2$ about the incident where he broke both his legs when he fell off one of the trees that are located behind his house. To ensure that $person_2$ has the very same tree in mind when $person_1$ make mention of the particular tree in question, person$_1$ can: (1) say something like, "the third tree from the house"; (2) describe any distinctive attribute or attributes of the tree; or (3) simply point at the tree. Doing so is, of course, made necessary by the fact that person$_1$'s backyard has more than one tree.

However, steering clear of bringing the wrong thing to the minds of those with whom one is communicating cannot be easily achieved, whenever words are used to refer to things that exist nowhere except in our minds, things such as: "happiness," "capitalism," "love," "soul," "freedom," "justice," et cetera. For example, when a teacher asserts that education is the key to success, does *success* bring the very same idea or thing to the minds of student$_1$, student$_2$, ... student$_{20}$? Perhaps. But such meeting of minds is unlikely.

Crossing Swords Over Words

When those who are pro-capitalism and those who are anti-capitalism argue about capitalism, do they always have the very same thing in mind? (As we all know, such a debate usually revolves around the question, "Is capitalism a good or an evil economic system?")

More often than not, when those who are for capitalism and those who are against it debate, the definition of capitalism, when defined by those who are for it, revolves around the "positive" aspects of capitalism, whereas that of those who are against it revolves around its "negative" aspects. As may be expected, such debates always end where they began.

Having said that, in many cases, the argument isn't really caused by opposing viewpoints. The disagreement is, unbeknown to those debating, caused by the discrepancy between what the two parties mean by whatever abstract thing that the debate is based on (capitalism, in our example's case).

I have seen and heard countless debates on countless subjects. But, believe it or not, I have never witnessed, not even once, a debate being preceded by the clarification of the definition of the word whose referent exist nowhere except in our minds—a referent that is about to be attacked by one side and defended by the other, or the word that is or words that are likely to mean different things to different people.

Let us use the previous example as an example. But, for the sake of simplicity, let us replace *capitalism* with *polygamy* (the practice or custom of having more than one wife or husband at the same time), something that is unlikely to mean different things to different people.

Although most people would be quick to attack or defend polygamy, if they were given the opportunity to take part in a debate that is based on the question, "Is polygamy good or bad?", such a question is meaningless as it stands. Before they share their take on polygamy, a semantics literate person would first ask, "What do you mean by 'good' and what do you mean by 'bad'?" (The answer to that will, of course, invite the question, "Good to who?" and "Bad for who?"). Having said that, a person who is semantics literate and mindful of some of the things that I will attempt to explore in this book's epilogue is unlikely to take part in a debate. More on that later.

Let us bring the debate between those who are for and those who are against an abstraction back into this.

I invite the reader to take any random dictionary, and then take a look at the definition of any random concrete or abstract thing. Chances are that the dictionary's definition does not say anything about that thing's "positive" and/or "negative" impact on anything or anyone (e.g., *New Oxford American Dictionary's* definition of *penis* does not say anything about the fact that a penis is sometimes used to rape and, as maybe expected, its definition of *vagina* does not say anything about the fact that some women use their vagina as a tool to control their man—more on that later). As a result, we end up with the dictionary's neutral definition and our biased take on the thing.

Perhaps that explains why an employer's definition of *employment* and an employee's are seldom the same. Similarly, a rapist and his or her victim's take on rape are unlikely to be the same.

Which is why it is advisable to ask what someone means by, say, polygamy, when they talk about polygamy. Because their definition of *polygamy* will, nine times out of ten, be contaminated by their experience and therefore their take on it. For example, a man who is relentlessly trying to convince his only wife to allow him to marry another woman is unlikely to define *polygamy* like someone who grew up with a very limited access to their father merely because their father had eight wives and eighteen other children to spend his limited time with.

Needless to say, the word *love*—like the word *capitalism*—does not have a particular thing *in the real world* to which it refers. The closest that we can get to seeing love is by having the rare opportunity of witnessing a man who claimed that he would, climb "the highest mountain," for the woman whom he claims to be in love with (as I once said, love songs are nothing without exaggeration). And the closest that we can get to touching love is by fiddling with a bouquet or a box of chocolates that a man bought or stole for the woman whom he claims to be in love with.

At any rate, we are so unmindful of the influence that our experience and our bias have on what things mean, are, or seem to us, that we almost always assume that when we use a word to refer to an abstract thing, the person listening to us, or reading what we wrote, will have the very same thing in mind. But, more depressing than that, we readily shout at and at times kill people over things that only exist in our minds: things like "capitalism," "equality," "freedom," "love," etc.

(Side Note: I am well aware that the aforementioned things' impact can be, and usually is, physical. That is to say, while, say, capitalism, might only exist in our minds, the lives of gazillions of people are affected by it. And while, say, hatred, might exist nowhere except in our minds, countless people's deaths are attributable to nothing but their killer's hatred towards them.)

Translation and Bloodshed

It goes without saying that having more than one language and, more important than that, our "need" to trade and as a result communicate with people from other tribes, countries, or continents led to the need of translation.

For two people with completely different tongues to communicate with each other without the help of a third party, i.e., a translator, $person_1$ ought to be able to communicate with $person_2$ using $person_2$'s native language, or vice versa. Or the two parties will have no choice but to communicate with each other using a *lingua franca*, that is, a language that is adopted as a common language between speakers whose native languages are different. Either way, translation is unavoidable. Seeing that $person_1$ will then be required to translate whatever that they wish to communicate from their native language into either $person_2$'s native language or the lingua franca of the two's choice. Obviously, if the two decide to communicate with each other using $person_1$'s native language, what one might call "the burden of translation" will be on $person_2$.

As we have seen in some parts of this chapter, it is easy for people who speak the very same language to misinterpret each other's words. Translation makes that more likely and easier than it already is.

At any rate, the price that we pay for a misunderstanding that is brought about by misinterpretation of other people's words differs from situation to situation and from relationship to relationship. For example, such a misunderstanding at worst leads to a quarrel, and maybe name-calling, should a man misconstrue his wife's words. However, such a misunderstanding can easily lead to bloodshed, when members of one tribe misinterpret whatever that has been said by a member of another tribe.

When translating carelessly, we do not concern ourselves with the figurative meaning that translation will add or remove from words or text. I would now like to demonstrate how literal translation, that is, the rendering of text from one language to another word-for-word with or without conveying the sense of the original, could easily communicate something completely different from what the writer or speaker of the original statement meant.

To English speakers, "break a leg!" is theatrical slang that is used to express wishes for success (it is, of course, an equivalent of "good luck!"). However, to Sepedi and Setswana speakers, when it is translated word for word "break a leg!" translates into "*roba leoto!*", which means "impregnate!" when it is interpreted figuratively, which it is likely to be.

So imagine, if you will, a very strict English-speaking man, the type that find smiling at their children as an invitation for their children to disrespect them. As he leaves the house with his good-looking female colleague, to go to a camp for their company's team building weekend for that year, his son, knowing that his father's weekend will revolve around nothing but games, shouts, "Break a leg!"

Now suppose that what the reader has just read is a passage from an English novel. I don't know about the reader, but I doubt that readers of the English version of that novel and those of the Sepedi or Setswana version (which carelessly translated "break a leg!" into "*roba leoto!*") will get the very same story. Because of nothing but the figurative meaning of what the man is told in the English version, readers of that particular version are likely to expect him to respond with a smile. However, readers of the Sepedi or Setswana version are likely to expect the man to respond to "*roba leoto!*" by breaking his son's leg or with an equally painful punishment.

(Side Note: The reader can, of course, argue that that is unlikely or even far-fetched, owing to the fact that readers of the Sepedi or Setswana version would have used the context to figure out what the man's son meant. Indeed. Having said that, that is only possible in cases where such readers can speak English.)

Niggers, Bitches, and Assholes

Finally, I would now like to touch on swear words and obscene language, while the previous example is still fresh in the reader's mind. After doing so, I will then share a few examples with which I hope to demonstrate to the reader that, believe it or not, one language's swear word or phrase is usually not offensive *to speakers of another language* when or even before it is translated into their language.

SBARTDA

One can, with reason, assume that the "word" that is formed by the above letters does not mean anything to anyone. What's more, it does not offend anyone. (Now, let us simply rearrange those letters.)

BASTARD

However, *bastard*, that is, an "illegitimate" child, somehow "has" the power to make an old educated man who has just been called that to either punch whomever that called him that, or to wish that his parents, the bastard's, used a condom during the particular sexual intercourse that led to him. Having said that, to a man who does not understand English, *bastard* is what it truly is (minus the meaning that English speakers have attached to that word); namely, either a particular arrangement of seven letters, or nothing but an unfamiliar sound. That, of course, depends on whether he is called that orally or in writing.

There is, of course, a habit of ours that is more ridiculous than the control that we allow swear words and obscene language to have over us. As the reader is likely to have noticed, we write "f@#k" instead of *fuck*, whenever we are trying to appear respectable or well mannered, or when our audience is made up of sensitive or respectable or well mannered people. Even though "f@#k" brings *fuck* to the minds of our audience. "The four letter word," too, brings *fuck* to their minds. Be that as it may, we sincerely believe that by saying or writing "The Four Letter Word" instead of *fuck* we are actually being polite or even clever.

That is, of course, the very same absurdity that Louis Szekely, who is professionally known as Louis C.K., tried to bring to our attention with the n-word joke; which basically revolves around the fact that most, if not all, black Americans are offended by the word *nigger*, whereas they are not offended by the term "the n-word." Even though the two refer to the very same race; in the same way that the so-called black people are, as one of the major divisions of humankind, a referent to which others refer with: "black people," "spooks," "niggers," "darkies," "coons" "spades," "shines," "negroes," etc.

At any rate, in some cases, the country in which one was born determines whether or not a swear word will offend one, even when that particular swear word is used to offend people who fall under the race under which one is classified. For example, most, if not all, black South Africans are not offended by the word *nigger*. However, calling them a kaffir is likely to spoil their weekend, if not the rest of their year. Chances are that the same happens with the so-called African-Americans. That is to say, while calling an African-American a kaffir, in your attempt to offend them, might be as ineffective as barking at them, in your attempt to terrify them, calling them a nigger is likely to offend them.

Swear words are arguably the best example that one can use in one's attempt to substantiate the seemingly absurd assertion that most of us believe that meanings of words are intrinsic to them. As promised, I will, in my attempt to bring our idiocy to our attention, conclude this writing with an example of how one's language determines what one is offended by. Here goes!

Bapedi, and of course, Batswana and possibly others, have an extremely amusing attitude towards the act of mentioning someone's genitals. The mere act of mentioning someone's genitals or anus is enough to make them extremely angry and offended. For example, "*marete a gago!*" (which loosely translates into "your penis") is likely to leave a man feeling extremely angry, not to mention disrespected. The likelihood of the poor man feeling so doubles when those words are said by someone who is younger than him; triples, when said by a female; quadruples, when said by a female that is younger than him.

Having said that, to infuriate someone way more than such a swear phrase would, the person doing the cursing would simply mention the other person's parent's genitals or anus instead of the other person's. For example, they would say "*mogwete wa mmago!*" instead of "*mogwete wa gago!*" The former loosely translates into "your mother's anus," whereas the latter translates into "your anus."

There is, of course, *asshole,* an English swear word that is likely to seem to be an equivalent of the latter to some people. However, there is a difference that is worth mentioning. When person₁ says *"mogwete wa gago!"* to person₂, all that they are saying is "your anus," whereas saying "asshole!" to person₂ would simply mean that person₁ is saying that person₂ is an asshole, instead of simply mentioning person₂'s anus, as is the case with *"mogwete wa gago!"* What's more, asshole would, in that context, simply mean that person₂ is irritating, detestable, or contemptible. Or so person₁ would have claimed.

Two other related Sepedi swear phrases are *"marete a papago!"* and *"nnyo ya mmago!"* The former loosely translates into "your father's penis," while the latter translates into "your mother's vagina."

I think that one can, with reason, assume that the reader does not need my help to compare the structure of Sepedi swear phrases that I have just touched on with that of similar English swear phrases.

Anyway, to see how ridiculous the notion of swear words and obscene language are—and to substantiate the assertion that words are intrinsically meaningless, and that it is people who mean, not words—take any random swear word from any random language, and then try to use that swear word to offend someone who does not speak or understand that language.

To further substantiate those two assertions, I will simply cite *New Oxford American Dictionary's* definition of *obscene*, "(of the portrayal or description of sexual matters) offensive or disgusting *by accepted standards* of morality and decency [italics mine]."

In closing, I would like to link what I have just touched on with two linguistic strategies or devices that I find relevant: (1) *political correctness*, i.e., the avoidance—often considered as taken to extremes—of forms of expression that are perceived to exclude, marginalize, or insult groups of people who are socially disadvantaged or discriminated against; and (2) *euphemism*, i.e., a mild or indirect word or expression substituted for one considered to be too harsh or blunt when referring to something unpleasant or embarrassing.

(Side Note: Granted, one could argue that the mere act of mentioning someone's "private parts" is "derogatory." Perhaps. Be that as it may, I think that the power that obscene language still have over us proves how intellectually underdeveloped and ignorant of semantics most of us are. For, as I once quipped, it is the invention of clothes, not "nature," that made "private parts" private.)

Invisible Technologies

Believe it or not, most of us are ignorant of the following facts about language: (1) as natural as it might seem, language is man-made; and (2) our languages shape how we think and how we see the world.

"Of course, most of us, most of the time, are unaware of how language does its work." Neil Postman is said to have written. "We live deep within the boundaries of our linguistic assumptions and have little sense of how the world looks to those who speak a vastly different tongue. We tend to assume that everyone sees the world in the same way, irrespective of differences in language. Only occasionally is this illusion challenged, as when the differences between linguistic ideologies become noticeable by one who has command over two languages that differ greatly in their structure and history."[2]

Although it is usually near impossible for most of us to see how our language shapes how we think and how we see the world, a brief scrutiny of the form of a question reveals how the manner in which one structures a question subtly determines how the question will be answered. To demonstrate that I will cite a passage from a chapter, whose title I borrowed, from *Technopoly*, a book that is said to have been written by Neil Postman.

"When even slightly altered, it [the form of a question] may generate antithetical answers, as in the case of the two priests who, being unsure if it was permissible to smoke and pray at the same time, wrote to the Pope for a definitive answer." Wrote Neil Postman. "One priest phrased the question 'Is it permissible to smoke while praying?' and was told it is not, since prayer should be the focus of one's whole attention; the other priest asked if it is permissible to pray while smoking and was told that it is; since it is always appropriate to pray."

Similarly, the order in which each of the two siblings tell their parent about the fight that they just had is likely to determine who, between the two, the parent will side with. This is, of course, not limited to parents and their children.

Allow me to conclude this writing with a citation of a story from the same book by Neil Postman. A story that Postman shared as an attempt to demonstrate that, to use his exact words, the form of a question may even block us from seeing solutions to problems that become visible through a different question.

"Once upon a time, in a village in what is now Lithuania, there arose an unusual problem. A curious disease afflicted many of the townspeople. It was mostly fatal (though not always), and its onset was signaled by the victim's lapsing into a deathlike coma. Medical science not being quite so advanced as it is now, there was no definite way of knowing if the victim was actually dead when burial appeared seemly. As a result, the townspeople feared that several of their relatives had already been buried alive and that a similar fate might await them. How to overcome this uncertainty was their dilemma.

"One group of people suggested that the coffins be well stocked with water and food and that a small air vent be drilled into them, just in case one of the 'dead' happened to be alive. This was expensive to do but seemed more than worth the trouble. A second group, however, came up with a less expensive and more efficient idea. Each coffin would have a twelve-inch stake affixed to the inside of the coffin lid, exactly at the level of the heart. Then, when the coffin was closed, all uncertainty would cease.

"The story does not indicate which solution was chosen, but for my purposes the choice is irrelevant. What is important to note is that different solutions were generated by different questions. The first solution was an answer to the question, How can we make sure that we do not bury people who are still alive? The second was an answer to the question, How can we make sure that everyone we bury is dead?

"Questions, then, are like computers or television or stethoscopes or lie detectors, in that they are mechanisms that give direction to our thoughts, generate new ideas, venerate old ones, expose facts, or hide them."

CULTURE

Culture: Contact Lenses We All Wear

Our cultures, that is, the totality of socially transmitted behaviour patterns, beliefs, institutions, et cetera, were gradually, not to mention subtly, sold to us when we were still too young to notice, let alone decide whether to accept or reject or even question whatever it is that we were being sold. As may be expected, it is difficult, if not impossible, for most of us to imagine, let alone see, life from the standpoint of those whose culture is vastly different from ours.

Furthermore, only those whose culture is vastly different from ours stand a chance of detecting the influence that our culture has on our perception of the world. For, as may be expected, we are generally blind to the subtle influence that our culture has on us. Owing to the obvious fact that we rely on the very same eyes, which are contaminated by our culture, when trying to see how our culture influences how we see things. That is, of course, analogous to attempting to see one's own eyes without the help of a camera or a reflective surface. Or attempting to stamp on one's left foot with one's left foot.

One can even go so far as to say that culture works as some sort of contact lenses—to every single sane person with at least one functioning eye, that is. Seeing that culture, like contact lenses, shapes our perception of the world. And, like contact lenses, culture is acquired. However, unlike contact lenses, our culture does not really better our perception. As a matter of fact, in some cases, our culture does the opposite: it worsens our perception; by making us see things that are not really there, and by making us blind to things that are really there.

Needless to say, only someone with immunity to culture, which is to say no one, sees clearly. The mere act of bringing ethnocentrism to the reader's mind, that is to say, the evaluation of other peoples and cultures according to the standards of one's own culture, is enough to substantiate the assertion that the closer to the limit of human lifespan one gets, the closer to impossible it becomes for one to see things as they really are—without one's perception being contaminated by one's cultural conditioning, that is. As I have already asserted, most of us are unaware of our culture's influence on our perception of the world, because we are so accustomed to our customs that they seem natural. Despite the fact that most of our customs, which we see as natural, are likely to come across as abnormal or even stupid or ridiculous when looked at through eyes that have been contaminated by a culture that is vastly different from ours.

Anyway, as may be expected, culture—like experience, context, literal translation, et cetera—can easily lead to a misunderstanding, when people from different cultures communicate with each other.

One gesture can mean different things to different people. Like words, gestures are intrinsically meaningless. What's more, like we do with words, we usually assume that a gesture will be interpreted as per what we mean by it—which is, of course, not always the case. For example, a well-meaning left-handed South African man is likely to be frowned upon, if he uses his left hand to shake hands with someone from, say, India, as a means to greet the latter. For, apparently, the left hand is considered to be "unclean" in countries such as India. "In India, as right across Asia," wrote someone in *The Rough Guide to India*, "the left hand is for wiping your bottom, cleaning your feet and other unsavory functions (you also put on and take off your shoes with your left hand), while the right hand is for eating, shaking hands, and so on."

As may be expected, members of cultures such as the aforementioned, like Bapedi and possibly Batswana, regard handing someone something, say, money or a plate of food, with one's left hand, as being disrespectful.

Needless to say, in some societies, being left-handed is seen as a curse. Having said that, in some societies, being left-handed is, believe it or not, seen as a blessing. For example, in such societies, while a talented right-footed soccer player's greatness is likely to be attributed to his talent, an equally talented left-footed soccer player's greatness is likely to be attributed to nothing but the fact that he is left-footed.

Finally, I would now like to, through an aphorism of mine, share two different interpretations of the very same gesture—interpretations that are obviously shaped by two different cultures. Here goes! "When conversing: a white kid that look their elder in the eye is seen as attentive; a black kid that does the same is seen as disrespectful."

(Side Note: I used contact lenses as a metaphor for culture with a purpose, namely, to remind the reader that we are usually unmindful of our culture's influence on our worldview, and that the very few who are end up forgetting. In the same way that, to use that metaphor for the last time, a man who wore contact lenses in the morning is unlikely to spend every single second of his day thinking about their presence, let alone their influence on his sight.)

Weird Cooks and Disgusting Meals

The fact that Mother Nature normally equips human beings with five toes per foot is, of course, the only logical basis for labelling a man who was born with eighteen toes as abnormal. However, labelling that man's behaviour as normal or abnormal would, in most, if not all, cases, be attributable to nothing but the cultural conditioning of those who would have labelled his behaviour as such.

Needless to say, a child that was born with three legs is labelled as abnormal by most people: owing to the fact that such people's *"frames of reference"* (a "normal" human being, in such a case) are "the same." However, because of nothing but the dissimilarity of their frames of reference (their cultures), a meal that was made from dog meat is labelled as "mouthwatering," by some people, and as "disgusting," by some. That is, of course, dependent on the cultural contact lenses through which such a meal is looked at. As I once quipped, "To most Americans, a dog is a potential mate. To some Chinese, a dog is potential meat."

At any rate, with the exception of those who do not eat meat at all, most of us who do not eat dog meat do not have a logical reason as to why we do not eat dog meat. The reason that we do not eat dog meat is a bit of a paradox, seeing that: the only reason that we do not eat dog meat is because we do not kill dogs for their meat; however, the only reason that we do not kill dogs for their meat is because we do not eat dog meat. There are, of course, those who do not eat dog meat because of religious or spiritual reasons. But that, too, could be classified as social or cultural conditioning. Anyway, if the fact that "dog meat has also been used as survival food in times of war and/or other hardships"[1] is anything to go by, then one can, with reason, assert that it is our cultural conditioning that is primarily, if not solely, responsible for us not eating dog meat. I mean, dog meat, too, has nutrients, and the last time I checked, that is exactly what we eat things for.

Cultural conditioning is so potent that most of us would probably vomit, if we were to be told that the meal that we have just devoured was made from dog meat, irrespective of whether or not the meal was really made from dog meat. (Note how what one believes is more potent than the truth. More on that in the chapter on religion.) As I have indicated, this is by no means limited to food. One can, with reason, assert that regarding a man's deeds as normal or abnormal, moral or immoral, appealing or appalling, is generally determined by the cultural conditioning of those who would have done the labelling. From how the man dresses during the day to the number of women he undresses in a day.

At any rate, because of nothing but their social and cultural conditioning, what members of society$_1$ (a people without a military force) would call a murderer, members of society$_2$ (a people with a military force) call a soldier. As I have admitted in the previous chapter, what we call people influences what we think of them and therefore how we treat them. For example, though both would have technically done the very same thing: a murderer is despised, whereas a soldier is adored.

One can, of course, add the influence of context to that.

Sense, a Box of Chocolates, and Romance

Like words, gestures are an attempt to convey or express an idea, meaning, one's feelings or intentions, et cetera, and as is the case when we communicate through words, the meaning that an observer of a gesture gets from the gesture is determined by what the gesture means to the observer, not on what the person who performed the gesture intended to convey or express with the gesture.

Needless to say, a gesture that is regarded as romantic by men from a particular culture could easily be regarded as foolish by women whose culture is vastly different from theirs. Fortunately, men rarely experience such potentially ego-deflating incidents, because they hardly ever woo women whose cultures are totally different from theirs. As we all know, the act of giving a woman flowers isn't, in itself, "sweet." The only intrinsically sweet thing about flowers is their scent, not the act of giving a woman flowers, or the man who gave a woman flowers.

At any rate, in this materialistic society of ours, it is not unlikely for a woman to permanently remove a man whom she likes a lot from her list of potential boyfriends, merely because the poor guy did not, say, buy her a gift on her birthday—simply because he, like me, does not find anything special about the so-called birthdays. Even though both her finding birthdays "special" and her finding being bought things by a man "sweet" are a result of cultural conditioning, not her own thinking or reasoning. I mean, there surely was an era when the calendar was not yet invented. Which makes it reasonable for one to suppose that there existed a time when the so-called birthdays were not "special." For a birthday was, before the invention of the calendar, seen as nothing but yet another day, not an annual resurrection of a particular set of twenty-four hours.

In closing, I would like to share a few aphorisms of mine that I find relevant to what I have just touched on, especially what I said about birthdays: (1) If every person were treated like they matter—everyday, birthdays wouldn't be so "special"; (2) If every single lover were treated like they matter—everyday, Valentine's Day wouldn't be so "special"; (3) If calendars were natural, then we would all die a day before our birthday; that is to say (4) Life is not a cycle of yesterdays.

Culture, Sex Appeal, and Erections

Are overweight men and women naturally sexually unattractive, or are we merely culturally conditioned to generally regard them so? Is finding a certain kind of men and/or women sexually attractive an end result of a natural or a cultural process? My guess is that both nature and culture shape whatever it is that is responsible for us finding some people sexually attractive whereas we find others sexually unattractive, and finding some people more sexually attractive than others. My interest is, of course, on culture. That said, I would like to share the reason why I believe that nature, too, plays a role in determining who we find sexually attractive, before I focus on how culture seems to play a role in determining the type of men and/or women that we find sexually appealing.

Mother Nature made us, I believe, to subconsciously prefer partners who are, more than anything else, likely to help us produce healthy offspring. Perhaps that explains why we are generally attracted to men or women who are fit, whereas we are repelled by those who are out of shape.

Let us now focus on how what we find sexually appealing is shaped by our culture.

It goes without saying that while a man's sexual attraction towards women might indeed be shaped by Mother Nature, one can, with reason, suppose that the things and the kind of women that the man finds sexually appealing was largely shaped by his culture.

At any rate, the region in which we live, and as a result culture, shapes our sexuality, particularly in the early stages of our development. In some, if not most, cases, what, and as a result who, a man finds sexually attractive is attributable to nothing but the country or region in which he was brought up. As we all know, it is not unlikely for, say, a Western man's "sex bomb" to be an Eastern man's "turn off." For example, as the stereotype goes, black men find women with gigantic buttocks sexually appealing, whereas white men find such women sexually unattractive.

Like I said, so goes the stereotype. More on that later.

Anyway, cultural conditioning is the only reason why we find some of what we find sexually attractive, sexually attractive. "Social institutions govern what we notice." Said Alan Watts. "An American male pays relatively little attention to the back of a girl's neck; and it is perfectly okay for her to grow her hair down long and covered. But to a Japanese, the back of a girl's neck is the most exciting sexual feature. ... they pay no attention, though, to breasts—which seem to so fascinate the American male. ... and the way that a traditional Japanese woman clothes herself is exposing the neck, but looking very flat in front and not at all showing the hips. She is willowy. She doesn't look very willowy underneath, as a rule, but she does when dressed in a kimono. Now, so you see, it isn't just that nature has built in to the human organism certain attractive features about other people. It's the social institution of what is to be attractive. ... of course, this comes out very, very strongly in the vagaries of fashion. ... how to do one's hair, paint one's face, et cetera, et cetera."

In other words, cultural conditioning has the power to dictate what gives and what does not give rise to a man's erection: healthy or not!

In closing, one can touch on the fact that materialism—which is, of course, attributable to nothing but cultural conditioning—also determines what, and as a result who, we find sexually attractive. As far-fetched as it is likely to sound, chances are that in a materialistic society, a broke man who, for whatever reason, appears to be prosperous in the eyes of a thousand women, is likely to leave about nine hundred and ninety-nine women sexually excited. For, in such a society, a man's bank balance plays the role of a chiseled physique.

THE MONETARY SYSTEM

Meaninglessness and Valuelessness

There are, of course, worthy similarities between money and words.

To start with, because of nothing but the different meanings that we have attached to them, the word *honey* and the word *bitch* do not "have" equal values and therefore the same influence or impact. Even though it takes the same number of letters and more or less the same amount of ink to write either. Similarly, although the two "have" different values, chances are that it takes more or less the same amount of ink and paper to print, say, a one-dollar bill, and, say, a hundred-dollar bill. As Tracy Chapman continues to remind us with one of her songs, "Money's only paper only ink."[1] At any rate, coins and bank notes are nothing but symbols with which we refer to the value that we have given, or rather attached, to them. In the very same way that a word is merely a symbol with which we attempt to refer to a thing or an idea or a feeling to which we have attached the word.

What's more, the value of money, say, a one-dollar bill, was and will still be changed by the passage of time. Similarly, as I have said in the first chapter, the meaning or meanings of some words were and will still be changed by the passage of time. One can, with reason, therefore assert that value is to money what meaning is to words. Hidden within the gist of that assertion is the fact that both money and words need those who use them to acknowledge their value or meaning for them (money and words, not their users) to be of any use.

In closing, contrary to popular belief, to be the rich's equals, all the poor have to do is think, not toil (as they have been indoctrinated to think). The simple act of refusing to acknowledge the value that we have given money will instantly make the poor the rich's equals. As I once quipped, "The poor would instantly be the rich's equals, if they were to stop acknowledging the value that we have given money." Similarly, as I wrote elsewhere, "VIPs are not-so-very-important without not-so-very-important-people's acknowledgement of the VIP area."

(Side Note: I will mostly, if not always, be referring to fiat money, not commodity money, whenever I use the word *money*. As the learned reader knows, fiat money derives its value from government regulation and/or the relationship between supply and demand rather than the value of the material that the money is made of, whereas commodity money is based on a commodity that has uses other than as a medium of exchange: e.g., gold, silver, salt, cocoa beans, alcohol, et cetera.)

The Cost of Convenience

I have never heard of someone who does not regard money as a creation of man. Both those who are for and those who are against the monetary system seem to agree that money is indeed man-made. What's more, every single "sane" human being that cares to think that far seems to acknowledge the convenience that we are afforded by the monetary system.

The monetary system certainly made trading much more convenient that it was in pure barter-based economies. Carrying, say, a few chickens, which one was going to use to buy, say, a bag of rice, was, I presume, quite a taxing, not to mention irritating, noisy, messy, and smelly inconvenience. And perhaps more inconvenient than that: one needed to be lucky enough to come across or patient enough to look for someone who (1) had what one needed; (2) needed what one was offering in exchange for what one needed; and (3) was willing to trade what one needed for what they needed.

Having said that, as I have already warned the reader, I will exclusively focus on what one might refer to as the "side effects" of the monetary system. Here goes!

I once jokingly complained that: "I hate coins. Granted, they do not get wet. But I think that their value does not justify their weight." From that, the alert reader is likely to have deciphered what I intended to suggest; namely, sometimes a convenience is accompanied by an inconvenience. In other words, a solution to one problem usually gives rise to another problem. For example, we have caused or worsened air pollution in the course of solving whatever problems to which fire, automobiles, factories, and cigarettes are a solution. One can, of course, also attribute the cause or exacerbation of conditions such as asthma and cancer to tobacco smoke.

As may be expected, most, if not all, of those who are for the monetary system argue that we should not entertain the idea of getting rid of the monetary system merely because money can and is usually used to better the lives of other people, particularly the poor. Perhaps. Having said that, that is a symptom of being ignorant of the fact that like crime and poverty, most social ills are side effects of our inventions. Which then means that using money in one's attempt to put an end to poverty is like erecting more borders in one's attempt to put an end to xenophobia. Or using law to put an end to crime. Or using religion to put an end to atheism.

(Side Note: I hope that the reader will, as I attempt to explore some of the side effects of the monetary system, bear in mind that the answer to the question as to whether or not an invention, a practice, or an institution is life-enhancing should be made the basis of any serious humanistic discussion concerning the invention, practice, or institution. For in some cases abolishing a system, practice, or institution is the only possible way to "improve" the system, practice, or institution. As we all know, most inconveniences are intrinsic to the system, practice, or institution that bred them. Hence he who is inconvenienced by having to defecate has no choice but to tolerate having to go to the loo. Unless, of course, he would rather starve than poo.)

Bags of Money and Starving Islanders

Imagine, if you will, a small island that has drinkable water, but no food. For whatever reason, we decide to send a few people to go live there. But instead of giving them boxes that are filled with food, we give them humongous bags that are filled with nothing but money...

I will not take that thought experiment further, not because I am too lazy to write, but merely because I believe that the reader isn't too lazy or too busy to think.

On second thought, I would like to, through an aphorism, spoon-feed readers who are reading this during their precious lunch break. Here goes! "When stranded at sea: a sailor that has food but no money is a billion times more likely to outlive the one that has money but no food." Owing to the obvious fact that, as is the case with words such as *food* and *bread*, a starving man cannot eat bank notes or coins to avoid starvation.

As I have asserted elsewhere: "People do not need jobs. As a matter of fact, they do not even need money; they need food."

Money Never Had Hands

Civilization, that is, the stage of human social development and organization that is considered most advanced, is usually the very first thing that comes to most people's minds, whenever they try to imagine the world without money.

Such people are generally of the opinion that things would not have been the way that they are, should we have not invented money. By "the way that things are" they are usually referring to nothing but man-made things such as skyscrapers, computers, automobiles, airplanes, houses, and the like.

Believe it or not, there are people who seem to either fail to grasp or refuse to acknowledge the following: money never did a thing. Granted, we pay other people to use their skills, their time, their energy and/or their tools to get things done. Be that as it may, it is the person that does the actual work, not the thing that is or was used to entice them into doing the work; e.g., money, food, experience, fame, sex, or similar strings with which this puppet called the civilized man is artfully controlled.

Although money undoubtedly played and still continues to play a pivotal role in getting civilized men to do whatever that those who have money desired or desire, every single man-made thing—bridges, clothes, jewelry, lipstick, condoms, makeup, nuclear weapons, false teeth, vibrators, et cetera—would have still been possible to make, should we have never invented money. It is worth reminding the reader that the access to or the lack of information and skills is probably the only significant difference between what we can invent and then produce today and what our great-great-grandfathers' grandfathers' great-great-grandfathers could have invented and then produced.

Perhaps sculpturing is the simplest analogy that one can use in one's attempt to make that assertion less confusing and more plausible. Let us use *David*, the well-known statue by Michelangelo, as an example. The particular block of marble that ended up as that statue existed before Michelangelo was even born. Which then means that it was possible for someone who existed hundreds of years before Michelangelo was born to carve an identical statue.

To sum up, whatever man-made thing that we make from, say, steel, was possible to make even before we knew that we could make steel by smelting iron ore. The same can, of course, be said about all the things that we make from man-made raw materials such as paper, polyester, glass, concrete, metal, and the like.

The Commodification of Copulation and Reproduction

All that animals intrinsically desire is, I believe, to survive. Apart from doing whatever that is necessary or possible to decrease the chances of it being killed, an animal achieves that by eating (to increase the chances of it seeing yet another day) and by having sex (to increase the chances of its gene seeing yet another generation). If that is indeed so, then one can, with reason, argue that apart from food, water, and protecting themselves from whatever that might harm or kill them, all that animals desire is to reproduce.

Human beings are, of course, not an exception. Although most, if not all, sane civilized men do not have sex with the aim of producing as many offspring as they possibly can. As is, I presume, the case with many if not most animals. Apparently, there are animals that, like us, sometimes if not mostly have sex for pleasure, not to reproduce.

Let us now bring money into this discussion.

With the exception of incidents of rape, all civilized

men's sexual activities are one way or another preceded by: (1) a promise or two; (2) a social ritual or three; and/ or (3) a dollar or twelve, especially the very first sexual intercourse with that particular woman.

It is certainly not an exaggeration to assert that every single sphere of every single civilized man's life is one way or another shaped by money. His love life and his sex life are, of course, not exceptions. As we all know, (1) In a materialistic society, there is no such thing as a "romantic" broke man; (2) There is a correlation between the number of digits that a man's bank balance is made up of and the number of things that his woman is willing to overlook or forgive him for; and (3) In a materialistic society, the sexiest (or most handsome) man is he with the deepest pockets.

In some if not most cases, money is the only deciding factor when it comes to the number of children that civilized couples "want" or decide to have. I am, of course, well aware that there are countless poverty-stricken couples who have more than three times as many children as countless couples who earn more than thirty, three hundred, or even three thousand times of what they earn. That topic alone deserves an essay, if not a book, of its own. Anyway, not only does money determine the maximum number of children that many, if not most, "responsible" civilized couples "can" have, money is, with or without their realization, used by some, if not most, civilized women as the deciding factor or as one of the deciding factors as to whether or not a man is worth dating and/or having sex with. For a man's *financial inability* to deposit money into a woman's bank account easily leads to his *social inability* to deposit semen into her womb, even though he is *biologically* able to do so. As I once generalized through an aphorism, "A civilized woman's demands: a man who will (1) make her come ... sometimes; but (2) pay the bills ... at all times."

As may be expected, most, if not all, civilized men spend most of their time and resources trying to acquire as much money as they possibly can. For whether for procreation or for recreation, the civilized man has to one way or another earn sex by acquiring whatever that the society in which he finds himself values the most, particularly women: things like education, fame, a chiseled physique, hunting skills, a French accent, deep pockets, et cetera.

Speaking of work and sex, a friend of mine recently tweeted, "Freud said, we live for work and sex," and I quickly replied, "I say, we work to live and for sex."

Anyway, perhaps that is why men generally seem to love (making) money more than women do. Having said that, I am, of course, of the opinion that it is because of the men's desire to be granted the opportunity to copulate and/or to reproduce that men seem to not only love money, but to love money more than women do; an opportunity that is, as I have argued, dependent on a woman's decision, which is one way or another influenced by the depth of the man's pockets.

In other words, whatever that their society values the most—particularly women, not the love for money, is what determined what civilized men are generally toiling to achieve or acquire. (Remember, as I have argued, apart from avoiding whatever that might kill them, all that men intrinsically desire is to have something to eat and someone to impregnate. That is, of course, a generalization. Owing to the fact that because of nothing but our faculty of reason or rationality, which gave us the ability to challenge or disregard whatever ultimate plan that Mother Nature has or might have with regard to the existence of human beings, there are countless men and women who can but genuinely do not want to have kids.) Anyway, I assert so merely because I strongly believe that in a society where women are conditioned to value, say, a man who risks his life to protect his country over the one with deep pockets, men who want their sexual appetite fulfilled and their gene to stand a chance of seeing yet another generation, which is to say virtually all "sane" men with functional genitals, will spend most of their time and resources trying to join the army instead of trying to deepen their pockets.

In addition to what we have just touched on, as we all know, money is one way or another used by those who have it to control those who do not have it. In the same manner that vaginas are generally used to control men who desire to copulate and/or to reproduce. To wit, money is to (most) rich people what a vagina is to (most) women: a tool that is used to control those who do not have it.

That is to some extent what made civilization possible: a handful of men's artful exploitation of inborn needs and desires of multitudes of men.

To sum up, a man-made thing is the primary and at times the only factor that is used by some, if not most, civilized women to decide as to whether or not a man is worth taking part in a natural activity or process of copulation and/or reproduction.

Finally, I would like to share three published aphorisms of mine, which I find relevant to what we have just touched on: (1) To a man who was required to marry *before* he was allowed to have sex with his lover, marriage is a "righteous" form of prostitution; (2) Marriage is the commodification of affection, copulation, and reproduction; and (3) Men marry for the womb. Women marry for their tummy.

(Side Note: I have, of course, sort of exclusively focused on men. I have an excuse for that. I did so merely because in most if not all societies, men generally play the role of "providers" or "hunters," whereas women play that of the provided for and/or the hunted. What's more, I have intentionally narrowed this to heterosexual relationships. I have two excuses for that: [1] I did so to save my precious ink and the reader's precious time; and [2] although an orgasm is, an offspring isn't a possible end product of sex between a man and a man or a woman and a woman.)

Paper Chasing's Impact on Trees

Man has become preoccupied with making as much money as he possibly can.

His society's economic system, because of the influence that it has on his way of life and his aspirations, has inevitably transformed him from a creature that persistently did its level best to live in perfect harmony with the environment and its fellow creatures into a creature that is forever trying its level best to make as much money as it can possibly make from the environment and its fellow creatures.

As may be expected, in an economic system where the primary goal is to make as much money as possible: money comes first. Everything else, which sometimes includes the lives of workers, those of other organisms, the environment, posterity, et cetera, is secondary; especially in instances where whatever negative impact that man's attempt to make as much money as he possibly can will have on society and/or the environment will only surface decades or even months after he has been paid or laid to rest.

Speaking of the lives of workers and our impact on the environment, allow me to cite a few passages from "The Destruction of Environment" and "The Degradation of the Worker," respectively, two relevant writings from *Technics and Civilization*, a book that is said to have been written by Lewis Mumford.

"The first mark of paleotechnic industry was the pollution of the air. In this paleotechnic world the realities were money, prices, capital, shares: the environment itself, like most of human existence, was treated as an abstraction. Air and sunlight, because of their deplorable lack of value in exchange, had no reality at all. ... The values of the paleotechnic economy were topsy-turvy. Its abstractions were reverenced as 'hard facts' and ultimate realities; whereas the realities of existence were treated ... as abstractions, as sentimental fancies, even as aberrations. So this period was marked throughout the Western World by the widespread perversion and destruction of environment: the tactics of mining and the debris of the mine spread everywhere. The current [1934] annual wastage through smoke in the United States is huge—one estimate is as high as approximately $200,000,000. In an all too literal sense, the paleotechnic economy had money to burn."

"Kant's doctrine, that every human being should be treated as an end, not as a means, was formulated precisely at the moment when mechanical industry had begun to treat the worker solely as a means—a means to cheaper mechanical production." Further wrote Mumford. "Human beings were dealt with in the same spirit of brutality as the landscape: labor was a resource to be exploited, to be mined, to be exhausted, and finally to be discarded. Responsibility for the worker's life and health ended with the cash-payment for the day's labor.

"The poor propagated like flies, reached industrial maturity—ten or twelve years of age—promptly, served their term in the new textile mills or the mines, and died inexpensively. During the early paleotechnic period their expectation of life was twenty years less than that of the middle classes."

To that I would like to add two relevant aphorisms that I have published elsewhere: (1) Retirement is a stage where an employer discards an employee that he cannot exploit further; and (2) Old Age homes are civilization's dumpsites for human beings who it cannot exploit further.

As an inevitable result of having bought the claims that his society's economic system has sold him, the civilized man foolishly demands infinite financial growth despite the fact that most of the resources whose extraction his economy is one way or another dependent on are finite.

In closing, I would like to share a relevant remark that Mahatma Gandhi is said to have said, "Earth provides enough to satisfy every man's need, but not every man's greed."

(Side Note: Although his economy's appetite is impossible to quench, the civilized man has, in his attempt to realize infinite financial growth, come up with economic tricks such as *planned obsolescence*, that is to say, a policy of producing consumer goods that rapidly become obsolete and so require replacing, achieved by frequent changes in design, termination of the supply of spare parts, and the use of nondurable materials.)

Scarcity, Boredom, and Infidelity

Pricing a product is a straightforward process. All that sellers have to do is add the cost of producing or buying and selling a product to whatever amount that they would like to earn as profit.

However, as we all know, that is seldom the case in cases where the product is scarce. In such cases, an auction of sorts occurs. For a similar phenomenon, one need not look further than an employer's yard. Seeing that a salary, the monthly cost of having an employee, too, is influenced, if not dictated, by the number of people, both those who are employed and who aren't, who meet the minimum requirements of that particular position.

Alternatively, one can direct one's attention to luxury goods. For while some luxury goods sure cost an arm and a leg to produce, some, if not most, luxury goods' scarcity, not their production cost, is the primary, if not the only, reason that they cost an arm and a leg. In other words, while a luxurious product, say, a car, sure is, well, luxurious, its prospect owners are, generally speaking, implicitly sold nothing but the ego-satisfying low odds of them coming across someone driving "the same" car, not the luxury that the car provides.

Enough about things. Let us now, while still exploring scarcity and value, move our focus from products to human beings.

Believe it or not, I did not really mean to imply that employees are products. Having said that, after reading the following aphorisms that I have published elsewhere, the reader is likely to doubt that that implication was honestly not intentional: (1) School is a factory where the raw material called a student is turned into a product called an employee; (2) School is a factory where employees manufacture employees; and (3) Education is a manufacturing process whereby raw materials called curious boys are turned into products called obedient men.

Anyway, as we all know, with regard to appreciation and boredom, man tends to value things and people whom he has a *limited access* to (e.g., a friend who he is only allowed to see for, say, an hour, once a month) over those that he has an *unlimited access* to (e.g., his wife). As may be expected, an unfaithful husband generally finds two minutes of sex with his mistress to be a billion times more pleasurable than all-night sex with his wife, even when there is absolutely nothing different or special about his mistress' body, vagina, or the things that she says or does to him during sex.

Speaking of relationships and scarcity, many a lover is bored to death by their other half, not because their other half "is" that boring, but merely because they have had "too much access" to their other half. In other words, because of nothing but "too much access to their lovers," those lovers inevitably miss missing their lovers.

At any rate, to keep her man (interested in her and in still being in a relationship with her), a woman needs to master the near impossible to master art of not sexually under- or overfeeding her man. For if she underfeeds him, he will or at least be tempted to cheat on her, because of his then sexual starvation. Likewise, if she overfeeds him, he will or at least be tempted to cheat on her, because of his then sexual boredom.

To sum up, many a man cheats on his woman with a woman who is not even half a quarter of the woman that his woman is merely because the other woman provides him with a scarce, not to mention forbidden, moment. As any marketer worth listening to will tell you, commodities, especially luxury goods, are made all the more desirable by their rarity. (I will, to add to that, borrow "Infidelity and Tap Water," an essay that I have published elsewhere.)

(Side Note: Speaking of scarcity and value, unlike its economic value, the life-enriching value of a thing has absolutely nothing to do with the thing's scarcity or the labour and the raw materials that were used to produce the thing.

"The rarity of gold, rubies, diamonds: the gross work that must be done to get iron out of the earth and ready for the rolling mill—these tended to be the criteria of economic value all through this civilization." Lewis Mumford is said to have written. "But real values do not derive from either rarity or crude manpower. It is not rarity that gives the air its power to sustain life, nor is it the human work done that gives milk or bananas their nourishment. In comparison with the effects of chemical action and the sun's rays the human contribution is a small one. Genuine value lies in the power to sustain or enrich life: a glass bead may be more valuable than a diamond ... the juice of a lemon may be more valuable on a long ocean voyage than a hundred pounds of meat without it. The value lies directly in the life-function: not in its origin, its rarity, or in the work done by human agents."[2]

Finally, I would like to share a passage that is relevant to what we have just touched on and, of course, the chapter that follows the following one.

"Much of the sacredness of holy texts doubtless used to come from their scarcity and inaccessibility," Daniel J. Boorstin is said to have written, "from the fact that the few existing copies were in the custody of holy priests."[3])

Infidelity and Tap Water

We have only we to blame for why we cheat. (One sentence I employed, two things I assert.)

Firstly, it is our invention, namely, fidelity, that has inevitably brought about its antithesis, namely, infidelity. In the same way that it is, as I have already argued, the invention of clothes, not "nature," that made "private parts" private. Secondly, the inevitable habit of classifying, as a "forbidden fruit," the act of having sex with someone other than one's lover or spouse, usually seduces us into infidelity.

It is the latter that I would like to touch on.

As we all know, *forbidden fruit* is defined as a thing that is desired all the more because it is not allowed. What is left of this writing will center around the part that qualifies that definition, namely, " ... *all the more because it is not allowed.*"

In one of his interviews, Jacque Fresco shared a story about his visit to some island that is home to some "primitive" tribe without clothes; an area where every single person is forever in his or her birthday suit. Such a way of life is so foreign to most of us, the so-called "civilized" people, that the mere thought of it is likely to leave some readers sexually excited. Anyway, Fresco concluded the story with something that is inconceivable to most of us: whenever men spoke with women, the men's eyes were forever on the women's faces, not on their nipples or their "private parts," as most of us would have expected.

For now, I ask the reader to allow me to digress, to bring, into this writing, the second part of its title.

At any rate, many a sexually active man sees having sex (for procreation, not reproduction) as much a necessity as drinking water is to his life and his well-being. Killing another person over a glass of water, in a village where there is a scarcity of drinking water, is, I believe, likely to be seen as more understandable than doing the same thing over the same thing in a city whose residents have access to plenty of drinking water. Indeed, our need to quench our thirst can be as intense as our want to quench our sexual desire. (That statement will, of course, come across as far-fetched to some readers. But that is, I believe, only because most of us who have access to running water have never really experienced, firsthand, thirst at its worst.) However, we, with access to running water, are not always drinking water. As a matter of fact, countless people who, believe it or not, have access to drinking water, are or were once hospitalized for dehydration—which, of course, occurs when water loss exceeds intake.

A likelihood too irresistible not to mention is that, as the alert reader is likely to have inferred, if we did not "invent" the institution of marriage and monogamy (which brought about infidelity), it is likely that we would have treated having sex with the same attitude that we have towards drinking water. In other words, we would not be preoccupied with having sex. Just like how we are not preoccupied with drinking water.

Let us now bring back our habit of classifying all human beings, except our lovers, as forbidden fruits.

People do not cheat only because their "accomplice" has or does whatever that turns them on, whereas their lover or spouse does not. Or because their "accomplice" does or says whatever that turns them on better than their lover or spouse. Many, if not most, people cheat because of either or both of the following: (1) the most obvious, sexual starvation or sexual boredom; and (2) the least obvious, the thrill that their knowing that they are not supposed to have sex with anyone other than their lover or spouse brings about, whenever they imagine having, or are about to, have sex with someone other than their lover or spouse.

At any rate, there is more to curiosity, with regard to infidelity and sex, than meets the eye. Such an assertion is, of course, substantiated by instances where a man who initially found a woman to be sexually irresistible suddenly finds her to be sexually resistible: a second or two after her clothes and her underwear hit the floor. (I am, of course, by no means implying that women do not experience the same sexual disappointment.) In such cases, clothes give rise to curiosity; curiosity makes the curious imagine; imagining (what the woman's clothes are employed to hide) leaves many, if not most, heterosexual men and homosexual women sexually excited. However, the mere act of walking around in an extremely short skirt, when performed by a woman who is amongst members of a forever-naked tribe, alone, is unlikely to be seen as "sexy" and/or as "provoking," by heterosexual men and homosexual women of that tribe who had the privilege of witnessing such a performance. As we, forever-clothed heterosexual men and homosexual women, are likely to.

To sum up, our having classified, as a forbidden fruit, the act of having sex with someone other than one's lover or spouse or spouses, subconsciously seduces, I believe, many a man into indulging in the forbidden fruit.

Heaps of Bank Notes and Heaps of Corpses

The government is, in more ways than one, the governed's saviour. Amongst other things, the government is an abstraction from which governed believers seek answers, while they are waiting for God to answer their prayers.

However, because of their "need" to make money, by means of an invention called tax, many a government inevitably prioritizes its chances of making more money from its people over its people's chances of living another decade. For example, it is widely known that cigarettes kill gazillions of people annually, yet many, if not most, governments do not ban the selling of cigarettes. Reason? Simple. Such governments make money from every single cigarette sold. The same can, of course, be said about alcoholic drinks. Although, I must say, banning the selling of liquor would be unfair to those who drink responsibly. Remember, there is no such thing as a "responsible" smoker.

In a word, many a government's impossible to fill pockets will become shallower, should it ban the selling of harmful things like cigarettes. Similarly, without (someone's) death, the family of an undertaker will starve to death. (The difference is, of course, that death is an inevitable price that we pay for having lived, whereas smoking isn't.) Interestingly, come to think of it, the latter, in a way, profits from the former's lack of the desire to ban the selling of cigarettes. Seeing that the death of countless undertakers' "clients" would not have been, should they have lived in a country where the government banned the selling of cigarettes.

At any rate, such a government is therefore faced with a dilemma. I have attempted to explore that with "The Ruling Party Dilemma," an essay that I have published elsewhere. In a nutshell, by eradicating one social ill, say, crime, another, say, unemployment, will inevitably be worsened. Owing to the fact that the services of jailers, jail cooks, those who make uniforms for jailers and prisoners, jail cleaners, those who supply jails with food, and the like, will then no longer be needed.

And as a result, that country's unemployment rate will skyrocket.

The Government's Skinny- and Fat-cats

Although I would also hate to live in a country where one party rules until hell freezes over (come to think of it, that isn't necessarily a bad thing), giving other parties a chance to rule seem to, in a way, work against the very same people in whose eyes that is meant to appear fair.

Granted, giving the ruling party a limited number of years in office sure impels its members to get things done. Or to at least appear to be doing so. What's more, that gives the people an opportunity to "fire" the ruling party come the next general election, should they find the ruling party to be corrupt or incompetent.

That is the good thing about any type of government where rulers are given a limited number of years to rule: unless, of course, they are kept in office through voting. Having said that, there seems to be a negative effect that is inevitably brought about by giving the ruling party a limited number of years in office. For example, a political party is put in office for, say, four years. Yet they are expected to eradicate, or at least make less harsh, social ills that require decades to eradicate or make less harsh. That is a seldom discussed issue that is, I believe, worthy of our immediate attention. For it brings about an attitude that unavoidably leads to despair and, in many a case, corruption.

At any rate, after realizing that they are only given, say, less than 4 years, to solve social ills that at times require at least, say, 40 years, to solve, many a politician stoop to taking as much money as he possibly can take from the government. For another term isn't guaranteed. So, they think, I assume, rather they, while they are still in power, steal from the government only to be elected back in office come the next general election, than be all holy only to be unemployed come the next general election.

Needless to say, it is impossible, for me at least, to imagine the monetary system unaccompanied by corruption. I am forever reminded of such a pipe dream whenever I hear of an attempt to "fight corruption." It is worth reminding readers who are tempted to challenge that that many a man works primarily to make a living, not because he enjoys his work, or because he likes his boss, or because he and his boss worship the same God or gods. For many a man, a job is first and foremost merely a means to some means called a full tummy.

In other words, money is some, if not most, employees' only incentive. Hence I strongly believe that almost all people who work primarily to earn a salary, which is to say most employees, can, with the right price, be bought. For example, an underpaid, overworked police-man who primarily works to earn a salary can easily be seduced—by simply being offered what he earns in 2 years—into performing the effortless 2-second long task of making some docket disappear, to ensure that some rich murderer walks free.

As the wise keep reminding us through a proverb, "Every man has his price."

The Profitability of an Intentional Misdiagnosis

It is difficult to trust a medical doctor whose primary goal, like that of the economic system that has molded his character and his aspirations, is to make as much money as possible. For, as I have already asserted, where making as much money as possible is a priority, everything else—including some human beings' lives or well-being, is of secondary importance.

As we all know, some infections can easily be cured by consuming something that many, if not most, kitch-ens have. For example, honey, ginger, garlic, lemons, cayenne pepper, green tea, and the like, can be used to cure a cold or flu. However, because doctors have a con-sultation fee to charge, and pharmaceutical companies have a profit to make, patients who suffer from a cold or flu are usually, if not always, referred to a pharmacy instead of their kitchens.

At any rate, many doctors occasionally prescribe unnecessary medication. Luckily, such prescriptions are usually harmless—in cases where the patient is lucky enough to have consulted a doctor that isn't "completely" immoral, that is. There is, of course, room for such a doctor's trial lawyer to, in their client's defense, argue that such prescriptions are only used as a placebo, not as a quick way to earn the doctor more money. Perhaps. But that is seldom the case.

Anyway, the thought of a doctor not referring a patient to the patient's kitchen, in cases where their kitchen would have effectively played pharmacy, isn't as horrifying as what lies in the following paragraph.

In this monetary system of ours, when a surgeon recommends surgery, it is usually impossible to (immediately) know for sure whether one's body really needs to be put under the knife, or whether the surgeon merely recommended that just so he will earn enough money to fund his extravagant third wedding, or to buy the newer model of the German car that he bought last year.

(Side Note: The alert reader can, of course, argue that many a surgeon recommends unnecessary surgeries merely because he needs to make money in order to increase the odds of him being able to keep his landlord's mouth shut, not because he wants to earn enough money to buy a faster car. Perhaps. But even so, such harmful and intentional misdiagnoses are one way or another brought about by such surgeons' "need" to make money: something that we have invented.)

One Man's Panic Funds Another's Picnic

Perhaps the primary, if not the only, reason why the reform of many, if not all, social, political, or economic institutions or practices is seemingly impossible is because the way that things are profit from the way that things are.

As may be expected, those who are profiting from the status quo use some of their profits to fight—through reason, propaganda, warfare, etc.—anyone and anything that attempts to reform any social, political, or economic institution or practice. For example, many a wealthy man decreases the chances of that happening by artfully using their money to keep those with shallow pockets too busy to think. That is, of course, mostly achieved through employment and/or entertainment. As I have already asserted, the rich are nothing without the poor's acknowledgement of money. What's more, nothing but thinking can make the poor realize that.

Anyway, as I once quipped, (because of the monetary system) an undertaker's kids will, without death, starve to death. In other words, some undertaker will someday see the reader's death as nothing but an income, not a loss.

But it is relatively easy for one to live with such a fact of life. For death is inevitable. However, the fact that there are countless men who pray that other men slaughter each other, just so they are able to buy, say, their tenth private jet, is disheartening. Seeing that war isn't unavoidable. (Although men usually fight over natural resources, war is neither an inevitable nor a natural phenomenon. One can, of course, link our killing each other over natural resources with what we have recently touched on with regard to scarcity and value.) What's more, a tenth private jet isn't really a life-enhancing necessity.

If the ills that are brought about by the monetary system, particularly our economic system's obsession with profit, are anything to go by, then one can reasonably assert that, like that to end corruption, our dream to confine war to history books is nothing but a pipe dream, not because war is inevitable, but merely because there are wealthy profit-driven people whose wealth is increased every single time someone buys a weapon.

Before I conclude this writing, I would like to leave the reader with a question that adds, to what we have just touched on, the dilemma that many a government that desires to make as much money as possible faces: What are the chances of country$_1$ sincerely wishing for its neighbours, country$_2$ and country$_3$, to end the war that they are engaged in, when country$_1$ will profit when a company that is based in country$_1$, a company that is supplying country$_2$ and/or country$_3$ with weapons, pays tax?

Finally, I would like to share an aphorism that is said to have been said by Bertrand Russell. Apart from its subject's obvious relevance to this writing, his exploitation of the meanings and ambiguities of the words *right* and *left* is, of course, relevant to what we have touched on in the first chapter. Here goes! "War does not determine who is right. Only who is left."

COUNTRIES

Made In China

Amongst gazillions other things, man invented cell-phones, microscopes, televisions, stethoscopes, automobiles, guns, statoscopes, airplanes, clothes, teaspoons, microwaves, fridges, contact lenses, bombs, stoves, money, debt, banks, sperm banks, pregnancy tests, condoms, morning-after pills, g-strings, monogamy, infidelity, poverty, crime, and Nigerians.

As we all know, the division of human beings by some natural border called an ocean is attributable to Mother Nature, not Her offspring. However, the division of human beings by some invention called a border is.

At any rate, it is unlikely for every single human being to regard the invention of countries as a blessing. For many a man's opinion as to whether or not the invention of countries is a blessing was primarily determined by what his country has or lacks. In other words, a border, a fence that has divided a concrete piece of land into abstract pieces of land, is a blessing to those who live in country$_1$—a country with an abundance of food, whereas the very same border is a curse to those who inhabit country$_2$—country$_1$'s neighbour—a country that is going through a famine.

As may be expected, when looked at through the eyes of country$_2$'s citizens, a border divides human beings. However, when looked at through the eyes of country$_1$'s citizens, a border protects human beings (from other human beings).

Still and all, security is a double-edged sword. For while a fence sure protects the fenced, it also imprisons the protected.

The Fear Our Invention Invented

It goes without saying that we would not have had xeno-phobia (i.e., intense or irrational dislike or fear of people from other countries) should we have not invented bor-ders. In the very same way that there would not be theft, and as a result no thieves, should we have not come up with the concept of ownership.

At any rate, xenophobia is not to be taken lightly. For unlike "ridiculous" phobias such as claustropho-

bia (extreme or irrational fear of confined spaces), ter-
dekaphobia (fear of the number 13 and avoidance to use
it), hippopotomonstrosesquipedaliophobia (the fear of
long words), and the like, the effects and ramifications
of xenophobia usually go beyond the minds in which
it occurs: I doubt that there was ever an instance were
someone committed suicide because of nothing but
their intense or irrational dislike or fear of someone or
people from another country. As we all know, gazillions
of homicides are attributable to nothing but xenophobia. Such killings are, of course, avoidable end results of
an unavoidable fear or dislike that is brought about by
the nonessential invention of borders.

In May 2008, the world watched as some black South
Africans slaughtered some of their fellow human beings
for being from the other side of the border.[1] The poor
foreigners (an abstraction that is, of course, a by-prod-
uct of the invention of borders) were victims of nothing but being from and on the wrong side of the border.
Interestingly, apparently not a single white person was
killed in any of the xenophobic attacks in question.

If that is indeed true, then one can, with reason, suppose that the invention of the concept of race, that of
class, and the attitude towards people who are classified
under a particular race and/or class are mainly respon-

sible for those riots' death toll of white foreigners. Seeing that many, if not most, black South Africans call black foreigners "foreigners," whereas they call white foreigners "tourists." (Note how such black South Africans omit the word *black* whenever they refer to black foreigners. If that isn't because the term "white foreigner" does not exist in their vocabulary, chances are that they subconsciously do so merely because though black South Africans and black foreigners are divided by the invention of borders, the two are, believe it or not, "united" by the invention of the concept of race.)

Lastly, as the reader is likely to have already noticed, the referent to which the word *foreigner* refers is relative. In other words, we are all foreigners to every single human being other than our countrymen. In short, as some protester's placard read, "EVERYONE IS A FOREIGNER SOMEWHERE."

The Region of Birth and the Religion of Choice

(This writing is, of course, also relevant to the following chapter on religion. Having said that, I find it to be more relevant to this part of this chapter. Seeing that I will, with this writing, touch on the part that one's

country of birth usually plays when it comes to one's decision as to which religion to adhere to—and as a result who or what to call God, whilst our slaughtering each other over a division that is brought about by the invention of borders is still fresh in the reader's mind.)

As we all know, man did not have the privilege of choosing the family that he was born into.

In many a case, the country or region in which a man was born is the only factor that determined the religion to which his family adheres. His family, in turn, gently sold him the religion that they believe in and whose practices they follow. Even though his being born into the family that he was born into was nothing but "randomness of nature." (Such an assertion cannot, of course, coexist with the belief in the will of God, that is, the concept that God has an ultimate plan for humanity, which implies that every single person was born to play a crucial part in the realization of that plan. As Paul Borthwick is said to have claimed: "There is a *you*-shaped hole in God's global mission. God has prepared good things *specifically* for you to do.")

Anyway, as I have already asserted, who or what man calls God is, for the most part, determined by the country or region in which he was born. In other words, the country or region in which a man was born, as random as it was, narrowed the "options" that he had with regard to which religion to adhere to—and as a result who or what to call God. What's more, although some, if not most, religious people are willing to die for the beliefs and practices that they have been sold by their religion, many would have been of the opinion that the religion that they currently adhere to isn't "the truth," should they have been born in any continent or country other than the one that they were born in. For chances are that they would have been adherents of that continent or country's most popular religion; a religion that they currently regard as not being "the truth" and whose adherents they secretly see as "religiously lost."

At any rate, as random as it might be, the continent or country in which a man is born plays such a dominant role when it comes to "his" choice as to who or what he will call God that a blind man can, from nothing but the name of the country that a stranger is from, correctly guess the religion that that stranger adheres to. For example, from me telling him nothing other than the fact that my friend is from India, he is likely to be correct in presuming that she is an adherent of Hinduism; South Africa, Christianity; Israel, Judaism. Obviously, the probability of his guess being correct gets lower and lower as more and more people leave their continent or country of birth to reside in another continent or country. Owing to the fact that, say, Hindus, rarely abandon their religious beliefs and practices when they migrate; even when they migrate to a country where Hinduism is not as popular as it is in their country of birth, a country that has successfully sold them Hinduism. Which then makes it more likely for the blind man in question to wrongfully guess that a Hindu that is South African by birth adheres to Christianity.

RELIGION

First Things First

Countless believers and innumerable nonbelievers have written numerous books on religion; books that they used as nothing but a platform to advocate and/or to defend their religious beliefs or lack thereof.

If truth be told, I have never read even one of the books in question. I have, however, browsed quite a few. Needless to say, in every single case, nonbelievers wrote with the primary, if not the sole, aim of justifying their disbelief in the existence of God and as a result prove believers wrong. Likewise, believers wrote to substantiate theism and as a result refute atheism.

Naturally, such books are generally contaminated by their authors' religious bias. Having said that, unlike the aforementioned authors, I aim to write this chapter as an impartial observer of the division of human beings by religion, not as a believer or as a nonbeliever. In other words, I am by no means, with this chapter, trying to sell religion to the irreligious or irreligiousness to the religious. My humble intention is to explore religion, not to prove who—between believers and nonbelievers—is wrong.

What's more, most, if not all, parts of this chapter will seem to exclusively focus on Christianity. I have two excuses for that. Firstly, Christianity is the only religion that I have had firsthand experience of adhering to. Secondly, Christianity is said to be the world's largest religion—apparently, its adherents constitute about a third of the world's population. Having said that, my primary intention is to explore religion—that is, the system of faith and worship—as a whole, not a particular system of faith and worship: e.g., Christianity, Islam, Judaism, et cetera.

Amongst other things, I will attempt to lucidly explore the symbols, beliefs, narratives, practices, claims, and, of course, the contradictions found within Christianity and its teachings.

Some writings will, of course, not be applicable or relevant to some "sub-religions." For example, though an exploration of the arguments for and/or against the belief in the existence of God will apply to, say, Christianity and Judaism, such an exploration will obviously not be applicable to Buddhism. For, apparently, Buddhism has no creator god (as Damien Keown is said to have said, "If belief in God in this sense is the essence of religion, then Buddhism cannot be a religion.") Some people even argue that Buddhism is a philosophy, not a religion—in the sense that the word *religion* is generally used, namely, the belief in and worship of a superhuman controlling power, especially a personal God or gods. Anyway, I trust that the reader will bear that in mind, as I attempt to explore this complex thing called religion.

If truth be told, in light of the very little that I know about religion, and what there is to know about religion, I know nothing. Be that as it may, I have failed to resist the urge to share my observations with regard to the mental and the physical impact that religion has on human beings. I pray that at least a quarter of the seemingly random statements with which I am about to propound, assert, question, speculate, et cetera, is plausible, if not true.

Lastly, I would first like to briefly explore the human race, before I explore religion. I find that absolutely necessary. Simply because I strongly believe that the role that religion plays and, perhaps more important, the value that human beings get from religion, is mainly, if not entirely, dependent on the (mental) state of the human race. As we all know, like all social constructs, religion is nothing without the human mind. In other words, if all human beings were to be extinct, there wouldn't be such a thing as religion, a country, money, theft, a sin, et cetera.

(Side Note: Like many facets of the civilized man's life that I am going to occasionally touch on in this chapter, the following scrutiny of the primary goal of most economic systems is likely to come across as unworthy of incorporating into an exploration of religion. Be that as it may, the reader will eventually understand why I found a brief exploration of the aforesaid facets of the civilized man's life pivotal. That is, of course, provided that I will, with this chapter, achieve what I am about to attempt to achieve.)

THE STATE OF MAN

With civilization came the invention of tools (that, of course, sort of invites the puzzling chicken-and-egg conundrum); and then later, the invention of machinery. With the introduction of machinery came the Industrial Revolution.

While the Industrial Revolution might not have

brought about money and the concept of and the lust for profit, in it capitalism found a fertile ground. If truth be told, I am a bit reluctant to use the word *capitalism*, as that is likely to contaminate many a pro-capitalism reader's take on the assertions that I am about to make. But I hope that such readers' emotional attachment to the economic system in question will not lessen the odds of them being logical when they scrutinize the following paragraphs.

In any case, as is the case with most words whose referent exists nowhere except in man's mind, the word *capitalism* is likely to mean different things to different people. Here is the simplest definition of capitalism that I have ever come across: "An economic system based on private ownership of the means of production with the goal of making profit." (That is, of course, likely to come across as an oversimplification to some readers. Anyway, note how, as I have said in the first chapter, nothing "good" or "bad" is said about whatever that is defined.) From that definition, I would like to emphasize: " ... *with the goal of making profit*." For I am about to attempt to link the civilized man's unhappiness with his society's (economic system's) obsession with making, at all costs, as much money as possible. From the last two sentences, the attentive reader is likely to have correctly supposed that I believe that any economic system whose primary goal is to make as much profit as possible, too, is likely to produce the unhappiness that the so-called civilized man is tormented by, should we replace capitalism with such an economic system. The civilized man's unhappiness is, I believe, a side effect, which I am about to attribute to capitalism's unattainable goal of filling up capitalists' bottomless pockets. Here goes!

In these industrialized societies of ours, never-ending consumption is a prerequisite for keeping the conveyor belt running and a handful of men's families smiling.

To deepen their pockets, capitalists needed to produce more things (by *more* I mean both quantity and variety), which they, of course, achieved with relative ease. However, that alone wasn't enough to earn them one-way tickets to the promised land. They were, of course, then left with the challenge of giving rise to consumption that will at worst match and at best exceed their forever-increasing production capacity. Owing to the obvious fact that to make more money and to have a valid reason to produce even more, whatever that they produced needed to be consumed.

When an economic system's priority is to make profit, merely meeting a demand, as many a man believes that to be the sole reason why businesses exist, becomes an obstacle to businesses' desire to make as much money as they possibly can. For that then means that capitalists' longing for infinite financial growth will be impractical. Hence producers need to produce and then sell more than consumers need—if they are to increase the odds of their pockets forever deepening, that is.

Because of that, the civilized man has been subtly molded into a materialistic creature that is forever preoccupied with the acquisition of possessions. As may be expected, the civilized man derives most of his happiness from buying things. Having said that, his happiness is seldom derived from the product or products in its- or themselves. Unbeknown to him, his happiness is usually derived from the act of buying. To substantiate such a seemingly absurd assertion, I will simply remind the reader of the activity to which we refer with the term "retail therapy." (Ironically, some, if not most, of the civilized man's unhappiness is attributable to nothing but debt: a hole which he got himself into while attempting to acquire happiness through buying things that he does not need, with money that he does not have.)

At any rate, the civilized man has been programmed to want things that he does not need. Capitalism, in its attempt to deepen capitalists' pockets, has successfully blurred, in most consumers' eyes, the very thin line between a need and a want. Perhaps that is the primary concern of many a man who criticizes capitalism: the fact that capitalism is not really an attempt to meet consumers' demand for things that they need. On the contrary, it is, for the most part, an attempt to manufacture consumers' demand for things that they (would then) want. That, of course, works in capitalists' favour. Because, like capitalists' appetite for even deeper pockets, consumers' appetite for wants is insatiable.

Anyway, advertising then became the primary instrument with which capitalists made the civilized man blind to the difference between a need and a want. In other words, in some if not most cases, buying moved from being a rational acquirement of a need to being an irrational acquirement of a want. In short, buying is, because of that, seldom an acquirement of a requirement.

"Advertising is more effective when it is irrational." Neil Postman is said to have written. "By irrational, I do not, of course, mean crazy. I mean that products could be best sold by exploiting the magical and even poetical powers of language and pictures. ... By the turn of the century, advertisers no longer assumed that reason was the best instrument for the communication of commercial products and ideas. Advertising became one part depth psychology, one part aesthetic theory. *In the process, a fundamental principle of capitalist ideology was rejected: namely, that the producer and consumer were engaged in a rational enterprise in which consumers made choices on the basis of careful consideration of the quality of a product and their own self-interest. This, at least, is what Adam Smith had in mind.* But today, the television commercial, for example, is rarely about the character of the products. It is about the character of the consumers of products. ... What the advertiser needs to know is not what is right about the product but what is wrong about the buyer. And so the balance of business expenditures shifts from product research to market research, which means orienting business away from making products of value and toward making consumers feel valuable. The business of business becomes pseudo-therapy; the consumer, a patient reassured by psychodramas [italics mine]."[1]

I have, up until now, attempted to link capitalism with the civilized man's unhappiness as a consumer, i.e., as the buyer of whatever that is produced. In closing, I would like to share an aphorism with which I attempted to link capitalism with the civilized man's unhappiness as an employee, i.e., as an employed producer of whatever that is produced. Here goes! "Capitalism has turned human beings into commodities. To the owner of a restaurant, the cook and a bag of potatoes are equally important."

My Mother Is Selfish (and so Is Yours)

Selflessness is, of course, an admirable thing to strive for. Having said that, I strongly believe that it is impossible for us to be selfless. For a human being is an intrinsically selfish creature. By *selfish* I mean, "concerned *chiefly* with one's own personal profit or pleasure," not the other sense that is usually referred to when the word *selfish* is used, i.e., "lacking consideration for others."

At the core of every single "sane" person's every single deed or lack thereof hides their loss or gain and/or their pleasure or pain. At the core of every single freedom fighter's fight hides the freedom fighter's desire for his people to be free, not his people or their freedom. Similarly, at the core of a woman's attempt to have her man dressed "properly" hides the odds of her looking good (in the eyes of her peers or their neighbours), not the man's.

The very same selfishness lies hidden at the core of the real reason why we are friends with, say, a humorous person. For we did not, in such a case, become friends

with a humorous person merely because they are humorous. We became friends with them primarily, if not
solely, because they make us laugh.

When an employer employs an employee, it isn't because the employer wants to play a part in lowering their
country's unemployment rate. Or to increase the odds
of the employee sleeping on a full tummy. He does so
merely because he believes that what the employee will
demand every four weeks is nothing compared to what
the employee will make for him every single workday.

When a woman supports her man and his business, it
isn't because she wants her man to experience the pleasure of having deep pockets. She does so merely because
she does not want to experience the pain of dating a
man that has shallow pockets. As I once quipped, "Most
women do not really want their man to become a king;
they merely want to be a queen."

When a reader buys a book, he does not really do so to
"support" the writer, as many a reader claims. He does
so as an attempt to appear to have taste or to be up to
date like those who bought the book, in cases where he
is under the impression that that book is on everyone's
lips. Or to become smarter or more knowledgeable, in
cases where he is under the impression that reading the
book will leave him so. Or to simply be entertained, in

cases where he is under the impression that reading the book will leave him so.

When an affluent, self-conscious twin encourages his destitute look-alike to get a job, it isn't because he likes his twin brother so much that he wants him to have a bank balance that many a civilized woman will find sexually appealing. He does so merely because he does not like having a worn-out-clothes-wearing person that looks like him. Lest he be mistaken for him. Or vice versa.

In other words, parents are not really supportive of their children because they want their children to succeed. Their supporting their children is merely their desperate, subconscious attempt to avoid appearing to have bred a failure, or failures, in the eyes of their friends, neighbours, and/or enemies. (That, of course, depends on their child's age. If their child is still too young to be expected to be a success, then their attempt is for the future. Whereas their attempt is for the present, in cases where their child is too old not to be expected to be a success.)

Like I concluded an essay titled "Why We Weep:" "After being told about the death of a friend or a family member or a lover, we cry; not because they left, but because they left us." I mean, last time I checked a dead person was not capable of being hurt, not even by their own death.

(Side Note: Many, if not most, readers of this essay read it merely because: [1] *they* failed to resist the curiosity that was brought about by its title; [2] they thought that this essay will make *them* laugh; [3] they thought that my thoughts will make *them* think, and as a result, inspire independent thought; or [4] they merely wanted to "kill time," and as a result, get rid of *their* boredom.

As the reader is likely to have noticed, at the core of all the above possible reasons hides the readers' loss or gain, or pleasure or pain, not this writing's writer or his at odds with the masses' opinions.)

Every Man for Himself

(I have, with the previous writing, attempted to link man's pleasure or pain, or loss or gain, with every single deed that he does or does not do. I will, with this writing, attempt to link man's selfishness with his religiousness.)

In his essay, "What is Man?", Mark Twain asserts that: (1) Man is merely a machine; (2) Man's mind is, by itself, incapable of producing anything new; it merely responds to external influences; and (3) Every single decision that man takes with regard to saying or not saying, doing or not doing, something is primarily determined by his desire to experience pleasure or to avoid pain.

With the last still in the reader's mind, I would like to share, "The Paradox of Selflessness," the shortest "essay" that I have ever published. Here goes! "Selfless people do not serve others merely because they love serving *others*; they serve others merely because *they* love serving others." In other words, a selfless person is not devoted to others merely because he cares more about *other people* than himself. He is devoted to others merely because *he* cares more about other people than himself.

As may be expected, man's selfishness is found in every single sphere of his life. As an example, let us look at his selfishness as an employee. An employee does not work merely because he likes working for his employer or because his employer is trying to "change the world." He does so primarily to make a living. (In the rare instance where an employee truly loves doing whatever it is that they are employed to do, and making a living isn't their primary incentive, one could argue that their love for their job, not their job itself or their employer's good heart, is the primary, if not the sole, reason that they do what they do.) Likewise, employers do not hire employees merely because the employees are in need of a source of income. They do so primarily, if not solely, because they believe that, as I have already argued, what the employees will demand every four weeks is peanuts when compared to the money that the employees will make for them every single workday.

Finally, let us now shift our focus from man's relationship with his financial saviour to his relationship with his spiritual saviour.

Man does not pray merely because he thinks that his God deserves it. He usually prays merely because of nothing but (1) a bad situation that he is in—in other words, to get God to get rid of whatever that is troubling him; or (2) a bad situation that he does not want to be in: in other words, to qualify for the sought-after walk through the Pearly Gates, and as a result, avoid being grilled until hell freezes over. The reader can, of course, argue that there are countless people who pray to thank God, not to ask Him for anything. Indeed. Having said that, one could then argue that such people pray merely to increase the chances of them continuing to experience the pleasure of having whatever it is that God has blessed them with. Or to decrease the chances of God taking away whatever it is that they think they will, in His eyes, come across as not being thankful for, should they not pray to thank Him for whatever it is that he has blessed them with—which will, of course, subject them to the pain of losing whatever it is that God has blessed them with.

Man does not help others merely to help others. He helps others, usually unbeknown to those that he is helping and at times himself, merely as a subconscious attempt to triple the odds of him being granted a one-way ticket to heaven.

Man adheres to religion as his (usually subconscious) attempt to either go to heaven or to avoid burning in hell, after he has breathed his last. That is to say, man's adhering to religion is by no means about or for God. It is one way or another about: (1) his desire to experience the pleasures that he believes are to be experienced in heaven; and/or (2) his fear of experiencing the pain that is said to await those who will find eternal residency in hell.

It goes without saying that many a reader will regard my assertion that man is a selfish creature as absurd. There are two possible reasons that I could come up with. Firstly, that assertion is too "unorthodox" for many a reader's liking. Secondly, and perhaps more unfortunate, I am just a 28-year-old boy. Or so claims my parents and, as a result, the identity number with which the Department of Home Affairs refers to me. (Like all human beings, I was not there when I was born—mentally, that is. So I'm not really sure as to whether or not I am as old as my parents claims.) Anyway, allow me to share a proverb by men who came centuries before my great-grandfather; a proverb that somewhat justifies my assertion. Here goes! "(the) Devil take the hindmost," which is said to mean that, "everyone should (or does) look after their own interests rather than considering those of others." In other words, "you should think of yourself and not be concerned about other people; look after yourself and let *the devil take the hindmost*" (with allusion to a chase by the Devil, in which the slowest will be caught).

According to *New Oxford American Dictionary*, that proverb is an equivalent of the proverb, "Every man for himself."

FAITH AND RATIONALITY

The Religion I Subscribe to

I strongly believe that human suffering would eventually be dramatically reduced, if not eradicated, if we invest in developing a society of Independent Thinkers.

Granted, thinking isn't everything: one might even go so far as to say that thinking alone will not solve anything. Having said that, I believe that at the core of most, if not all, causes or forms of human suffering lies: (1) *Thinking*, i.e., human deeds, which were brought about by our thinking or lack thereof; and/or (2) *Perspective*, i.e., the attitude that we have towards things that cause human suffering, e.g., death; an attitude that is, of course, attributable to nothing but our thinking. I mean, who the hell decided that death should pain those who are left behind? Anyway, I believe that pain, unless it is physical, was sold to us (by our culture). For it only exists in our minds.

So my intention, with the seemingly random, not to mention silly, things that I usually say, isn't to teach anyone anything. Unlike most teachers, I do not think that human suffering is, for the most part, due to the lack of knowledge. My humble attempt is merely to make those who are fortunate or unfortunate enough to come across what I think, think. Anyway, I will not attempt to further give grounds for my seemingly excessive, not to mention overrated, advocacy of Independent Thinking. For I believe that what I have just disclosed is sufficient. By the way, I only use "Independent Thinking" for emphatic purposes. That term is somewhat tautological—to me at least. For I do not think that the mental activity that we usually refer to as "thinking" deserves to be called that if it isn't done independently.

In closing, it goes without saying that bringing thinking into my attempt to explore religion is likely to come across as unnecessary to some readers, despite the fact that beliefs are acquired, not inborn—which means that both the acquirement and the rejection of a belief are mental processes. What's more, like all social constructs, although it has brought about countless concrete things (churches, religious books, church badges, uniforms, photographs of church leaders—which are hung on the walls of some believers' homes, etc.), religion is an abstraction, that is, it exists nowhere except in our minds.

Faith and Rationality: Oil and Water?

Believe it or not, 90% of the people whose intellectual capacity I revere happen to be nonbelievers. (I urge the religious reader not to be angered by that statement's implication and not to be intimidated by such a high percentage. After all, I could be referring to nine [of the ten] people [whom I regard as remarkable thinkers, not legions of men].)

At any rate, when looked at through eyes that have been purified by reason, there are two kinds of human beings: (1) *thinkers* — those who think and then arrive at a conclusion that isn't contaminated by the rest of the world's opinions or worldview; and (2) *parrots* — those who, through the use of a linguistic veil called paraphrasing, parrot popular opinions of men who thought for themselves and at times opinions parroted by other parrots).

There are, as far as I can see, only two factors that determine whether or not one will accept whatever it is that one is told or sold: (1) *reasoning* — carried out by whomever that is told or sold whatever; and (2) *authority* — the trust, respect, fear, et cetera, that whomever that is told or sold whatever has with regard to whomever that told or sold them whatever.

I mentioned that merely because being a believer or a nonbeliever seems to, as I am about to attempt to illustrate, be determined by either of those two factors.

Finally, let us end this writing with its beginning.

Before and while writing this book, I came across innumerable articles that are relevant to what we have just touched on. Some questioned whether there is, whereas some asserted that there is, a correlation between intellect and ignorance and religious beliefs and lack thereof. For example, Stephen J. Dubner asked, with the title of an article that was published on Freakonomics.com, "Does More Education Lead to Less Religion?"[2] Whereas Chris Barker, with the title of an article that was published in the *Freethinker*, asserted that, "Atheists Are More Intelligent Than Religious People."[3]

Labelling: By Belief or Lack Thereof

When looked at through eyes that have been contaminated by religion, there are only two kinds of human beings: namely, believers and nonbelievers.

Having said that, there are, as far as believing in a god and our habit of labelling is concerned, three major kinds of human beings: (1) *theists*, namely, those who believe in the existence of a god or gods; (2) *atheists*, namely, those with the theory or belief that God does not exist; and (3) *agnostics*, namely, those who claim neither faith nor disbelief in God. As I once quipped, "An agnostic is someone who has low self-esteem and an equal number of theist and atheist friends."

At any rate, religion is by no means natural. It is, as I have already said to believe it to be, a social construct. In other words, religion, like culture and language, was fed to us. So, technically, every single human being is born an agnostic. Which then means that an agnostic is either someone who has rejected both theism and atheism from the word go or someone who, after being a theist or an atheist or both, has returned to man's "default" religious standpoint.

Needless to say, any literature that does not touch on the belief and the disbelief in the existence of God, while it aims to cover the most important aspects of religion, would be incomplete. For religion "is," to borrow *New Oxford American Dictionary's* definition, "the belief in and worship of a superhuman controlling power, especially a personal God or gods."

Anyway, with the following writings on faith and rationality, I will attempt to shed light on some of the reasons as to why it is impossible to concurrently be rational and religious. Or so it seems. As may be expected, I would like to begin with the never-ending infamous debate between theists and atheists. But before I do, I would like to share, "The Lifespan of a Miracle", an already published essay with which I attempted to explore the concept of miracles.

The Lifespan of a Miracle

(This writing is partly made up of my reply to a friend of a friend with whom we were conversing. By the way, this is the very same guy whose attempt to define "love" I shared in the first chapter. Anyway, I believe that the subject of this writing is relevant to what I am about to explore because, as we all know, most, if not all, theists use "miracles" as proof that God does exist.)

We were talking about religion—the existence of God, to be precise.

Friend Y asked Friend X, the aforementioned guy, as to what makes him so sure that there is a God. Friend X confidently replied that question with the following question, "How do you explain miracles?"

For some reason, Friend Y's mouth remained shut. I

then asked Friend X, as any student of semantics would, what he means by *miracle* and he simply replied that a miracle is any event whose cause we do not know. I then asked him if that then means that a miracle is dependent on its observer's ignorance.

After that question, which Friend X treated as a rhetorical question, I told him that: "It is said that there once existed a primitive tribe whose members believed that lightning was God's way of telling them that they have infuriated Him. Because of that, whenever lightning struck, they sacrificed the life of one member of their tribe. And as may be expected, in instances were the lightning persisted despite the fact that they have just slaughtered one member of their tribe, they then sacrificed the life of a child. For they, like many a man does, believed that children are 'pure.' However, as we gathered more and more knowledge with regard to how the physical world functions, we learned that lightning is by no means brought about by the fact that God is mad at us. For a simpler example, let us use the process of evaporation. To a primitive tribe that had water on the ground after a heavy rainfall, the disappearance of the rainwater in question was a miracle. For they did not know what evaporation is. We, too, the so-called civilized beings, would have labelled such a natural phenomenon as a miracle, should we have existed before the process of evaporation was known, understood, and, more importantly, believed by man."

Anyway, I have shared that anecdote merely to: (1) share two simple examples that reveal the flaw in Friend X's argument; an argument that is usually used when many, if not most, believers attempt to justify their belief in the existence of God; and (2) show or remind the reader that miracles are dependent on their observers' ignorance with regard to the observed. In the same way that perfection is dependent on the observer's success or failure to notice the observed's defects.

Back to my conversation with Friend X and Friend Y.

Friend X's definition of *miracle* does not differ from *New Oxford American Dictionary's*, namely, "A surprising and welcome event that is not explicable by natural or scientific laws and is therefore considered to be the work of a divine agency." The part that this writing revolves around is, of course, " *... and is therefore considered to be the work of a divine agency.*" Obviously, if you do not know what electricity is and how it functions, then pressing a switch and "there being light" will be a miracle to you. Well, that is until you come across a physical science textbook. The birth of a child, too, is a miracle to an observer that is ignorant of the biological processes of conception and childbirth.

At any rate, as we live, experiment, experience, and learn, we know more and more as to how the natural world functions. The acquirement of the collective knowledge that we, human beings, have was, still is, and will forever be, a gradual process, not a single event. Which then means that if a miracle is merely an event whose cause we do not understand or cannot account for, then a miracle is a relative and, perhaps more important, a temporary phenomenon: in many, if not most, or even all, cases. In other words, we know, today, more than we did, say, a thousand years ago. Which then means that we should have, today, fewer miracles that we had a thousand years ago.

In a word, the more we know, the fewer miracles there are or ought to be.

A relevant remark that Robert G. Ingersoll is said to have said comes to mind: "Ignorance worships mystery; reason explains it: the one grovels, the other soars. No wonder that fable is the enemy of knowledge."

In closing, I would like to cite a relevant passage from *The Tyranny of Words*, a book that is said to have been written by Stuart Chase. "A savage has little knowledge of natural causes. Tribes exist to whom the part played by the father in the conception of a child is unknown. It is held that a demon enters into the mother's womb. It is not quite fair to call savages superstitious in such cases, for no better explanations are available."

The Burden of Proof

As the patient reader will find out when I conclude this chapter, I strongly believe that "the truth" isn't a prerequisite for religion's fruitfulness. Having said that, I would still like to share a few opinions with regard to the truthfulness of some religious claims, especially that of the existence of God.

Like I attempted to do with the anecdote about Friend X's use of events that he or we do not understand or cannot account for, that is, "miracles," as evidence that God does exist, I will merely touch on the flaw or flaws found in arguments that are usually used to prove or defend the belief in God's existence. Like I disclosed, my intention is not to convert believers into nonbelievers or vice versa. Anyway, I hope that the mere act of touching on some irrationality that is found in some claims and some teachings of some "sub-religions" will help some theists better understand why it is inevitable for some people to be atheists.

The burden of proof is a phrase that is usually associated with a Latin maxim, which is said to translate to, "The necessity of proof always lies with the person who lays charges." In law, the plaintiff, i.e., the person who brings a case against another in a court of law, is responsible for providing the court with evidence that supports his or her allegation against the defendant, i.e., the individual, company, or institution sued or accused in a court of law. For example, if I were to accuse the reader of having stolen from me, the burden of proof would then be on me to provide the evidence that the reader indeed stole from me. It wouldn't be the reader's obligation to provide the evidence that the reader did not steal whatever that I would have accused the reader of having stolen.

At any rate, one can, with reason, assert that the claim that God does not exist would not have been asserted, if the claim that He does were never asserted. Which then means that the burden of proof is on theists. (As far as the existence of God debate is concerned, what theists did is—to employ an analogy—claim that there exists a snake that has seven heads. But instead of substantiating their bold claim by simply showing atheists that particular snake, they, contrary to expectations, demand that atheists, that is, those who are not convinced by their claim, prove that such a snake does not exist.) Having said that, there is a "revelation" that I would like to touch on.

Looking at what atheism is, that is, the theory that God does not exist, theists could argue that the burden of proof is also on atheists. Seeing that atheists, like theists, are making a bold claim; a claim that they, too, cannot prove. Having said that, an atheist with a functioning mind can counterattack that with the argument that atheism is the antithesis of theism; which means that, as I have just said, atheism would not have been, should theism not have been. In the very same way that soldiers did not invent war; war invented them. Perhaps that is the reason why agnosticism seems to be the most intellectual religious standpoint. While I understand why atheists do not believe that God exists—as I am about to attempt to illustrate with some of the following writings, I find their spending their valuable time and mental energies on trying to reason theists out of theism to unfortunately make one question their intellect. As someone once said, you cannot reason someone out of a position that they did not reason themselves into.

By the way, from what I said earlier on, the alert reader is likely to have correctly supposed that I believe that not believing that God exists isn't necessarily the same as believing that He doesn't.

What's more, there is another issue: namely, atheists' inability to refute theism does not necessarily strengthen the claim that makes theists, theists. For example, person$_1$'s inability to refute person$_2$'s claim that person$_2$ once ran into a snake that spoke Swahili does not necessarily make person$_2$'s claim true or more plausible.

(Side Note: It would, of course, be a lie to say that theists do not provide atheists with proof that substantiates their claim of there being a God. As we all know, they actually do. Having said that, their "proof" is nine times out of ten akin to Friend X's use of miracles to prove that God definitely exists.)

God's Dad's Mom's Dad's Mom's Dad

Atheists demand proof that God exists. While theists demand proof that God does not exist.

One can, with reason, suppose that if the two were to employ a court of law, the latter would lose. Having said that, the challenge with the existence of God debate, or any debate that revolves around beliefs, is that being rational is usually equivalent to not saying anything at all.

At any rate, the chances of that debate producing a winner were lessened, if not eradicated, by atheists' opposing assertion: namely, the claim that God does not exist. For if atheism was merely the disbelief in the existence of God, as opposed to being the belief that God does not exist, the existence of God debate would have been put to an end by simply asking theists to prove their claim. Granted, that would not necessarily mean that God's existence would be proved or provable. Having said that, that would make this infamous debate less complex. Seeing that theists wouldn't easily evade their responsibility, not to mention inability, to provide evidence that supports or proves the truth of their claim that God does exist, by demanding that atheists provide evidence that supports or proves the truth of their claim that He does not exist.

As we all know, in their attempt to convince atheists, countless theists use the beauty, order, and wise arrangement of the universe—which they, of course, regard as a miracle—as evidence that proves their claim of there being a God. In philosophy, such an argument is called a Teleological Argument, i.e., the argument for the existence of God from the evidence of order, and hence design, in nature. In Christian theology, it is referred to as the Argument from Design, i.e., the argument that God's existence is demonstrable from the evidence of design in the universe.

Anyway, if that is anything to go by, then one can, with reason, claim that theists' bold claim of there being a God wasn't really brought about by the beauty of and the order in the universe. Their belief that God exists seems to rest upon another belief: namely, the belief that something—the universe, in this case—cannot come from nothing; that someone or something must have created it. Perhaps that is the logic behind God's other name; namely, "the Creator."

As may be expected, the belief that something cannot be made from nothing invites the following question: If something cannot come from nothing, then who or what created the Creator? Obviously, if one happens to be one of the few people who have, if not the only person that has, the "correct" answer as to who created the Creator, their answer, too, will invite the following question: Who or what created the Creator's creator?

Those who are bored and intellectually shortsighted enough to answer that question will, of course, inevitably invite the question: Who or what created the Creator's creator's creator?

Clergy Robes versus Lab Coats

An exploration of the debate on the existence of God would be incomplete without touching on the role that science plays in the existence of atheists. What's more, it goes without saying that the Book of Genesis's narrative as to who created the world and science textbooks' theory as to what created the world have divided the world: both physically and mentally.

At any rate, one can, with reason, suppose that while science did not bring about atheism, it has brought about some atheists. "When the new technologies and techniques and spirit of men like Galileo, Newton, and Bacon laid the foundations of natural science, they also discredited the authority of earlier accounts of the physical world, as found, for example, in the great tale of Genesis." Neil Postman is said to have written. "By calling into question the truth of such accounts in one realm, science undermined the whole edifice of belief in sacred stories and ultimately swept away with it the source to which most human beings had looked for *moral* authority."[4] (Note how, as I have attempted to illustrate with "The Lifespan of a Miracle," the progress made in science inevitably undermines the claims made by religion.)

"[The invention of] glasses not merely opened people's eyes but their minds: seeing was believing. In the more primitive stages of thought the institutions and ratiocination of authority were sacrosanct, and the person who insisted on seeing proof of imagined events was reviled as the famous disciple had been: he was a doubting Thomas." Lewis Mumford is said to have written. "Now the eye became the most respected organ. Roger Bacon refuted the superstition that diamonds could not be broken except by using goat's blood by resorting to experiment: he fractured the stones without using blood and reported: '*I have seen this work with my own eyes.*' The use of glasses in the following centuries magnified the authority of the eye."[5]

In closing, I would like to share two passages that are relevant to the gist of this writing. "The printing press placed the Word of God on every family's kitchen table, and in a language that could be understood." Neil Postman is said to have written. "With God's word so accessible, Christians did not require the papacy to interpret it for them. Or so millions of them came to believe."[6]

As we all know, science is, amongst other things, an ongoing process of acquiring new and getting rid of some old "beliefs," whereas religion is static with regard to its claims and principles. Or so it seems. "Principles are not tools by which discoveries are made, for they tend to close the mind against free enquiry." Stuart Chase is said to have written. "When men observe the world in the light of ideals which they consider sacred and timeless, they tend to develop priests rather than scientists."[7]

As may be expected, there is, or so there seems to be, a war between science and religion; a never-ending war where theists shoot atheists with labels such as "damned," while atheists retaliate with terms like "intellectually backward."

(Side Note: Although both sure have their own usefulness, I would like to end what we have just touched on by reminding the reader of the fact that religion and science can, in countless cases, be blamed for the deaths of gazillions of human beings. As I have generalized elsewhere, "Religion makes people kill each other. Science supplies them with weapons.")

Believing is Seeing

Contrary to what the learned reader is likely to have assumed, the above "mistake" is intentional. Even though the proverb: "Seeing is believing," which is said to mean that you need to see something *before* you can accept that it really exists or occurs, is relevant to what I am about to attempt to explore with this writing: namely, believers' use of what they see or have seen as events or incidents that confirm God's existence.

Getting what one has prayed for is perhaps the second most common "evidence" that theists use in their attempt to prove their theory of there being a God. But, like all non-scientific theories, that theory cannot be falsified.

Allow me to cite a passage from *Technopoly*, a book that is said to have been written by Neil Postman. By the way, this passage is from, "Scientism," a chapter with which Postman, amongst other things, argued that "social science" is a misnomer because what "social scientists" (viz., sociologists, anthropologists, psychologists, economists, political scientists, etc.) do does not qualify to be called science. For, as he justified his remark, what we may call science, then, is the quest to find the immutable and universal laws that govern processes, presuming that there are cause-and-effect relations among these processes. It follows that the quest to understand human behavior and feeling can in no sense except the most trivial be called science. "The status of social-science methods is further reduced by the fact that there are almost no experiments that will reveal a social-science theory to be false. Theories in social science disappear, apparently, because they are boring, not because they are refuted. But, as Karl Popper has demonstrated, science depends on the requirement that theories must be stated in a way that permits experiments to reveal that they are false. If a theory cannot be tested for its falsity, it is not a scientific theory—as, for example, Freud's theory of the Oedipus complex. Psychiatrists can provide many examples supporting the validity of the theory, but they have no answer to the question 'What evidence would prove the theory false?' Believers in the God theory (sometimes called Creation Science) are silent on the question 'What evidence would show that there is no God?'"

Let us now bring many a believer's use of answered prayers as an indication of God's existence back into our exploration.

In incidents where, say, parents who are desperately in need of a "miracle" to save their newborn whose life is slipping away with every single breath that he or she takes pray, but their child dies nonetheless, such incidents are seldom, if not never, seen as proof that God does not exist. As a matter of fact, most, if not all, believers are likely to regard them as part of God's ultimate plan for humanity.

That is, of course, by no means limited to "bad" things like death.

As is almost always the case when it comes to our successes, chance is seldom considered as a possible cause. As we all know, man readily considers the possibility of chance being the cause only when it comes to his failures, whereas he almost always attributes his successes to himself, or to be more specific, his education, skills, charm, experience, looks, or intellect, and—if he is excited enough—God. Such a phenomenon is, of course, called a self-serving bias; which refers to our habit of attributing our successes to internal or personal factors, whereas we attribute our failures to external or situational factors. In the former instance, the bias is a mechanism that is used to enhance the successful person's self-esteem. In the latter instance, the bias is used to protect the failure's self-esteem.

At any rate, when a theist man that has been unemployed for years gets a job, it is seen as normal. When an agnostic man that has been unemployed for years gets a job, it is seen as normal. When an atheist man that has been unemployed for years gets a job, it, too, is seen as normal. However, when a nonbeliever that has been unemployed for years becomes a believer, and then it happens that he gets a job, a few days or months after that, his then having a payslip will, nine times out of ten, be attributed to nothing but his having converted to a believer. The same claim would have, of course, been made if the opposite happened. In other words, if an employed believer quits believing, and then it happens that he loses his job, a few days or months after converting from a believer to a nonbeliever, his having switched to the other side of the theistic fence will, nine times out of ten, be blamed for his then lack of a payslip.

Which then means that if one gets what one has prayed for, then that proves that God exists. However, if one does not get what one has prayed for, then that merely proves that it is not the right time for one to get whatever it is that one has prayed for. What's more, more often than not, the person who did not get whatever it is that they have asked God for, and at times their family and friends, will be of the belief that God is delaying whatever it is that they have prayed for merely because He has something better in store for them; e.g., a bigger house, a better job, a faster car, a longer-tempered lover, a less talkative mother-in-law, et cetera.

To sum up, while seeing might lead to believing, believing usually leads to not seeing. For man mostly sees what he is looking for. Seldom what he is looking at.

That is, of course, attributable to his beliefs, cultural and religious conditioning, expectations, et cetera.

In closing, allow me to share, "The wish is father to the thought," a relevant proverb that is said to mean that we believe a thing because we wish it to be true.

Who or What Does "God" Refer to?

Finally, let us now bring semantics into our exploration of the existence of God debate.

I have had the privilege of witnessing numerous debates on the existence of God. What's more, I partook in a few. Because of that, I have heard all kinds of arguments, by both intelligent and not-so-intelligent debaters. Believe it or not, as I have lamented in the first chapter, I have never heard a single debater demand that the abstraction that is about to be debated be defined before it is debated (and that includes debaters whom most, if not all, people would label as "intelligent").

Now the question is, by the word *God*, are all those who are taking part in the existence of God debate really referring to the very same thing, being, or phenomenon? In other words, is theists' assertion that God does exist, and atheists' assertion that He does not, really based on the belief, on the one hand, and the disbelief, on the other, in the existence of the very same thing or being?

At any rate, it is worth reminding the reader that language, say, English, did not make, say, a red car, red. As a matter of fact, English did not even produce the object to which we refer with the word *car*. In the same way that language did not invent, or should not have invented, God. Or rather, the thing or being to which we refer with the word *God*. That is to say, if God really exists, then he or she or it would have still existed, should we have not come up with a name with which we refer to him or her or it. Like I said in the first chapter, the existence of organisms to which we refer with the word *trees* are the reason that we came up with the word *tree*: the word *trees* isn't the reason that organisms to which we refer with that word exist. As it is said in Genesis 2:19, KJV, "And out of the ground the Lord God formed every beast of the field, and every fowl of the air; and brought them unto Adam to see what he would call them: and whatsoever Adam called every living creature, that was the name thereof." In other words, God created the animals, *and then* Adam named them, not the other way around.

As I have said a thousand times already, while words only exist in our minds, there are concrete things to which we refer with words like *car, tree, chair, mountain*, and the like. In other words, not only can we see the referents to which such words refer, we can also touch them. However, the same cannot, of course, be said about whomever or whatever it is that we use the word *God* to refer to.

At any rate, most of those who partake in the existence of God debate are so blinded by their eagerness to prove their opponents wrong, that they always disregard what I believe ought to be central to their debate: namely, the answer to the question, What do you mean by "God"?

Perhaps having created the universe is the most common thing that is to be found in most, if not all, definitions of the word *God*. As I have already presumed, that explains the origin of, or the logic behind, "the Creator," God's other name. The one thing that those who argue for creationism and those who argue for the Big Bang theory agree on is, of course, that the universe was one way or another created. In other words, existence had a genesis. So, technically, there is or was such a thing or being as "the Creator." That is, of course, assuming that there was indeed a period when the universe did not exist. (Notice how the mere act of changing "God" to "the Creator" seems to change everything.) The dispute seems to start as soon as we attach a thing, process, or being to the name "the Creator." Seeing that, to a creationist, the name "the Creator" refers to whomever or whatever that they refer to with the word *God*. Whereas, to those who believe in the Big Bang theory, "the Creator" refers to whatever that they refer to with the term "the Big Bang."

Finally, although I have exclusively focused on religion's and science's theory with regard to our creator and origin, I find it worth reminding the reader of the obvious: namely, while either creationism or the Big Bang theory might be true, both cannot, of course, be so, and, perhaps more important than that, both might actually be wrong. Having said that, despite the fact that I have witnessed gazillions of debates on the existence of God and as a result our origin, I have never heard a single debater remind those involved that both theories might actually be wrong. Reason? Simple. The debaters, blinded by their emotional attachment to the theory that they are defending, and their eagerness to refute the theory that their opponent is arguing for, fail to consider the seemingly obvious fact that both theories might actually be wrong.

(Side Note: In addition to the fact that the theory of there being a God is not provable or disprovable, like with almost all debates, the debaters' "ego" and "identity" play a tremendous role in leaving the debaters where they were before the debate began, with regard to their opinions and beliefs. I will, when concluding this book, come back to that.

By the way, the reader will be pleased to hear that this was the last writing with regard to the existence of God debate. I will, with what is left of the second part of this chapter, attempt to explore the incompatibility between some religious teachings and rationality.)

Writing in Tongues

Although I have already attempted to do so in the first chapter, I find it necessary for me to touch on the problem that is brought about by misinterpretation. Before I attempt to explore the incompatibility between some religious teachings and rationality.

At any rate, it matters not whether God wrote the Bible by Himself (as some people believe) or through the hands of a chosen few men. What matters is that the Bible was written to be read by human beings. What's more, as I have already asserted in the first chapter, readers' interpretation of a text matters more than what the writer meant to convey with the text.

As we all know, whenever two Christians have different and at times conflicting, say, lifestyles, thanks to their dissimilar interpretation of a biblical command, they, nine times out of ten, consult the Bible to prove each other wrong. However, not only does the Bible continuously fail to settle the debate between Christian theists and atheists, in many a case, a reference to the Bible fails to settle a dispute between two Christians—people whose deeds and thoughts are supposedly governed by the very same book.

Misinterpretation is one of the things, if not the only thing, that makes it impossible for the Bible to be an authoritative manual to which Christians go for rules of behaviour. Such a claim is, of course, substantiated by the countless instances where two Christians with incompatible beliefs use the very same religious book in their attempt to prove the each wrong.

Let us, as an example, touch on the infamous debate as to whether or not Christians are permitted to eat pork.

In Leviticus 11:7-8 (ESV), the third book of the Bible, which is said to be regarded as a handbook for priests (perhaps because it contains the details of law and ritual), the Lord is quoted as having said the following to

Moses and to Aaron with regard to "clean" and "unclean" animals: "And the pig, because it parts the hoof and is cloven-footed but does not chew the cud, is unclean to you. You shall not eat any of their flesh, and you shall not touch their carcasses; they are unclean to you."

Such a divide is by no means only attributable to incompatible translations of the very same verse. In some cases, Christians actually interpret the same verse the same way. However, in some instances, the divide is brought about by two contradictory verses, not by two incompatible interpretations of the very same verse. For example (with the two verses that I have just cited still in the reader's mind), some people, in their attempt to prove to Christians who do not eat pork that eating pork isn't forbidden, cite, 1 Timothy 4:1-5 (NIV), "The Spirit clearly says that in later times some will abandon the faith and follow deceiving spirits and things taught by demons. Such teachings come through hypocritical liars, whose consciences have been seared as with a hot iron. They forbid people to marry and order them to abstain from certain foods, which God created to be received with thanksgiving by those who believe and who know the truth. For everything God created is good, and nothing is to be rejected if it is received with thanksgiving, because it is consecrated by the word of God and prayer."

Speaking of eating pork, allow me to share a comment that was anonymously left on some online forum's debate as to whether or not eating pork is forbidden: "It's OK. That's the Old Testament. So, it doesn't count." Another remark (also voiced anonymously, but relevant and interesting nonetheless) went as follows: "It is not a sin to eat pork. The law was only for the Hebrews. Anyways, Jesus did make all foods clean."

It goes without saying that what one could reasonably call "hetero-interpretation" of the very same verse or verses is by no means the only thing that divides men who are seemingly united by Christianity. In addition to the ambiguity that our everyday languages are full of, the fact that the Bible is divided into the Old- and the New Testament is usually responsible for some divide between some Christians. As the learned reader is likely to have detected, the two books, Leviticus and 1 Timothy, which I have cited as an illustration of how Christians are typically divided by the Bible, also serve as an illustration of the incompatibility between some parts of the Old- and some parts of the New Testament.

Believe it or not, as if the fact that our everyday languages are usually open to interpretation and the fact that the Bible is divided into the Old- and the New Testament were not confusing and divisive enough, some people believe that some words in, and therefore some parts of, non-Hebrew Bibles were mistranslated into whatever languages that the non-Hebrew Bibles are in. (Side Note: I am well aware of the fact that some assertions that I would have penned come the end of this chapter, are likely to be untrue. Owing to nothing but my misinterpretation of a verse or two. Be that as it may, such seemingly disadvantageous instances will actually demonstrate, and as a result substantiate, at least one of the countless assertions that I have stated: namely, the assertion that the ambiguity that non-technical languages are overpopulated with leads to at best a misconstruction and at worst division between many a man.

What's more, I am confident that I am by no means the only person who misinterprets the following scriptures and notions. Actually, I will, in some writings, argue for the one side of an interpretation that has divided Christians.

By the way, I will, in some of the subsequent writings, continue to occasionally cite a few scriptures. But I beg the reader not to allow the mere act of quoting scriptures to be the sole reason that the reader finds my reasoning reasonable. For, as the saying goes, "the devil can quote scripture for his purpose.")

Love is Conditional

*(Like when I made the assertion that a human be-
ing is an intrinsically selfish creature, I, thanks to the
claim that that title is made up of, will, of course, be
disagreed with by most, if not all, readers. Because, in
addition to having been brought up to regard love as a
sacred thing, the implication that is to be drawn from
that title is that we, the people to whom other people's
love is directed, are not as special as being loved made
us believe.)*

Why do you (or did you) love your mother? If she were
still the very same person, but not your mother (or a
relative), would you have loved her (the same way that
you do or did)?

Although most of us have never really given this
much thought: we love our family members merely because they are our family members. And that is generally because society subtly hints that it is "normal," or
even obligatory, for one to love one's family members.

One can, with reason, assert that we love people because of their having met a condition or two, not because of their being them. Conditions that a man needs
to meet before some, if not most, women can love "him"

are to be gathered from statements such as: "I am into tall guys," "I don't want to live in the ghetto for the rest of my life," "Intelligent men are such a turn on," "I love shopping," "Potbellies are such a turn off," "Being a pedestrian sucks," et cetera.

So, technically, a person cannot really be loved, the closest that we can get to that is loving something, or if we are lucky: some things, about that person. If that is indeed the case, then isn't love conditional? If love isn't conditional, then why doesn't everybody love everybody? If your love for your lover were attributable to nothing but their being, say, a comedian or a trial lawyer, and then, after a few months or years, they stopped joking or lying for a living, would you then still love them?

Let us briefly focus on the assertion that a person cannot be loved: we can only love something or some things about them.

Let us, as an example, use the reader's ex-lovers.

What do they have in common? Your answer to that is probably what you loved, and probably still love, not them. (It goes without saying that the answer to that question is by no means limited to a person's so-called character. For, as we all know, a man's deep pockets are, in countless cases, the only reason that a woman truly believes that she is deeply in love with him.) That is to

say, one can only love, say, a thing, for, say, its usefulness, its beauty, or the social status that having the thing
elevates one to, not the thing in itself. So, what one really loves, when one claims to love, say, sushi, is either the
taste that is and/or the nutrients that are to be derived
from eating sushi, or the image that eating or listing
sushi as one's favourite dish creates or maintains, not
the dish in itself. Like I once quipped, "Eating a salad
(in public) is an overweight person's (subconscious) attempt to appear to be in control of their weight."

In other words, gluttonous people do not really love
food. What they love is the comfort, as short-lived as it
might be, that they derive from eating. Similarly, porn
addicts do not really love porn. What they love is the
"excitement" that watching porn gives rise to and, maybe, the orgasm or orgasms that doing so usually bless
its audience with. In short, a thing is a means to an end.
What people love is the end, not the means or the thing
in itself.

To further substantiate my seemingly ridiculous
claim, let us examine how a romantic relationship
typically begins: A stranger meets another. No love is
claimed or felt. But after a few months, weeks, or even
minutes, of "getting to know each other," the two "feel"
what they call love (for one another). Now the question

is, if it is indeed possible to love a person, not something or some things about that person (e.g., their character, their intellect, their sexual performance, their beliefs, their job title, their penis size, their looks, their bank balance, their bra size, et cetera.), then why do we regard the getting-to-know-each-other phase that precedes or preceded many, if not most, relationships as pivotal or necessary? Aha!

It goes without saying that the thing or emotion or process to which we refer with the word *hatred*, too, substantiates my claim. Owing to the fact that we are told that hatred is the antithesis of love. Now the question is, can you really hate someone or something without any reason at all? While we are at it, can you really love someone or something without any reason at all?

To sum up, whether intentional or not, subconsciously or not, we earn both being loved and being hated. For love is, as I have just attempted to argue, nothing but an end result of a condition or conditions met. In other words, to be loved is to have met a condition or six.

(Side Note: This writing, like some herein, is from a collection of writings that I have already published. The reason that I shared it is, of course, because I find it relevant to this part of this chapter. Even though I am well aware that some people are of the opinion that the idea of "unconditional love" is not a religious invention, whereas others are of an opposing opinion.

Likewise, the opposing interpretations of the theme of the following writing, which I also borrow from my collection of already published writings, has divided Christians in the very same manner that Leviticus 11:7-8 has.)

In Defense of Divorce (and Breakups)

Part of what attracts us to our ideal other half is their looks. For example, their six-packs, unwrinkled skin, bow-legs, chiseled physique, gravity-defying breasts, ruler-and-milk-jealous-making teeth, and the like. Having said that, as we all know, their worldview and their beliefs—which, of course, usually shapes their so-called personality—play the foremost role.

Or so many a lover claims.

Anyway, like all organisms, a human being is a creature that is forever evolving. Its worldview and its beliefs are, of course, by no means exceptions. Which then means that one is never really the "same" person, from the beginning until the end of their being. (Of course, a change of one's worldview or beliefs does not necessarily lead to a change of one's so-called personality.)

At any rate, while a man and a woman or another man who are deeply in love with each other might have the same, or at least compatible, say, beliefs or lifestyles, it is possible for them to develop into individuals whose beliefs or lifestyles are no longer compatible. Or for them to simply grow apart.

In other words, "good" people do break up. Rather that, than force a relationship that isn't working out to work out. For that is rarely a fruitful exercise. Besides, "forever" is a very long time to promise someone.

(Side Note: As the alert reader is likely to have already noticed, one can, of course, argue that a woman can use, say, the fact that her man has lost his bodily shape or money or teeth, as a reasonable reason to break up with him; in instances where a man's physique or money or teeth was what his woman loved instead of "him.")

A Man's Other Half

We are told (by society and by the Bible) that a woman completes a man. (By the way, I strongly believe that the former's take on homosexuality was, in many cases, molded by the latter's. Owing to the fact that, although

I have heard gazillions of arguments against homosexuality, I have never heard a single argument as to why someone disapproves of homosexuality that isn't one way or another based on Christian teachings or claims.)

Well, I have a problem with that claim. Depending, of course, on what is meant by "complete." What needs to be asked is, "What can't a man be or do or get without a woman?" For a man can get, from any of his friends, almost everything that he gets from his woman: somebody to talk to; somebody to laugh with; somebody to eat with; somebody to listen to; somebody to cry with; somebody to starve with, et cetera.

Any of a man's friends or family members, good-looking or not, tall or short, old or young, male or female, can be that to him.

At any rate, a woman can only logically be said to be a man's missing other half if and only if having sex and/or reproducing is the two's sole objective. On second thought, I would like to take "having sex" out of the last sentence. For whether we like it or not, turn a blind eye or not, there are countless men who satisfy their sexual desire by having sex with another man. As we all know, in such cases, the anus plays vagina.

The same can, of course, be said about women getting sexual pleasure from sleeping with other women.

Granted, those women would have used an artificial penis. Be that as it may, an orgasm or two, they would have realized. For as far as sexual pleasure is concerned, our bodies cannot really differentiate between a penis that is made of flesh and one that is made of silicone or stainless steel. Which then means that, as I have already asserted, a woman can only be said to be a man's missing other half if and only if reproduction is the only object of all romantic relationships. Otherwise, both the man and the woman are easily replaceable by any random person of any random gender. Seeing that amongst a billion other things: A man can cook for another. A man can take a walk with another. A man can clean for another. A man can eat with another. A man can watch a movie with another. A man can choose an outfit for another. A man can satisfy another ... sexually.

To sum up, the claim that a man and a woman complete each other can only be said to be logical if and only if making babies is the ultimate reason that people get into romantic relationships. As I once quipped, the phrase "You complete me" is nonsensical. A couple is a "we," not a complete "me." And as John Lennon is said to have said, "They made us believe that each one of us is the half of an orange, and that life only makes sense when you find that other half. They did not tell us that we were born as whole, and that no one in our lives deserve to carry on his back such responsibility of completing what is missing on us: we grow through life by ourselves. If we have a good company it's just more pleasant."

(Side Note: I have absolutely no desire to get into this whole debate as to whether or not homosexuality is immoral. For I find a human being that hates another merely because of the gender of the people whom the other prefers to have sex with to be nothing but an end result of prying. As I once aphorized, "Man cannot be homophobic without having concerned himself with another's sex life." Another aphorism of mine that I find relevant goes as follows, "Homophobia is the ignorant and arrogant assumption that copulation and reproduction is all there is to a relationship."

What's more, there is yet another division, amongst literate human beings with access to the Bible, as to whether or not homosexuality is forbidden. I would like to, as an example, cite *Wikipedia's* page on Christianity and homosexuality, "The Bible refers to sexual practices that may be called 'homosexual' in today's world, but the original language texts of the Bible do not refer explicitly to homosexuality as a sexual orientation. For example, passages in the Old Testament book Leviticus prohibit 'lying with mankind as with womankind' and the story of Sodom and Gomorrah (Genesis 19) has been interpreted by some as condemning homosexual practice. ... Other interpreters, however, maintain that the Bible does not condemn homosexuality, arguing any of several points: (i) that the passages [Matthew 15:19, Mark 7:21, Acts 15:20, et al.] yield different meanings if placed in historical context, for instance the historical interpretation of Sodom's sins as being other than homosexuality; (ii) there may be questions surrounding the translation of rare or unusual words in the passages that some interpret as referring to homosexuals; (iii) both the Old Testament and New Testament contain passages that describe same-sex relationships."[8]

Anyway, I am confident that the alert reader was quick to notice the divisive role that context and mistranslation play in the division between those who believe that homosexuality is forbidden and those who argue otherwise.)

Love Thy Neighbour as Thyself

In his book, *Civilization and Its Discontents*, Sigmund Freud shared his take on Mark 12:31. Not only do I find

Freud's rational exploration of the commandment interesting, I also find his analysis to be relevant to this part of the chapter.

His remark went as follows, "We will adopt a naïve attitude towards it ['Thou shalt love thy neighbour as thyself'], as if we were meeting it for the first time. Thereupon we find ourselves unable to suppress a feeling of astonishment, as at something unnatural. Why should we do this? What good is it to us? Above all, how can we do such a thing? How could it possibly be done? My love seems to me a valuable thing that I have no right to throw away without reflection. It imposes obligations on me which I must be prepared to make sacrifices to fulfil. If I love someone, he must be worthy of it in some way or other. ... He will be worthy of it if he is so like me in important respects that I can love myself in him; worthy of it if he is so much more perfect than I that I can love my ideal of myself in him; I must love him if he is the son of my friend, since the pain my friend would feel if anything untoward happened to him would be my pain—I should have to share it. But if he is a stranger to me and cannot attract me by any value he has in himself or any significance he may have already acquired in my emotional life, it will be hard for me to love him. I shall even be doing wrong if I do, for my love is valued as a privilege by all those belonging to me; it is an injustice to them if I put a stranger on a level with them. But if I am to love him (with that kind of universal love) simply because he, too, is a denizen of the earth, like an insect or an earthworm or a grass-snake, then I fear that but a small modicum of love will fall to his lot and it would be impossible for me to give him as much as by all the laws of reason I am entitled to retain for myself. What is the point of an injunction promulgated with such solemnity, if reason does not recommend it to us?"

As is the case with the remarks—mine and others'—that I have shared with regard to religious commands and rationality: it matters not whether Freud, with the aforementioned remarks, is "right" or "wrong." What matters is that, as I have attempted to demonstrate, some people have (what they believe to be) valid reasons not to believe and/or not to believe some people's interpretation of some parts of the Bible.

(Side Note: One can, of course, use some of Freud's remarks to further substantiate my assertion that at the core of man's decision to do or not do something hides his loss or his gain and/or his pleasure or his pain.)

Predestination, the Will of God, and Free Will

Are we free to speak and free to act as per our desires, or are our words and our actions merely part of the fulfillment of God's plan for humanity?

In other words, was the decision to write this book brought about by my own desire, or was it predetermined—more than 6000 years before my father's mother met his father—that I will, at this very moment, find this taxing book worth spending my time and energy on and sacrificing my social life? Is your reading this book an end result of your own decision, or was it decided—centuries before I could even spell "i"—that you will be reading this book at this very moment?

At any rate, whether or not they are true, nothing is as comforting as religion's major claims. While, at the same time, what many a man infers from what they believe the doctrine of predestination to be or mean is arguably the most depressing thing to ever occupy man's mind. For predestination is, to some people at least, the belief that everything that will happen has already been decided by God or fate and cannot be changed.

As may be expected, that belief invites the following question: if every single thing that we did and will do was and is indeed already decided by God or fate, shouldn't we then absolve ourselves from the burden of being responsible for our own actions? Owing to the fact that predestination implies, to some people at least, that we are merely puppets whose strings were pulled in advanced by some puppet master called God; puppets whose actions are nothing but a means to realizing God's plan for humanity. As I once quipped, "If we really exist merely to fulfill God's plan for humanity, then life is a drama; God is the scriptwriter, the director, and the audience."

As I have already said, what the doctrine of predestination implies, to some people at least, is that man cannot reasonably be held accountable for the "bad" things that he did or does. Or be praised for the "good" things that he did or does. For everything that happened or is happening was already decided by God before it happened. Which then means that if predestination is anything to go by, then there is no such thing as a competent surgeon. In other words, all the people who died while they were being operated by a drunk or incompetent or absentminded surgeon died merely because their "character" has reached the end of its part in the script of life that was penned by some playwright called God, not because of the surgeon's deed or lack thereof.

Now the question is, if every single thing that we did

and will do was and has already been predetermined by God, shouldn't a rapist or murderer's deed be excused, for the poor rapist or murderer was merely acting as per the Almighty's script?

In a nutshell, predestination unwittingly implies that God, in his attempt to actualize whatever plan that He is said to have for humanity, makes some people kill some people. Yet, it is the poor killers that are arrested or killed. And as if that isn't enough, God, the very same being whose desire to actualize His own plan turned non-killers into killers, is going to judge the poor killers and then possibly punish them by sending them to hell come Judgment Day.

(Side Note: It goes without saying that, as many anti-science adherents of religion never forget to remind us, as depressing as what predestination unwittingly implies might be: when it comes to that inevitable time when one has no choice but to deal with the death of one's lover, friend, or family member, religion's claim of there being life after death is a billion times more comforting than the best that science can offer: namely, sleeping tablets, a rope, a razor, a gun, a bottle of whiskey, et cetera.)

The Purpose of Life

Naturally, with man's faculty of reason came the question, What is the purpose of life?

Perhaps religion is one of the very few things that human beings consult in their pursuit of the answer to the question as to what the purpose of life is—a question that, to this day, continues to leave countless thinkers with sleepless nights.

At any rate, the belief in the existence of God excuses those who believe in that claim from the intellectually burdensome mental voyage of seeking the answer to the question as to what the purpose of life is. While the idea of there not being a God, which implies that life is purposeless (as many, if not most, theists are quick to remind those who believe that God does not exist), is too much for the average human being to handle. Hence, I believe, many a man readily accepts whatever is claimed to be the purpose of life.

As we all know, most, if not all, of those who adhere to religion are of the belief that we are here merely to earn a one-way ticket to heaven ... or hell. Two aphorisms that I have already published come to mind: (1) If heaven really exists, then—technically—life is an activity that we keep ourselves busy with, while we wait for our death; and (2) If heaven really exists, then heaven is the job; unemployment is hell; and life is merely an interview.

As may be expected, many a rational man is then haunted by the following question, If life here on earth is merely a process by which God decides who goes and who does not go to heaven, then why didn't the Creator just create those who will come Judgment Day be seen as worth sending to heaven? (Since He is said to be omnipotent and because He is said to have already decided every single thing that we would have all done come the end of our lives.) What's more, if qualifying for a one-way ticket to heaven is indeed what the purpose of life on earth is, reason will inevitably inspire many a rational man to ask, What then is the purpose of heaven?

As the alert reader is likely to have noticed, similar to how the answer to the question, Who created the Creator?, invited the question, Who created the Creator's creator?, the answer to the question, What is the purpose of heaven?, will inevitably invite the question, What is the purpose of the purpose of heaven?

Preachers and Teachers

One of the most common mistaken impressions that are brought about and then perpetuated in church is that preachers are more knowledgeable than every single person that they preach to; in school, that teachers are more knowledgeable than every single person that they teach.

Those two assumptions are, of course, understandable and usually truthful in cases where the congregation or class is made up of children. However, as we all know, that isn't always the case. What's more, as those very few people who are knowledgeable enough to be humble with regard to their knowledge know, teaching is one of the best ways to learn. Like I once aphorized: To teach, learn. To learn, teach.

At any rate, whether or not it is intentional, most preachers and most teachers, by virtue of their method of preaching and that of teaching, teach those whom they preach to and those whom they teach to be nothing but passive consumers of whatever it is that is preached or taught.

Although the rest of this writing also applies to school, I will, to save the reader's time and my ink, narrow what's left of this writing to church.

It is unlikely for a member of a congregation to witness another congregant raise their hand, while the preacher is busy preaching, to ask the preacher whether or not what he or she is saying does not contradict what he or she said the previous Sunday; even many, if not all, of those who have been going to church every single Sunday for the past 5, 20, 50, 70 years, have never witnessed that. Even though preachers, too, are human. Which means that they, too, are not infallible. Surely there were countless instances where at least one member of a congregation interpreted a scripture better than their preacher did and, more importantly, instances where at least one member of a congregation got, as a result of their interpretation, a message that contradicts the one that their preacher got because of his interpretation of the scripture; with the member of the congregation being right.

At any rate, the intellectual submissiveness of the average member of a congregation was, before the invention of the printing press, excusable. For, apart from the then prevalence of illiteracy—which was in part attributable to the rarity of books, including the Bible—priests enjoyed a "knowledge monopoly." As Neil Postman is said to have written, "The mass-produced book, by placing the Word of God on every kitchen table, makes each [literate] Christian his own theologian—one might even say his own priest, or, better, from Luther's point of view, his own pope. In the struggle between unity and diversity of religious belief, the press favored the latter."9 Be that as it may, the role of preachers and, more importantly, the structure of a typical sermon, do not seem to have been altered by the colossal increase in the number of literates and the fact that the Bible and other religious books are now ubiquitous. For the congregations' intellectual submissiveness is as omnipresent as ever.

Lastly, I would like to, in concluding this part of this chapter, share unanswered questions that have been troubling me since I was a teenager; questions that, I believe, direct our attention to the irrationality of one of religion's major claims. Here goes! "If hell really exists, then how the hell are souls going to be burned? Will it hurt (like we are told it is supposed to)? And, more importantly, if hell will indeed be a painful experience, don't you need a nervous system for pain to stand a chance of being?"

MAN AND BELIEFS

I have, thus far, attempted to explore: (1) this complex creature called the civilized man; and (2) the discrepancy between some religious teachings and claims and rationality.

As we all know, the aforementioned incompatibility is, in some, if not most, cases, the only reason why some people abandon the religion that they were fed by their parents, as soon as their parents' control over them come to an end; and why some people who were raised by nonbelievers remain nonbelievers, even though they were and are still free to believe.

With this last part of this chapter, I will share my analysis, and as a result my understanding or misunderstanding, of religion, its adherents and their beliefs. While I cannot promise to be right, I promise to at least make sense. Here goes!

Religious Faith: a Need or a Want?

In addition to looking at Mother Nature for inspiration, and to constantly remind myself of how insignificant this creature named Mokokoma Mokhonoana is when compared to what is, I also turn to Her whenever I need to differentiate between things that are imposed on us by nature and those that are imposed on us by man, especially laws.

Let us take, as an example, the concept of monogamy, something that is, of course, relevant to religion and what I have just said with regard to things that were brought about by Mother Nature and those that were brought about by Her offspring. For the sake of saving the reader's time and my ink, I will simply share an already published aphorism of mine that sums up what I would have written: "If monogamy were really natural, then every single penis would fit exclusively into a maximum of one vagina. And vice versa." (I am almost certain that most, if not all, polygamists who will come across that assertion will shout, "Amen to that!")

At any rate, we, human beings, like every single animal and every single plant, have no choice as to whether or not to obey, say, the law of gravity and the law of birth and death. However, as we all know, we have a choice as to whether or not to obey the law of the land and the laws that we have been fed by our religion. In other words, man-made laws are made up of dos and don'ts; natural laws are made up of cans and can'ts. As I have asserted elsewhere, laws are nothing but society's attempt to force or inspire man to behave as per its desire.

Anyway, I intend not, with this writing, to argue—as many a reader is likely to have wrongly assumed—that believing is unprofitable. As a matter of fact, I will, in a few writings' time, touch on the profitability of believing. Having said that, allow me to share an assertion that is at the core of this writing: Believing isn't a prerequisite for living. For Mother Nature does not demand that we believe for us to live. In other words, there are dead believers and live nonbelievers.

Speaking of the need for religious faith, allow me to touch on one of the primary functions that churches are said to be responsible for. As we all know, there are people who believe that the state needs churches to help it to minimize, if not avoid or eradicate, the conflict between those who have more than they need and those who have less than they need; a conflict that is, I believe, inevitably brought about by the inevitable social inequality that is inherent to any economic system that is centered around the concepts of ownership and private property. "As long as the tables were set for only a minority, and the majority had to serve the minority's purposes and be satisfied with what was left over, the sense that disobedience is sin had to be cultivated." Erich Fromm is said to have written. "Both state and church cultivated it, and both worked together, because both had to pro-tect their own hierarchies. The state needed religion to have an ideology that fused disobedience and sin; the church needed believers whom the state had trained in the virtues of obedience. Both used the institution of the family, whose function it was to train the child in obedience from the first moment it showed a will of its own (usually, at the least, with the beginning of toilet training). The self-will of the child had to be broken in order to prepare it for its proper functioning later on as a citizen."[10]

In a nutshell, if what Fromm is said to have claimed is anything to go by, then one can, with reason, assert that religious teachings, and as a result religious faith, are needed, by the state, to keep most people believing that disobedience is a sin and that obedience is a virtue; lest they endeavour to dramatically change the status quo and/or to overthrow the powers that be. As Seneca is said to have said, "Religion is regarded by the common people as true, by the wise as false, and by rulers as use-ful." And as Lucretius is said to have similarly asserted, "All religions are equally sublime to the ignorant, useful to the politician, and ridiculous to the philosopher."

Morality and Religion: Which Came First?

When it comes to the need and as a result the marketing of religion, the most commonly held assumption, by many, if not most, believers, is, perhaps, the belief that man would run wild without religion—religious teachings, to be precise. That is probably because such people strongly believe that religion is not only the source but also the only source of morality.

Naturally, that invites the question, Are human beings moral because they are religious, or are they religious because they are moral?

One can, seeing that morality is taught and advocated by many a religion, reasonably suppose that some, if not many, believers are moral merely because they are religious, not the other way around. Having said that, that does not necessarily mean that religion is the only source of morality and, more importantly, that every single moral human being who happens to be religious would have been immoral (not conforming to accepted standards of morality) or amoral (lacking a moral sense; i.e., unconcerned with the rightness or wrongness of something), should they have not been religious.

While it is probably impossible to know how a moral person who happens to be religious would have turned out with regard to morality, should they have not been religious, one can attempt to confirm or refute the claim that man would have run wild should he have not been fed religious teachings by simply looking, as one's samples, at nonbelievers' morality, particularly those who became nonbelievers at a young age and those who have never been believers. Obviously, it is unlikely to be difficult or even unlikely to find a few "bad" nonbelievers in one's endeavour to support or strengthen the claim that we owe our morality to nothing but religion. Similarly, one can simply mention a few of the countless allegations and the innumerable convictions of child sexual abuse crimes that were committed by priests and nuns against boys and girls as young as three years old in one's endeavour to debunk that belief.

At any rate, as is the case with the debate as to whether or not God exists, the debate as to whether or not we owe our morality to nothing but religion and whether or not we would have run wild should we have never had religion, is unlikely to produce a gold medalist. Because of that, I'm not going to spend more of my ink on that debate, I will, instead of doing that, conclude this writing by touching on the fact that morality is, to me at least, a social construct.

New Oxford American Dictionary defines morality

as, "principles concerning the distinction between right and wrong or good and bad behavior." If that definition is anything to go by, then one can, with reason, assert that morality is a concept that was brought about by man, not Mother Nature. Seeing that morality is, according to that definition, based on concepts that were brought about by man: namely, "right and wrong" and "good and bad." Sounds far-fetched? Perhaps. Having said that, I believe that the following premise is well founded: Nature does not have the concepts of "right and wrong" and "good and bad." Otherwise life would not have "bad" things such as floods, volcanic eruptions, earthquakes, tsunamis, or even death. Nothing is, in Mother Nature's eyes, right or wrong, or good or bad.

Speaking of death, as we all know, there is, to worms and the soil at least, "goodness" to be derived from a "bad" thing such as a human being's death. For nature does not have the concept of waste: every single living thing is destined to someday be eaten by some living thing.

(Side Note: It goes without saying that there are countless beneficial occurrences that would not have occurred should we have never had the concepts of "right and wrong" and "good and bad"; concepts that are, of course, necessitated by nothing but the fact that we live as groups, as societies, as opposed to every man being an island. Anyway, my intention was merely to convince the reader that morality is our invention, not to convince the reader that morality is of no use to humanity.)

Our Bodies' Needs vs. Our God's Wants

Although I have neither the ink nor the desire to argue for or against the claim that we have the so-called free will, I would like to argue that we, like all animals, are not as free as we would like to believe. Sometimes our own desire isn't the reason or the only reason that we act or do not act in a certain way.

For example, the reader will sooner or later have no choice but to eat, irrespective of whether or not the reader wants to eat or likes eating. In addition to that, the reader will, a few hours or days after eating, have no choice but to stop whatever that the reader would be doing to go to the bathroom to defecate, irrespective of whether or not the reader desires to do so.

One can, in light of that, assert that we are, by virtue of how we were made, somewhat mechanical. Obviously, one can decide to ignore the signal with which our bodies tell us that we need to eat something. I am, of course, referring to the sound that is emitted when our digestive muscles contract. Having said that, I am almost certain that the reader will agree with the assumption that, although it is possible, it is unlikely for a sane person to starve themselves to death merely because they want to go against our need to eat: something that was, of course, imposed on us by whomever or whatever that has created us.

Let us now attempt to link what we have just touched on with the "Thou shalt not steal" commandment.

Naturally, sometimes (or some) unnatural laws conflict with man's natural instincts. In such instances, a Christian man's instincts easily overpower his sincere desire to be in the Good Book's good books. But despite that, many, if not most, religious people are—because of nothing but the aforementioned commandment—always quick to condemn people who steal. Even in cases where someone stole to fund a need, e.g., to avoid starvation, as opposed to stealing to fund a want, e.g., to buy what would be their thirtieth pair of shoes. (It is, of course, easy to judge the deeds of a starving man while you are on a full tummy.)

At any rate, when a man is hungry—that is to say, when his stomach dictates that he eats something, lest he die from starvation—his body does not care about where or how what he will eat to quieten his stomach was acquired. As I have asserted elsewhere, "Fish forks are for the rich. When you are poor, fish is fish." That is to say, morally acquired food is a worry for those who live above the poverty line. When you live below the poverty line, a stolen loaf of bread, too, is a loaf of bread. That statement sums up, I believe, the almost never discussed conflict between the "Thou shalt not steal" commandment's aspiration and man's innate desire to avoid starvation.

In a nutshell, religious dos and don'ts exist nowhere except in our minds. Which then means that religious people "think" before they "act," preferably as per their religion's rules of behaviour. Having said that, instincts are—as I have attempted to demonstrate—forever disregarding such commandments. As O. Henry is said to have said, "Love, business, family, religion, art, and patriotism are nothing but shadows of words when a man is starving."

Heartbeats In Heaven

"Everybody wants to go to heaven, but nobody wants to die," so quipped someone.

In addition to providing its adherents with the claims as to how we came here and why we are here, like many religions, Christianity promises—based on its claim of there being heaven and hell, and therefore, life after death—to give its adherents what almost every single human being subconsciously desires: namely, to live forever. (Obviously, if heaven and hell really exist, then even those who will be sent to hell will attain immortality. But as we all know, we are predisposed to gravitate towards things that will or are likely to give us pleasure, not pain.)

"The need to have has still another foundation, the *biologically given desire to live*." Erich Fromm is said to have written. "Whether we are happy or unhappy, our body impels us to strive for *immortality*. But since we know by experience that we shall die, we seek for solutions that make us believe that, in spite of the empirical evidence, we are immortal. This wish has taken many forms: the belief of the Pharaohs that their bodies enshrined in the pyramids would be immortal; many religious fantasies of life after death, in the happy hunting grounds of early hunter societies; the Christian and Islam paradise. In contemporary society since the eighteenth century, 'history' and 'the future' have become the substitutes for the Christian heaven: fame, celebrity, even notoriety—anything that seems to guarantee a footnote in the record of history—constitutes a bit of immortality. The craving for fame is not just secular vanity—it has a religious quality for those who do not believe in the traditional hereafter any more. (This is particularly noticeable among political leaders.) Publicity paves the way to immortality, and the public relations agents become the new priests.

"But perhaps more than anything else, possession of property constitutes the fulfillment of the craving for immortality, and it is for this reason that the having orientation has such strength. If my *self* is constituted by what I *have*, then I am immortal if the things I have are indestructible. From Ancient Egypt to today—from physical immortality, via mummification of the body, to mental immortality, via the last will—people have remained alive beyond their physical/mental lifetimes. Via the legal power of the last will the disposal of our property is determined for generations to come; through the laws of inheritance, I—inasmuch as I am an owner of capital—become immortal."[11]

Let us now bring back my attempt to link man's religiousness with his selfishness.

Adhering to religion is, as far as one can tell, the only route to some celestial territory called heaven. As may be expected, he who: (1) has the desire to live forever; and (2) believes the claim that God, thus, heaven, exists; has no choice but to adhere to religion. For religion is not only the only route to the Pearly Gates, as I have just supposed, but also the only way for one to be reunited with one's dead family members and friends. Hence it isn't surprising that the majority of human beings are religious. I mean, who in their right mind wouldn't want to not only live forever, but to also meet their great-great-great-grandfather's great-great-great-grandmother's father?

To sum up, man does not adhere to religion for the sake of God, he does so merely as a selfish means to earning a one-way ticket to heaven. Remember, it is man, not God, who will be sent to either heaven or hell come Judgment Day. Or so goes the claim.

The Role of Prayer

New Oxford American Dictionary defines *prayer* as, "a solemn request for help or expression of thanks addressed to God or an object of worship," whereas many a man simply defines *prayer* as, "a conversation with God."

Allow me to share a few already published aphorisms of mine that I find relevant: (1) A prayer is a poor man's credit card; meaning that (2) A credit card is a rich man's prayer; (3) The bank is a rich man's church; meaning that (4) Church is a poor man's bank; (5) The Bible is a poor man's bank statement; meaning that (6) A bank statement is a rich man's Bible; (7) A priest is to a poor man what a financial advisor is to a rich man; meaning that (8) A financial advisor is a rich man's priest; (9) Closing one's eyes when praying does not increase the odds of one's prayer being answered; it merely decreases the odds of one being distracted; and (10) When the going gets tough, the poor close their eyes; the rich open their wallets.

Now, allow me to share a theory of sorts that I have with regard to religion and its usefulness: (1) Religion breeds faith; (2) Faith breeds perseverance; and then (3) Perseverance gets the civilized man through a harsh today into a hopefully less harsh tomorrow.

At any rate, whether man prays because he has faith or he has faith because he prays, is a conundrum that I am not intelligent enough to even attempt to figure out. Having said that, I am intelligent enough to realize that praying plays a colossal role in at best deepening and at worst maintaining believers' faith.

Finally, to substantiate my opinion that praying does not make anything happen (it merely increases the chances of one holding on until what one wants to happen happens), I would like to share a relevant statement that Frederick Douglass is said to have said: "I prayed for freedom for twenty years, but received no answer *until* I prayed with my legs."

(Side Note: Because of its relevance, I believe that what I have asserted earlier deserves to be reiterated: The seemingly selfless act of thanking God through prayer is for the sake of believers' pleasure, not God. I assert so merely because I strongly believe that many a seemingly thankful man prays, not because he is thankful, but merely because he is fearful that if he thanks God not, he will be punished for being unthankful.

Speaking of being thankful, one can, with reason, argue that God does not deserve to be thanked by countless believers who thank Him every single morning, for allowing them to see yet another day. Well, that is if what is inferred from the concept of the will of God, by many a rational man, is anything to go by. Seeing that, according to what the aforementioned concept unwittingly implies, every single living person's still being alive is about God's plan for humanity, not them. Which then means that live men aren't really "luckier" than dead ones, as many a believer believes; the latter just happens to no longer be of any use to God's endeavour to actualize whatever plan that He is said to have for humanity.)

A Refuge from the Present

I am of the opinion that the average civilized man does not have, without the help of "intoxicants" such as alcohol and religion, the mental stamina to face life; the stamina that life demands from those who are lucky enough to be able to see it for what it really "is." As I once quipped, "Religion is a non-alcoholic man's alcohol; alcohol is a non-religious man's religion."

Anyway, it would be unfair, and perhaps untruthful, to attribute the civilized man's discontentment to civilization alone. For the assumption that primitive men, too, had their fair share of discontentment does not sound far-fetched.

Having said that, one can, with reason, presume that civilization changed what primitive men meant by contentment, thus, discontentment. And that many, if not most, things that bring about the civilized man's discontentment are nothing but side effects of the so-called civilization. (An exploration of "civilization and its dis-contents" necessitates a book of its own. Hence I have painfully resisted the temptation to undertake such an analysis within this chapter; a chapter to which I find the aforementioned topic relevant.) Naturally, the civilized man needs or wants something to believe in: something that will at worst provide him with the mental stamina that is required to survive an unpleasant today to see a hopefully less unpleasant tomorrow and at best pro-vide him with a vehicle that will transport him to and through the Pearly Gates.

At any rate, as I have asserted earlier, the civilized man is seldom satisfied. He is seldom satisfied with what he is, who he has, who he is, and what he has. Grant-ed, there are satisfied people out there. However, most people's satisfaction is nothing but a fleeting, recurring opinion. Such people's mood is akin to a drug addict: (extremely) high one minute, (extremely) low the next. Until, of course, another fix comes to their rescue. An-other fix being, in many a civilized man's case: a new job, a better salary, a less evil mother-in-law, a bigger house, a bigger TV, a faster car, a lover with a higher sex drive, a lover with a lower sex drive, et cetera.

Religion is, to the eternally anxious civilized man, a refuge from the harsh side effects of his and his forefathers' handiwork: namely, the so-called civilization. In addition, religion comforts the isolated civilized man by providing him with two things that he desperately longs for: (1) *a sense of belonging* — which is subtly reinforced by things like church uniforms; and (2) *a sense of purpose* — which is, of course, implied by the concept of the will of God. So, while employment might, for eight or so hours a day, isolate the civilized man from his family and friends, religion will, come Sunday, unite him with his fellow believers. And while his employer might see him as nothing but a replaceable commodity, religion constantly reminds him that he, too, like every single human being—believer or nonbeliever, rich or poor, giant or dwarf, good or evil, overweight or underweight, educated or uneducated—is playing an irreplaceable part in the actualization of God's plan for humanity; therefore, his life isn't replaceable or without a purpose.

Coincidentally, I, while writing this part of this chapter, came across an article with the following title: "Churchgoers Live Longer."[12] Allow me to cite the article's second sentence. "A new study finds people who attend religious services weekly live longer." If truth be told, I have neither the expertise nor the desire to prove or disprove that claim, that is if that claim is falsifiable. Having said that, if that claim is true, then the findings of that study substantiate the assertions that I have stated with regard to the profitability of religion. How so? Well, unbeknown to many a man, stress is silently killing, or at least contributing to the deaths of, gazillions of so-called civilized men.

Anyway, if I were certain that the claim that was made by whomever that conducted the study in question is true, then this is the theory that I would propound in my attempt to substantiate the proposition that people who attend religious services weekly live longer: (1) religion makes the religious "faithful"; (2) faith makes the faithful "hopeful"; (3) hope then becomes their antidote for stress—one of the top "silent killers" of many civilized men; and as a result (4) less stress, (increases the chances of the hopeful believer seeing) more tomorrows. So regardless of how unpleasant the present might be, the thought of the future possibly being more pleasant than the unpleasant present is pleasant enough to inspire one to have the will to survive the unpleasant present.

In a nutshell, religion is primarily, if not entirely, future-centered. It makes its adherents a billion times more obsessed about the future than they are about the present. Well, that is if two of its seductive, not to mention irresistible, claims are anything to go by: namely, a less harsh tomorrow for today's sufferers and the sought-after spot in heaven—something that those who do not believe and those who believe but do not behave as per their religion's commandments are to be deprived of.

Holy Water and Tap Water

New Oxford American Dictionary defines *placebo* as, "a harmless pill, medicine, or procedure prescribed more for the psychological benefit to the patient than for any physiological effect." And *placebo effect* as, "a beneficial effect, produced by a placebo drug or treatment, that cannot be attributed to the properties of the placebo itself, and must therefore be due to the patient's belief in that treatment."

To cut to the chase, I strongly believe that holy water can, with reason, be classified as a placebo. That is to say, it is a believer's belief that holy water has healing power, not the water in itself, that leads to the actual or perceived improvement or even healing of whatever medical condition that they are or were in.

Sounds far-fetched? Perhaps. Having said that, I believe that the mere act of reminding the reader as to what, or rather who, makes holy water holy should be enough to substantiate that seemingly absurd theory.

To do so, I will simply cite the simplest definition of *holy water* that I have ever come across: (holy water is merely) "water that has been blessed by a priest."[13]

Truths, Contexts, and Facts

Like many a philosophical debate, the debate as to whether or not there is such thing as "absolute truth" is yet to produce unanimity.

Suppose person$_{1769475930}$ kills your best friend. Nobody except the two is around to witness that. Person$_{1769475930}$ then burns your best friend to ashes before he buries their remains. As may be expected, nobody reports the homicide. (For the sake of saving the reader's time and my ink, I will, in a few sentences' time, speak as if that homicide actually happened.)

Allow me to digress for a moment.

New Oxford American Dictionary defines *truth* as, "the quality or state of being true." And the truth as "that which is true or in accordance with fact or reality." *Wikipedia* defines *fact* as, "something that has really occurred or is actually the case." At any rate, facts can, as far as I can see, be divisible into two kinds: (1) *historical facts*; and what one might call (2) *scientific facts*. With the former, I refer to events that *really happened*, whereas, with the latter, I refer to events that *really happen*. For example, the fact that person$_{1769475930}$ killed the reader's best friend is a historical fact, whereas the fact that a cobra's bite is deadly is a scientific fact.

Let us bring back the scenario that I have digressed from.

The fact will always remain that person$_{1769475930}$ killed the reader's best friend, irrespective of whether or not the reader's best friend's disappearance is seen as profitable enough to be granted a space in an international, national, or local newspaper. In other words, a fact's being isn't dependent on human beings' awareness. From that statement, the alert reader is likely to have correctly guessed what I am about to assert: namely, how the universe came to being is a historical fact, whereas the "fact" that God exists isn't. For God is claimed to be, not to have been.

Let us now bring truth into this exploration.

At any rate, truth, like meaning, is usually dependent on context, that is, the circumstances that form the setting for an event, statement, or idea, and in terms of which it can be fully understood and assessed. For example, while 2 + 2 might be said to be 4, 4's being "true" or "false" is dependent on the answer to the question, "4 of what?" Owing to the fact that 2 liters of water + 2 liters of milk amounts to only 4 liters of liquid, not 4 liters of water or that of milk.

For a simpler example, let us attempt to "add" things that are not as easy to mix as water and milk are:

3 Apples + 9 Socks + 4 Condoms = ?

But I trust that the sharp-witted reader gets the point.

Anyway, I find that conundrum to be a great demonstration of how a word's meaning is easily changed by context and, perhaps more important, how truth sometimes depends on context. For while one can sure put 3 apples, 9 socks, and 4 condoms in a bag or box, thus "add" them, such a deed would change what I meant by the word *add*. In short, 2 kilograms of sand + 2 liters of water does not amount to 4 of anything. Which then means that in such a case: $2 + 2 \neq 4$, and therefore, $2 + 2 = 4$ is untrue.

"It is context that defines contradiction." Neil Postman is said to have written. "There is no problem in someone's remarking that he prefers oranges to apples, and also remarking that he prefers apples to oranges—not if one statement is made in the context of choosing a wallpaper design and the other in the context of selecting fruit for dessert."[14]

Lastly, I strongly believe that this writing would be incomplete, if I were to conclude it without touching on how the invention of the microscope changed what primitive men meant by "reality", "fact", and "truth."

At any rate, although every single person who died before the invention of a microscope has never seen, say, animal cells, animal cells were already a reality. What's more, the claim as to or the belief in their existence would have still been a fact, should we have never invented a microscope. That is to say, the inventor of a microscope did not bring about any of the countless things whose existence we started believing in or being aware of only after a microscope revealed them. I find that to be a fairly good example that shows how knowledge or "reality" or a belief can easily be broadened or challenged or refuted by one simple question or, in this case, one simple invention.

(Side Note: I could have, of course, labelled the second type of facts as "verifiable facts" instead of "scientific facts." Having said that, I have a reason for labelling them as scientific: namely, to annoy readers who are both pro-religion and anti-science. I will, in a few writings' time, come back to that.)

The Uselessness of Truthfulness

"The mind is its own place, and in itself can make a heaven of hell, a hell of heaven." — Khaya P. Okonko

Finally, I would like to conclude this chapter with a bold assertion, an assertion that the alert reader is likely to have inferred from my seemingly far-fetched claims as to how the religious profit from religion: God does not need to really exist, for religion to bear whatever fruits that the religious are reaping.

Similarly, a woman does not need to really be present for a man to experience an orgasm. For when masturbating, a man's penis does not require "the truth" (viz., a "real" vagina, if he is heterosexual; a "real" anus, if he is homosexual; or either, if he is bisexual), or that the claim that he would be making by stroking his penis be a fact, as a prerequisite for his sexual activity to bring about an orgasm. Owing to the fact that when a man masturbates, his hand pretends to be a vagina or an anus; his penis gets deceived; and then an orgasm is realized.

The same can, of course, be said about things like a treadmill. Seeing that you do not need to really run a kilometer across land in order to burn whatever number of calories that a run of that distance burns. That is why those who run a kilometer on a treadmill burn more or less the same amount of calories as those who run a kilometer across land.

Before I share another example with which I will substantiate the claim that I began this writing with, I would like to make a similar claim: a story does not need to be truthful, for it to be fruitful or successful.

Think of a novel. A novel is, I believe, the most fitting example. Owing to the interesting fact that the fact that the reader is aware that the story is fictitious does not make it impossible for the novelist to achieve whatever that he or she desires to achieve with the novel; i.e., make the reader think, cry, laugh, act, et cetera. The same can, of course, be said about movies. For as "fictitious" as all movies are, countless movies still manage to make countless viewers think, cry, laugh, act, et cetera. (Technically, all movies are not "real" or "true." Even those who are "based on a true story.") Having said that, the difference between the cause of religion's fruitfulness and that of work of fiction is worth remarking upon, namely, the religious truly believe that God really exists, whereas readers of a novel merely suspend disbelief. "*Suspension of disbelief* or *willing suspension of disbelief* is a term coined in 1817 by the poet and aesthetic philosopher Samuel Taylor Coleridge, who suggested that if a writer could infuse a 'human interest and a semblance of truth' into a fantastic tale, the reader would suspend judgment concerning the implausibility of the narrative. Suspension of disbelief often applies to fictional works of the action, comedy, fantasy, and horror genres. *Cognitive estrangement* in fiction involves using a person's ignorance or lack of knowledge to promote suspension of disbelief."[15]

Lastly, I began this writing with words that many a reader is likely to have found profound. Allow me to, through a revelation, substantiate the claim that this writing revolves around, i.e., the claim that religion does not really need God to really exist, for it to be fruitful to the religious: the only thing it needs is that the religious truly believe that God really exists. Here goes! The words that I began this writing with were not really said by Khaya P. Okonko. As a matter of fact, I fabricated that name. Chances are that there exists no one so named. Be that as it may, one can, with reason, assert that whatever impression that that quotation had on the reader was by no means affected by the fact that those words were not really said by Khaya P. Okonko. Anyway, those words of wisdom are said to have been said by Satan in, "Paradise Lost", an epic poem by John Milton. I have intentionally misled the reader into believing that those words were said by Khaya P. Okonko merely to substantiate the seemingly absurd assertion that in many an instance, truthfulness isn't really a prerequisite and facts do not really matter.

(Side Note: To further substantiate the bold conviction that the belief in God is the only thing that is needed to make religion fruitful to the religious, I will simply remind the reader that countless men and women have successfully robbed many a shop using nothing but a toy gun. In such instances, the belief that the gun being used to rob is "real" brings about the very same paralyzing fear that being threatened with a "real" gun triggers.)

EPILOGUE

The End Is Near

I must say, this was an extremely difficult book to pen. Apart from it being made up of nothing but abstractions, the seemingly easy task of deciding where to explore what was uncommonly challenging. For, as the observant reader is likely to have observed, many a writing is relevant to many a topic that I have attempted to explore herein.

If truth be told, I find the topics that I have attempted to explore thus far and those that I am about to attempt to explore to be too complex to tame into a logically ordered book. But I trust that the sharp-witted reader will at least make sense of the writings herein individually; should the reader find the topics herein to be too many, not to mention too complex, for me to have penned sequentially.

Anyway, I will, with this last part of the book, share writings with which I will attempt to: (1) account for some of the things that I have already attempted to explore; and (2) link some of the things that I am about to attempt to explore with some of those that I have already attempted to explore. Here goes!

The Observer and the Observed

(I would like to start with an already published writing. Apart from its relevance to this part of the book, I find it to be a good introduction to the point that I will attempt to make with the following writing.)

More often than not, whether or not a love song is "sweet" depends on the state of the listener's love life, not the song in itself.

Likewise, whether or not someone or something is "bad" depends on the observer's taste, preferences, expectations, worldview, understanding, cultural conditioning, et cetera, not the observed person or thing per se. That is to say, to tell me about a "bad" person or a "good" thing is to tell me more about yourself (your taste, preferences, expectations, worldview, understanding, cultural conditioning, et cetera) and almost nothing about the person or the thing. For "evil" is the last thing that a serial killer sees herself or her deeds as. What's more, rape is a "bad" thing to only me, you, the victim and their family and friends, and other "good" people, not the rapist. (As I have already asserted, death is "bad news" to only the deceased's family and friends. For, because of nothing but the monetary system and our desire to make as much money as possible, the very same death is "good news" to an undertaker, his family, his business, and consequently, his landlord.) As a matter of fact, the very same eight minutes that were probably a "painful" experience to the victim of rape were probably a "pleasurable" adventure to the rapist.

The same can, of course, be said about some books— any book whose author's only goal is to leave readers more knowledgeable with regard to the book's subject, to be precise. For, in such a case, its contents, its structure, and how it was written aside, whether or not a book is "a waste of time" or "a must-read" depends on what the reader knew and what they did not know before they read the book. For example, "An Introduction to Geology" textbook is unlikely to be of equal use or importance to a first-year geology student and a geologist with thirty years experience.

That is, of course, half of the issue in question, namely, the ratio of a reader's knowledge to their ignorance with regard to a book's subject. The other half is, of course, attributable to the intellectual demands of a book. As an example, I will simply remind the reader that there are countless "great" philosophy books and innumerable "great" mathematics textbooks that are labelled as "a waste of time," merely because readers who labelled them so do not have the brainpower required to comprehend such books.

Anyway, those are the main reasons why I am not really a supporter of "book reviews." For what a book was to $reader_{188074}$ isn't necessarily what the book will be to $reader_{5388003}$. What's more, the thing that makes it near impossible to objectively judge a book whose author's goal is to leave its readers more knowledgeable with regard to its subject is that, as I once claimed through an aphorism, "Once acquired, knowledge comes across as a product of having used one's common sense." So, because of nothing but those two reasons, I will only start taking book reviews seriously from the day that books are able to review readers. For sometimes it is the reader that sucks, not the book.

To sum up, nine times out of ten, when someone tells you that they love your work, they are merely telling you something about themselves, not your work. "A book review, good or bad, can be far more descriptive of the reviewer than informational about the book itself." Nassim Nicholas Taleb is said to have written. "This mechanism I also call Wittgenstein's ruler: Unless you have confidence in the ruler's reliability, if you use a ruler to measure a table you may also be using the table to measure the ruler. The less you trust the ruler's reliability, the more information you are getting about the ruler and the less about the table."[1]

A Red Rose Isn't Red, It Looks Red (to Some People)

As may be expected, our being blind to the illusion that is usually bred by our careless use of the word "is" has left most of us convinced that descriptions exist within the person or thing that is described. For, as Kenneth G. Johnson is said to have said, "The structure of language obscures the role of the observer."

We habitually assume that every single person's mind will, when they look at the very same object that we are looking at, form the very "same" mental image that our mind has formed. (That can, of course, be easily refuted by reminding those who believe so of optical disorders such as colour blindness and nearsightedness.) In addition, we somehow expect every single person to "be," to every single person, whatever that we see, and as a result label, them as. To prove that that is so and that that will always be so, I will simply remind the reader that a woman is easily a "sweetheart" to her current boyfriend but a "bitch" to her former boyfriend.

The former is, of course, with reference to objects, e.g., a person. Whereas the latter is with reference to abstractions, e.g., a personality.

At any rate, language is one complex phenomenon. We sometimes use a word, a symbol that is meaningless in itself, to describe an object, a thing that does not possess its description. Let us use a red rose as an example. First of all, the word *red* is meaningless in itself. Secondly, the organism to which we refer with the word *rose* isn't "red." It merely appears so ... to *some* people.

Anyway, because of nothing but our being unmindful of such a seemingly obvious fact, we often hear statements such as: "Gym *is* a waste of time", "Blow jobs *are* disgusting", and "Mokokoma's essays *are* boring."

For such statements to bring about a heated argument, the person to whom such a statement is directed needs to be of an opposing opinion and, more importantly, ignorant of semantics. Someone who isn't ignorant of semantics would: (1) remind him- or herself that such a statement is contaminated by the perspective, taste, expectations, cultural conditioning, et cetera, of the observer, that is, the writer or speaker; and then (2) attempt to find out—before they attempt to refute that statement, should they find it worth refuting—what the writer or speaker means by "a waste of time", "disgusting", or "boring." What's more, those statements would have been phrased differently, should they have been expressed by someone who isn't ignorant of semantics. For example, "Gym *is* a waste of time" would have been phrased as follows: "*I think* that gym is a waste of time." "Blow jobs *are* disgusting" would have been phrased as follows: "Blow jobs disgust *me.*" And, lastly, "Mokokoma's essays *are* boring" would have been phrased as follows: "*I found* all of the twelve essays that are said to have been written by Mokokoma boring." ("That are said to have been written by..."? I know that that sounds pretentious, but yes! The fact that a writing or book is attributed to someone does not necessarily make that claim a fact. As we all know, almost all readers have never witnessed a writer write—yet many would be quick to assert that such-and-such a book was authored by so-and-so. What's more, seeing someone write does not necessarily make them the writer of whatever that they would have written. Seeing that they could be merely copying someone else's writing, which they have memo-rized, from their mind to a piece of paper, a book, or a computer.)

One can, from the rephrased statements, tell that the writer or speaker is conscious of the fact that their taste, understanding, expectations, cultural condition-ing, et cetera, have contaminated or molded their judg-ment, and as a result their labelling or description, of gym, blow jobs, and Mokokoma's essays. As may be expected, those to whom such an opinion is directed are seldom inspired to argue or debate with the person whose opinion is phrased in such an honorable manner. For the manner in which such an opinion is phrased re-minds the reader or listener that the writer or speaker acknowledges that that is how whatever that he or she has labelled or described feels or tastes or appears or sounds to them, that is, the writer or speaker.

(Side Note: In addition to preventing unnecessary ar-guments and unnecessary debates, I believe that such an honorable manner of phrasing opinions—that is, hinting one's acknowledgement of the role that one's percep-tion, preferences, expectations, cultural conditioning, et cetera, have played in molding one's opinion—leaves one intellectually humble.)

Sometimes: The Truth + Time = An Untruth

I concluded some essay on branding with the assertion that if the best team were really what soccer fans are after, then they would change the team that they support come the end of each and every single season—with, of course, the exception of the seasons whose championship is won by the team that they were supporting that particular season, that is, last season's champions.

Although the essay in question is about brand loyalty, I find its conclusion relevant to this writing. For within that assertion hides a seldom thought of fact: namely, in some cases, a statement's truthfulness depends on the time or date that it was or is stated. For example, the truthfulness of "Curtis Mayfield is alive" depends on when it was or is stated. For it to qualify as truthful, that statement needs to have been stated between Curtis Mayfield's birthday, i.e., 3 June 1942, and his deathday, i.e., 26 December 1999.[2]

I would now like to bring, as another example, soccer back into this discussion.

Although gazillions of people would be quick to do either, it is intellectually childish to attempt to prove or disprove the statement that "Manchester United is the UEFA Champions League champion" as it stands.

For without a date to qualify that statement, one cannot, with reason, accept or reject that claim. Unless, of course, Manchester United has never won the UEFA Champions League.

If that statement was stated (for simplicity's sake, on the last day of the year) in 1968, 1999, or 2008, then that statement is true, and any year other than those, then that statement would be false.[3] (Obviously, proving or disproving that statement would have been straightforward if that claim were expressed through a mouth instead of a hand. For all one would have had to do is to simply recall that day's date.) At any rate, a date can be used in two different but equally effective ways in order to make such statements easy to prove or disprove. Firstly, one could simply add a date to that statement. For example, "Manchester United is the 1968 UEFA Champions League champion." Or, alternatively, one could use a *dating device*. For example, "Manchester United is the UEFA Champions League champion$_{31\text{-December-1968}}$." (The dating device's function is, of course, to inform the reader that that statement was stated on the 31st December 1968.) What's more, one can even go as far as including the time of the day and one's time zone, in instances where doing so makes a difference. For example, "Manchester United is the UEFA Champions League champion$_{\text{31-December-1968-13h08-CAT}}$."

Speaking of time zones, while it might sure be, say, 3 p.m., where one is, the truthfulness of one's statement, i.e., "It is 3 p.m.," is confined to one's time zone. For that statement is, of course, an untruth to those who are outside one's time zone. Unless, of course, that statement was accompanied by one's time zone. For example, "It is 3 p.m. CAT."

To sum up, sometimes contexts change and organisms develop, and as a result, some of yesterday's truths are today's untruths.

I See It, Therefore It Is

Between an observed object and the mental image of that object hides the central nervous system of that object's observer—the observer's visual system, to be precise. Literally, that is. (By "mental image" I refer to the image that one's mind forms when one is looking at an object.) Figuratively, there usually hides one's perspective, background, taste, cultural conditioning, et cetera, between an observed person, event, or thing and what the observer sees, thinks, or feels with regard to the subject of their observation.

At any rate, without assuming, a stroll that usually takes you an hour would take you hours, if not the entire day. Owing to the fact that you would then have to painstakingly test to confirm whether or not the spot where your next step will place you is as solid as the spot on which your last step has placed you. The same can, of course, be said about visual perception. Seeing that when we see, say, an object that was not there yesterday, we seldom touch it just to confirm that what our mind is feeding us is really there. But even if we did, after a few instances of confirming the actual existence of the object whose mental image our mind is feeding us, we would eventually replace the demanding task of *verifying* the actual existence of every single object whose mental image our mind is feeding us with the undemanding task of *presuming* that what our mind is feeding us is really there.

The process of seeing is, of course, analogous to that of "abstracting." ("*Abstracting*, in the context of Korzybski's model, refers to physiological-neurological activities, or *processes*, that occur on *non-verbal* levels. Put another way, *abstracting* is something that your body-brain-nervous-system is continually *doing*, without respect to whether or not you're aware of it."[4]). Seeing that when one looks at something, not every single seeable thing about that thing is seen.

Anyway, this is more or less what happens when we abstract. For that, allow me to cite Steve Stockdale's book, *Here's Something About General Semantics*: "(1st ...) Something happens ... (then 2nd ...) I partially sense what happens ... (then 3rd ...) I describe what I sense ... (then ... etc.) I make meanings, inferences, beliefs, theories, judgments, etc."[5]

More often than not, an observer is blind to at least one observable thing about the observed. In other words, when we look at something we seldom see every single seeable thing about whatever it is that we are looking at. Yet, some, if not most, people are willing to defend their beliefs, theories, opinions, worldview, understanding, et cetera, with their lives.

At any rate, our common forgetfulness or ignorance of the fact that Mother Nature has placed limits on our senses has inevitably left most of us arrogant. In many a case, instead of saying that, "that *appears so to me*," those who are ignorant of general semantics assert that, "that *is* so." For example, instead of humbly saying that, "that car *looks* red *to me*," such people assert that, "that car *is* red." (Again, I am well aware of the convenience that our habit of speaking in such an arrogant manner affords us. Seeing that "that red car" demands half the time and half the ink that "that car that appears red to me" demands. Having said that, such an honorable habit of hinting one's acknowledgment of one's role as an observer when expressing oneself is pivotal when attempting to intelligently engage in a debate or discussion, especially those that revolve around an abstraction or abstractions.)

Lastly, I would now like to bring hallucinations into this exploration.

How the hell do we know for certain that the mental image that we see when we look at an object is not merely an end result of a hallucination—bearing in mind that, as I have just said, we do not verify the actual existence of every single object whose mental image our mind is feeding us? The answer is simple. To check whether or not what our mind is feeding us actually exists, we rely on what other people see when they look at what we are looking at. Although one person is usually sufficient for such verification, one can, in light of that, assert that reality is nothing but a hallucination shared by most sane men.

(Side Note: For the simplest illustration of what I hope to have reminded the reader about with this writing, I will simply remind the reader of *optical illusion*, i.e., the experience of seeming to see something that does not exist or that is other than it appears; a visual phenomenon that is, of course, relevant to what we have just touched on. "Let us recall, in this connection, the familiar example of a rotary fan, which is made up of separate radial blades, but which, when rotating with a certain velocity, gives the impression of a *solid disk*." Alfred Korzybski is said to have said. "In this case the 'disk' is not 'reality', but a nervous integration, or abstraction from the rotating blades. We not only see the 'disk' where there is no disk, but, if the blades rotate fast enough, we could not throw sand through them, as the sand would be too slow to get through before being struck by one of the blades.")

The Exploitation of Everyday Languages' Defects

In some cases, a trial lawyer's job is to look for a loophole or loopholes in the law, not honesty in their client. As we all know, trial lawyers usually exploit loopholes, that is, ambiguity or inadequacy in the law, in their attempt to achieve whatever that their client has hired them to realize.

Advertisers are also notorious for exploiting ambiguity. "You will find text of the advertising sections," Stuart

Chase is said to have written, "devoted almost solidly to a skillful attempt to make words mean something different to the reader from what the facts warrant."[6] Advertisers and trial lawyers are, of course, by no means the only people whose livelihood relies, partially or entirely, on the exploitation of the ambiguity that is easily found in our everyday languages. Book publishers, too, have the same habit. Countless book publishers habitually put the word "bestseller" on the cover of many a book that they publish, in their attempt to make such books appear popular, and as a result, worth reading.

At any rate, it is either most of us are not rational or we are merely too lazy (or too busy being entertained or too busy trying to be or remain employed) to be so. Perhaps that explains why a book publisher's simple mechanical act of "untruthfully" labelling a book as a "bestseller" alone is enough to make us buy a book that we would have not bought, should it have not had the word "bestseller" on its cover. "*In his Economic Survey of the Book Industry* in 1931," Daniel J. Boorstin is said to have written, "O.H. Cheney called best-sellerism 'an intolerable curse on the industry.' But, he explained, there was (and there remains) a substantial commercial basis for the institution: one way to make a book a best seller is to call it one. Then many potential book buyers 'want to join the thousands—or hundreds of thousands—of the inner circle of the readers of the book. As soon as everybody thinks that everybody else has read it—or should read it—a best seller gets talked about—and talk leads to the ringing of the cash register.' A buyer going into a bookstore is apt to ask for the best seller; even if he doesn't, he is apt to be urged to buy a book because it is one."[7]

I hope I have, with that passage, reminded the reader about our habitual reliance on a "lie" (the word "bestseller") when we decide on whether or not a book is worth our time and/or our money. I would now like to cite, from the very same page as the passage that I have just cited, a passage that justifies my labelling most claims made by most book publishers (calling some books "bestsellers") as nothing but fabrications. "One of the most interesting features of the institution," further wrote Daniel J. Boorstin, "is how flimsy is the factual basis for calling any particular book a best seller. To speak of *a* best seller—to use the superlative to apply not to one item but to a score of items—is, of course, a logical contradiction. But the bookstores are full of 'best sellers,' just as the media world of celebrities is full of 'the biggest,' 'the best,' and 'the greatest.' The factual basis for calling any book a best seller is not so much a statistics as an amalgam including a small ingredient of fact along with much larger ingredient of hope, intention, frustration, ballyhoo, and pure hokum."[8]

Let us now bring another linguistic "trick" that most, if not all, book publishers' livelihoods rely heavily on. More often than not, a book publisher cites (usually on the book's cover) esteemed people's remarks with regard to the book, as the publisher's attempt to turn potential readers of that book into readers of that book. I am, of course, referring to what is usually called a blurb. As an example, allow me to cite the cover of a book that I have randomly chosen from my bookshelf. The back cover of *Mathematics for the Million*, a book that is said to have been written by Lancelot Hogben, cites two esteemed beings: (1) "'It makes alive the contents of the elements of mathematics.' — Albert Einstein"; and (2) "'A great book, a book of first-class importance.' — H.G. Wells."[9] (The fact that not a single book has a negative or unfavourable review on its cover does not seem to make most people suspicious of blurbs.)

At any rate, such blurbs are seldom "lies." They are merely artfully taken out of context; just so they mean, to the reader, something slightly or totally different from what the book reviewer meant. Let us use this book as an example. The blurb on this book's front cover (which

I fabricated in my attempt to make the reader experience instead of merely reading about an example of how parts of a book review can easily be taken out of context to give potential readers a message that is different from what the book reviewer meant), namely, " ... the most important book in the world." could have simply been an artful omission of "I believe that Mokokoma has terribly failed to turn the great idea behind *Divided & Conquered* into..." from the review "I believe that Mokokoma has terribly failed to turn the great idea behind *Divided & Conquered* into *the most important book in the world.*" And "that's not all." Here is another disturbing thing: legally, there isn't really anything that the reader can do about that half-truth.

Last but not least, allow me to cite a relevant remark that is said to have been said by Erving Goffman. "Communication techniques such as innuendo, strategic ambiguity, and crucial omissions allow the misinformer to profit from lies without, technically, telling any. The mass media have their own version of this and demonstrate that by judicious camera angles and editing, a trickle of response to a celebrity can be transformed into a wild stream."[10]

"Twins" Is Made up of Two Individuals

It goes without saying that categorizing is more convenient than not categorizing. For example, saying "my children" is eight times more convenient than having to say "John, Salim, Jakobus, Dalingcebo, Mmakoma, Baingana, Barack and Majakathata," whenever a woman refers to all her children.

Having said that, when done thoughtlessly, as is often the case with most of us, placing people or things into a particular class or group can be detrimental. For when categorizing people or things, one's attention is drawn to their *similarities*, while their *differences* almost always go unnoticed and/or not taken into consideration.

General semantics pioneers recommend the use of a simple yet profitable tool called *indexing* (which is one of the devices to which they refer with the term *extensional devices*), whose function is to attempt to remind readers that no two people or things are identical. In instances where it is successful, indexing reminds readers that every single human being who is placed under the category that is referred to with the word *women* is a unique individual, regardless of how alike their reproductive organs are to those who are placed under the same category. That is to say, woman$_1$ and woman$_2$ are unique individuals, even though both have the "same" characteristics; namely, breasts, a vagina, an ovary, a womb, et cetera. So, while the word *women* highlights the similarities between the two individuals who are each categorized as a woman, those unique indexing numbers highlight the two individuals' uniqueness. Which then means that to assert that all women are bad drivers is to imply that womanhood is all there is to human beings who are categorized as women, and that being a "good" or a "bad" driver is determined by nothing but the possession or absence of nipples, a vagina, an ovary, and a womb.

Let us now touch on the example that we started this writing with.

That woman's children, namely, John, Salim, Jakobus, Dalingcebo, Mmakoma, Baingana, Barack and Majakathata, are not made identical by their being, as a whole, the referent to which "my children" (which is, of course, limited to their parents) and "so-and-so's children" (so-and-so being their mother, their father, or both) refer.

At any rate, teachers are forever reminded of the fact that although their students are categorized into the same group, they differ with regard to things like the number of times that facts, theories, dates, theorems, et cetera, need to be repeated before they can successfully commit them to memory.

A teacher's failure to take his students' uniqueness into account isn't as detrimental as a doctor's failure to do the same with regard to her patients' uniqueness is. To start with, some disorders have multiple possible causes. As is the case with, say, stress and the disorders that usually accompany stress (e.g., migraines, weight loss, depression, etc.). Secondly, while $patient_1$ and $patient_2$ might sure be classifiable into the same category, say, "AIDS patients," disregarding the two patients' uniqueness (e.g., their age, allergies, overall health, CD4 count, the presence of other viruses, the depth of their pockets, et cetera) inevitably inspires the doctor to, through a prescription, advice the two patients to take the very same medication. As may be expected, it is at best ineffectual and at worst deadly to treat $patient_1$'s condition as if it has the very same cause or causes as $patient_2$'s. Or to treat the two patients as if their bodies were invaded by not only the very same but the very same number of viruses (even if they were, their immune systems are unlikely to be equal with regard to their strength).

In a nutshell, generalizing generally leads to the *fallacy of composition*, i.e., the error of assuming that what is true of a member of a group is true for the group as a whole. While assuming usually inspire us to *extrapolate*, i.e., extend the application of a method or conclusion to an unknown situation by assuming that existing trends will continue or similar methods will be applicable. (I will, with the following writing, attempt to show the reader how and why such seemingly harmless errors have led to gazillions of people's deaths.)

"All Generalizations Are Dangerous, Even This One."

The implications of generalizations or stereotypes such as "Men are dogs," "Tall men have a gigantic penis," "Women are bad drivers," "Good-looking men are heartbreakers," "Men who have small feet have a minuscule penis," "Women who have big lips have a humongous vagina," and "Ugly women are good in bed" are not as detrimental as generalizations or stereotypes such as "Whites are racists," "Jews are wealthy," "Black men are thugs," "Foreigners are here to take our jobs and our women," and "Gentiles are a threat to Judaism."

This book would, of course, be incomplete without an exploration of genocide. For genocide is, I believe, one of the best things that one could refer the reader to as an attempt to show the reader how deadly social constructs can be.

The Rwandan genocide, like all genocides, can be used to show us: (1) how unintelligent a human being can be; and (2) how intelligent a human being can be. For it requires at least one extraordinary mind for a man or a handful of men to inspire millions of men to move their daily struggle from trying to make a living to taking the lives of other human beings. Alas, such in short supply mental equipment are usually used to feed a handful of men's insatiable appetite for power over other human beings instead of being used to attempt to better or replace social systems whose side effects many a civilized man's anxiety and unhappiness are attributable to.

Needless to say, ethnicity is a social construct. At any rate, to start some bloody inferno called genocide, colonizers usually use some fuel called ethnicity, to turn a group of men into groups of men. Such a tried-and-tested strategy is, of course, called *divide and conquer* or *divide and rule*, which *New Oxford American Dictionary* defines as "the policy of maintaining control over one's subordinates or subjects by encouraging dissent between them." The strategy's object is, of course, to break a united group of people into less powerful groups of people. The divide and conquer strategy is so powerful that there isn't really a correlation between the strategy's effectiveness and the ratio of those dividing to those being divided. In other words, a group of twelve men can easily divide and conquer a nation of twelve million united people with the very same speed and effectiveness as a group of twelve thousand men.

For the claim as to who and what caused the Rwandan genocide, and how the genocide was brought about, I would like to cite the introduction of *Sometimes in April*, a film that is said to have been written and directed by the Haitian filmmaker Raoul Peck.[11] Here goes! "For centuries, the Hutu, Tutsi and Twa of Rwanda shared the same culture, language and religion. In 1916, Belgium took control of Rwanda from Germany and installed a rigid colonial system of racial classification and exploitation. By elevating the Tutsi over the Hutu, they created deep resentment among the Hutu majority. In 1959, the Belgians handed control of Rwanda to the Hutu majority. With independence came decades of institutionalized anti-Tutsi segregation and massacre. Hundreds of thousands of Tutsis and moderate Hutus were forced into exile. In 1988, some of these refugees formed a rebel movement called the Rwandan Patriotic Front (RPF) to reclaim their homeland. In 1990, from their base in Uganda, the RPF launched an offensive against the Hutu regime that was stopped with French and Belgian military support. A deadly cycle of war and massacre continued until 1993, when the United Nations negotiated a power-sharing agreement between the two sides. To protect their power, hard-line Hutu extremists resisted the implementation of the agreements and planned one of the most terrifying genocides in history."[12]

From that introduction, one readily notices: (1) how relatively easy it is for the divide and conquer strategy to divide and conquer a united people; (2) how relatively easy it is to indoctrinate and to control the minds and the behaviour of human beings; and (3) the role that language plays in genocides; technically, genocide cannot happen without the preceding process of categorizing, generalizing, stereotyping, et cetera (a qualification is in order: *New Oxford American Dictionary* defines *genocide* as "the deliberate killing of a large group of people, especially those of a *particular* ethnic group or nation." I trust that the sharp-witted reader had no trouble spotting the part of that definition that qualifies my claim that language plays a role in genocides.). In addition, as the attentive reader is likely to have noticed, one can also see the part played by social constructs such as ownership and private property. And that it is possible to use a social construct to further divide a subgroup that was brought about by dividing a group through the aid of another social construct. For example, one can further divide the Hutus by simply drawing their attention to the fact that some Hutus have deeper pockets than others. Or that some Hutus have more money than they need whereas others have less money than they need.

(Side Note: As the learned reader knows, such mass killings of a particular ethnic or religious group are usually euphemistically referred to as "ethnic cleansing," a term that was, I presume, fabricated to subconsciously make such killings seem more justifiable and less inhumane, particularly in the eyes of those who will be doing the killing.)

The Reason Why The Sight Of A Poor Obese Man Is Puzzling

A man and his son are in a car on a road trip. They get involved in a fatal car accident. The father is killed instantly. The son is only injured, but he needs immediate surgery. The son is rushed to a hospital. The doctor rushes into the emergency room, looks at the patient, freezes for half a minute or so, and then says: "I can't operate on this boy, he is my son."

Now the question is, how is that possible? Bearing in mind that the boy's father was killed. (This has nothing to do with adoption.)

That is one of my favourite riddles. I came across it nine or so years ago. Anyway, the answer to that riddle is that the doctor is the boy's mother.

Most, if not all, readers who found that riddle puzzling are victims of a gender stereotype and the assumption that the doctor is a man. Anyway, the goal of that riddle is, I believe, to show us how and to remind us that stereotypes and generalizations easily make us blind to the obvious.

At any rate, as I have already claimed, genocide (like xenophobia, sexism, racism, etc.) would be impossible without at least one of the following processes: categorization, generalization, stereotyping, et cetera. Such mental processes are either made possible by language or they are merely perpetuated by how we think: something that is, of course, molded by the structure of our everyday languages. Either way, language plays a tremendous role in dividing human beings. Not only because it made it possible or easier for us to categorize each other (a process that is deadly), but also because it has given us some deadly tools called swear words.

Perhaps the only person or thing that is unlikely to be a victim of a generalization or a stereotype is someone or something that the observer knows absolutely nothing about. (Having said that, the observer is likely to already have a prejudice against people and things that he knows that he does not know.) In such rare instances, the observer is likely to see and judge the subject of his observation for what it "is" or how it appears to him, not what it is said to be or how it ought to appear. For man is usually blinded by his expectations from whatever that he is looking at.

Let us use fat people as an example.

A person who has accepted the truth of the claim and stereotype that fat people are forever eating is unlikely to get rid of that stereotype. For he is likely to seem to always see a fat person eating whenever he sees one. Or he will notice a fat person's fatness only when he sees a fat person eating. As I have already said to have already said through an aphorism, "Man sees what he is looking for; seldom what he is looking at."

Anyway, once a stereotype's truthfulness is "confirmed" a few times, or at times once, the claim that it is based on is then labelled as a fact. For example, when a white man who was sold the stereotype that blacks are intellectually inferior to whites (something that he regards as a fact) comes across a black man who is and seems to be more intelligent than all the white people that the white man in question knows, he is likely to merely regard that black man as merely a not-so-unintelligent black man, without reassessing the stereotype that he was fed when he was 14. Having said that, if that white man were fed the opposite, that is, the stereotype that blacks are intellectually superior to whites, all that it is likely to take is for him to come across one unintelligent black person for him to reassess that stereotype.

Reason? Simple. His ego will profit from proving the latter stereotype wrong, while it profits from his subconscious decision to ignore instances that refute the former stereotype.

In other words, coming across a million men whom he regards as bad drivers is unlikely to make a man who bought the stereotype that women are bad drivers reassess that stereotype, even if it only took one bad female driver for him to confirm that the claim that that stereotype is based on is a fact.

At any rate, although doing so is likely to prevent gazillions of deaths, we do not really need to stop categorizing and generalizing. That is if that is even possible. Anyway, when dealing with abstractions, being conscious of the fact that our debate or discussion is based on an abstraction or abstractions reminds us that what we mean by, say, the word *capitalism*, and what the word *capitalism* means to those with whom we are conversing might not be the same. Similarly, our being aware of the fact that we are categorizing or generalizing will remind us, whenever we need to do so, that not all wise people are old and not all old people are wise. Or that, to use deadly stereotypes, not all whites are racists and not all racists are white. And that not all blacks are thugs and not all thugs are black.

Anyway, life is too fast, not to mention too complex, for the civilized man that it is practically impractical for him to see every single person and every single thing as a unique individual or entity. That is why categorizing, generalizing, and stereotyping help him avoid a nervous breakdown. Having said that, as understandable as that might be, such processes inevitably bring about a habit of looking at things through the eyes that were contaminated by yesterday. (That is, of course, a wise habit when it comes to how a man who once witnessed another being killed by a cobra behaves when he is around a cobra. As I have said elsewhere, "Wisdom is finding out that a cobra is deadly; without first having to lose one's life.")

Beliefs Are Believers' Facts

(I have attempted, with a few writings in the last chapter, to remind or show the reader how powerful beliefs can be. I will, with this writing, attempt to remind or show the reader how deadly beliefs can be. And how a judge's "conviction" easily results in the life imprisonment of an innocent man.)

For the 2008 South African xenophobic attacks to stand a chance of taking place, South Africans who took part in the slaughtering of their fellow human beings had to believe that: (1) people from country$_1$ are naturally different from those from country$_{2, 3, 4, 5, etc.}$; and/or that (2) the so-called foreigners are or were really stealing "their" jobs and "their" women.

It goes without saying that it mattered not whether or not the so-called foreigners were really stealing jobs and/or women from South Africans, particularly those who took part in the killings in question. All that mattered was that South Africans who took part in the aforementioned attacks believed that to be so. Similarly, men whose bodies are covered with tattoos need not really be thugs for them to be seen and treated as thugs. And the defendant does not need to really be guilty for them to be sentenced to two life sentences. All that is needed is for the judge to believe that the defendant committed whatever it is that he or she is accused of having committed. That is, of course, not limited to the imprisonment of countless innocent men. A guilty man, too, can easily be sent back home to the house in which he raped and killed his neighbour's three-year-old son. All that he needs is for the judge to believe that he did not commit neither of what he is accused of having committed: namely, rape and murder.

As may be expected, most of many a trial lawyer's energy and working-hours revolve around tripling the odds of the judge's belief with regard to the defendant's innocence working to the advantage of the defendant; irrespective of whether or not the defendant, the trial lawyer's customer, is innocent.

At any rate, as I have attempted to remind the reader earlier, in a society where most people's priority is to at best make as much money as possible and at worst earn a living, "petty" things such as the possibility of a trial lawyer succeeding in persuading an initially suspicious judge into finally believing that a murderer is innocent, and as a result free the killer, are not terrifying enough to impel us to rethink the ideologies and social systems that we have inherited from our forefathers.

In essence, the court of law revolves around the judge's belief with regard to the plaintiff's claim, and as a result the defendant's innocence, not the truth. As a matter of fact, in many a case, a trial lawyer's job is to deceive the judge.

Let us now attempt to link that with the monetary system and our desire to make as much money as possible. As may be expected, the rich seem to always get away with murder. Owing to the fact that they afford to hire the best trial lawyers that money can buy. What's more, if the court of law were indeed a place where the truth is sought, then all trial lawyers who have just lost a case would be banned from ever entering the court of law. For they would have tried to convince the judge to believe a lie and as a result free a criminal—a criminal whom they attempted to set free primarily, if not solely, because he or she had enough money to pay them, not because they believed that he or she is innocent. That is, of course, provided that the judge's belief that the trial lawyer's client committed whatever it is that they are accused of having committed is a fact.

Disheartening? Certainly!

Finally, I would like to cite a relevant passage from *The Tyranny of Words*. "The human element, says [Jerome] Frank, in the administration of justice by judges is irrepressible." Stuart Chase is said to have written. "The more we try to conceal the fact that judges are swayed by prejudices, passions, and weaknesses, the more likely we are to augment the fact. Legal systems have been reared on the beliefs (1) that a judge centers his attention on impersonal rules of law; (2) that his decision is the product of his application of those rules to the facts of the case; and (3) that as a consequence the human element is practically boiled away—as if one were working out a problem by following the rules of algebra. These beliefs enhance the bad effects of the judges' prejudices, passions, and weaknesses, for they tend to block self-examination by judges of their own mental processes. Judges develop a kind of oracle complex. 'It has become compulsory and respectable for judges to give explanations of their decisions in so artificial a manner as to insure, to the maximum, the concealment from the judges and from others of judicial biases and predilections.'"

Needless to say, some impartial readers will regard my conviction that the court of law revolves around the judge's belief with regard to the defendant's innocence, not the truth, as an exaggeration, if not a lie. Perhaps. Anyway, the passage that I am about to cite is likely to leave such readers with the same opinion as me. Either that, or they will at least understand why I am of such a seemingly far-fetched opinion. (By the way, within the passage that I am about to cite hides another conviction: namely, in many a case, a well-read judge can easily find, within the books of law, principles that he can use to substantiate his belief with regard to the defendant's innocence.) "Chancellor Kent of New York State, a great legal authority," further wrote Stuart Chase, "in a charming burst of frankness once wrote: 'I saw where justice lay, and the moral issue decided the court half the time. I then sat down to search the authorities. ... I might once in a while be embarrassed by a technical rule, but I almost always found principles suited to my view of the case.' The learned judge used his best judgment, came to a decision, and then ransacked the fat books for authority to support him. He almost always found it. I would be willing to take his decision, if he were a good judge, without the ornament of citations. The decision constitutes the reality of legal machinery; the citations contribute to the magic."

As the saying goes, I rest my case.

(Side Note: I refer to the basis of many a judge's conviction as a belief instead of a fact owing to the fact that, technically, the defendant is accused of having done, not doing, something. Hence an accusation rests upon a historical fact. Moreover, I am by no means ignorant of the fact that in many a case what the judge believes to be a fact is in fact a fact, even though they weren't there to witness the crime. For that the judge is, of course, indebted to the application of scientific methods and techniques to the investigation of crime.

Speaking of forensics, allow me to share an aphorism with which I attempted to draw our attention to the fact that some of our inventions would not have been necessary if it weren't for the side effects of some of our inventions: "Science gave us forensics. Law gave us crime.")

The f.Law of Law

(Speaking of law, allow me to lend myself an already published writing of mine that I find relevant. In addition to law, the writing touches on assumptions, something that I have attempted to explore with some writings herein.)

As soon as traffic lights turn red, each and every single driver of a car that is headed in the red lights' direction is supposed to stop the car that they are driving. But one might not. And some undertaker might have to undertake a burial.

The person next to you, be they a friend, stranger, or foe, is not supposed to kill you. But he or she might make the last time that you saw your family the last time that you saw your family.

In such cases, an assumption is deadly.

In a word, laws do not prevent unlawfulness; they merely encourage lawfulness.

The f.Law of Identity

He who wrote last year will still be called a writer next year (even if he does not write anything that year).

He who spoke yesterday will still be called a speaker tomorrow (even if his mouth remains shut the entire day).

He who stole ten dollars ten years ago will still be called a thief in ten years' time (by she who the ten dollars were stolen from and they who know of the theft).

She who broke a heart in 1985 will still be called a heartbreaker in twenty-eight years' time (by he whose heart she shattered twenty-eight years ago).

Needless to say, as useful as they usually are, words with which we describe or identify each other are usually unfounded or the claim that is hidden within them is no longer truthful. Owing to the fact that many are based on what one did (sometimes what one did only once) instead of what one is doing. For example, someone who has committed a crime once and then stopped doing so and someone who has committed crimes and still continues to do so are both individually labelled as a criminal.

At any rate, the problem with the concept of "identity" is that it demands that we assign fixed labels or categories to man: a creature that is, like all organisms, more of a process than an object. A creature that is, from birth until death, forever developing—something that we seldom consider before we bitterly accuse our soon-to-be-ex to have "changed" or to no longer be "the same person."

(Side Note: In closing, allow me to share a remark that I find somewhat ad rem. "Loyalty to any one sports team is pretty hard to justify." Joked Jerry Seinfeld. "Because the players are always changing, the team can move to another city, you are actually rooting for the clothes when you get right down to it. You know what I mean, you are standing and cheering and yelling for your clothes to beat the clothes from another city. Fans will be so in love with a player but if he goes to another team, they boo him. This is the same human being in a different shirt, they hate him now! Boo! Different shirt! Boo!"

I will, with the next writing, briefly remind or acquaint the reader with another conundrum that the concept of "identity" inevitably brings about.)

How Many Bricks Make a House, a House?

Some, if not most, readers are likely to wrongly suppose that that question is equivalent to the following question: How many bricks does it take to build a house? But I trust that the sharp-witted reader knows that the latter is meaningless as it stands.

Anyway, here is the knotty conundrum that is at the core of this writing's title: At what point does a group or pile of bricks become a house? In other words, at what point does removing a brick from a house turn the house into a group or pile of bricks? Needless to say, the answer to that question will inevitably invite the question, What "is" a house? And the answer to that will, of course, invite the question, What makes a house, a house?

Such a conundrum is, of course, not limited to houses. An example is in order. How many body parts make a body, a body? Or rather, what makes a person, physically? In other words, is there a point where removing a body part from a corpse turns what is left of the corpse into "body parts"?

At any rate, the identity conundrum that this writing revolves around is, as the learned reader is likely to have noticed, equivalent to The Heap (The Bald Man, The Sorites, Little-by-Little Arguments). To familiarize those who are not familiar with the aforementioned paradox, I would like to cite a passage from a book that is claimed, by its cover, to have been written by Michael Clark.[13] "10,000 grains suitably arranged make a heap. But, at no point can you convert a collection of grains that is a heap into one that is not, simply by removing a single grain. So it follows that a single grain makes a heap. For if we keep removing grains over and over again, say, 9,999 times, at no point does it cease to be a heap. Yet we obviously know that a single grain is not a heap."

There is, of course, another paradox whose relevance to the concept of identity makes it worth citing. So allow me to cite, from the aforementioned book, The Ship of Theseus Paradox. "Over a period of years, in the course of maintenance a ship has its planks replaced one by one – call this ship A. However, the old planks are retained and themselves reconstituted into a ship – call this ship

B. At the end of this process there are two ships. Which one is the original ship of Theseus?"

Finally, let us now bring semantics into this conundrum.

We often hear of people whose dream is to "change the world." There is, of course, absolutely nothing wrong with that. But what exactly does that entail? What do *they* mean by "change" and by "the world"? If by the latter *such people* mean "the earth, together with all of its countries, peoples, and natural features" and if by the former *they* mean, "make different," then the mere act of starting or ending a tree or person's life, intentionally or not, makes one a "world changer."

Judging Kids with Kids

Most, if not all, attributes that are attributable to human beings cannot really be seen with the naked eye.

That is to say, one cannot, from the mere act of gazing at a portrait of a stranger, see what that person is said to "be," e.g., calm, humble, decisive, generous, reliable, punctual, realistic, spiritual, mature, honest, adventurous, intelligent, disciplined, sincere, sympathetic, polite, selfless, tolerant, ambitious, courageous, kind, trustworthy, open-minded, friendly, tenacious, imaginative, unpretentious, alert, et cetera. (I have intentionally limited that list to "positive" attributes. More on that in the following writing.)

At any rate, one can see such attributes only through some microscope called behaviour—the behaviour or actions of whomever that is the subject of one's observation, to be precise. In other words, a person's qualities or features, which are each regarded as something that is inherent in that person, can only be assumed from their actions or behaviour and at times from their appearance.

For example, although we can easily see that an "immoral" fifteen-year-old girl whom we are seeing for the first time had sex without a condom six or so months ago—thanks to some conspicuous "blemish" called an occupied womb, we cannot, from the mere act of gazing at her, see that the seemingly "moral" fourteen-year-old girl whom we are comparing the pregnant one with had an abortion ... thrice.

(Side Note: I will, with the following four writings, attempt to remind or show the reader how the impression that the observer gets from the observed's behaviour or deeds or appearance is easily molded by the observed as per the impression that the observed desires to give;

an impression that is, of course, admired or expected or demanded by the observer.)

The Hardships of Womanhood

I am not a woman. I have never been one. And I doubt that I will ever be one. Having said that, I think that being a woman is extremely hard, especially when it comes to romantic relationships.

As we all know, three out of every five men with a functioning penis tell every fourth woman that they come across that they are in love with her, while it is her vagina that they are really after, not her heart.

Sad to say, in some, if not most, instances, the only time when a woman can know for certain whether or not a man merely wants to get into her pants is after he got into her pants.

(Side Note: As short as this writing is, I find it to be a good reminder of the fact that it is easy for someone to deceive us with regard to "who" or "what" they are and what is truly going on in their "heart" by simply behaving or speaking in a manner that they know is likely to give us whatever impression that they desire to give us. Two things come to mind [1] the commonly insincere smile of a salesperson; and [2] a horny man's most overused tactic: namely, chivalrous behaviour when he is around a woman whose dress he would like to be granted the permission to undress.

Finally, let us now bring the "positive" personality attributes from the previous writing into this.

As we all know, some, if not most, women are programmed to "love" men who are honest, intelligent, friendly, mature, ambitious, understanding, et cetera. Be that as it may, as the sharp-witted reader is likely to have noticed, a man can easily pretend to "have" any of the attributes that countless women value and use as a deciding factor as to whether or not a man is worth dating or sleeping with.

Let us take "understanding," an attribute that is demanded by almost every single sane woman, as an example. A man can easily pretend not to mind waiting the 90 days with which a woman whom he just met tests the seriousness of a man whom she just met—before she gives him the permission to undress her, while he is having sex with seven other women or even her best friend behind her back.

What's more, to win brownie points, all the man has to do is to simply suggest that they wait an extra week or two before they have sex; just to make sure that the woman is sure that she is ready to have sex with him.

Last but not least, let us now bring language into our desire and tactics with which we attempt to mold the impression that others have of us.

To come across as intelligent, to an unintelligent woman who is into intelligent men, an unintelligent man can simply alter his diction. Apparently, to be regarded as intelligent by unintelligent people, all one has to do is to include, within every second or third sentence, a word or phrase whose meaning those with whom one is communicating do not know.)

True Colours of a Politician

Needless to say, the only time when the people can find out whether or not a political party will do as it has promised to do while it was desperately trying to win their votes is after they have voted for the political party.

That is to say, after the political party has won the general elections: after they have put the members of the political party in power. What's more, if and when the people realize that the political party promised them heaven and earth and heaven on earth just so its members are put into power, it would then be too late for the people to do anything about it. For they would have then given the political party the power to use the people's money, i.e., the state's deep pockets, to try to keep themselves in power for as long as possible (by means of propaganda and the like).

In a nutshell, a greedy political party that was foolishly put into power could use its then power to quadruple the likelihood of it ruling until hell freezes over.

(Side Note: Speaking of voting and the illusion of having power that it gives voters, allow me to cite a relevant passage from *Amusing Ourselves to Death*. "You plan to do nothing about them [NATO, the CIA, affirmative action, crime and unemployment rates, and the monstrous treatment of the Baha'is in Iran.]. You may, of course, cast a ballot for someone who claims to have some plans, as well as the power to act." Neil Postman is said to have written. "But this you can do only once every two or four years by giving one hour of your time, hardly a satisfying means of expressing the broad range of opinions you hold. Voting, we might even say, is the next to last refuge of the politically impotent. The last refuge is, of course, giving your opinion to a pollster, who will get a version of it through a desiccated question, and then will submerge it in a Niagara of similar opinions, and convert them into—what else?—another piece of news. Thus, we have here a great loop of impotence: The news elicits from you a variety of opinions about which you can do nothing except to offer them as more news, about which you can do nothing."[14])

I Am, Therefore I Act

How man is perceived, which almost always determines how he will and will not be treated, is mainly shaped by the following: (1) the manner in which he behaves; (2) the manner in which he dresses; and (3) what others think of and as a result say about him; which is, of course, mostly determined by the former and the latter.

Needless to say, with the exception of children, all sane human beings are fully aware of that. Hence a sane man is nothing but an actor. That is to say, to be certified as "sane" by one's society is to have and to continue to role-play. By *role-play*, I mean what is usually meant by that term in psychology, namely, "the acting out or performance of a particular role, either consciously (as a technique in psychotherapy or training) or unconsciously, *in accordance with the perceived expectations of society with regard to a person's behavior in a particular context.*"

"When the individual presents himself before others," Erving Goffman is said to have written, "his performance will tend to incorporate and exemplify the officially accredited values of the society, more so, in fact, than does his behaviour as a whole." Man's acting is, of course, by no means limited to individuals. In some cases, the performance is carried out by a team. "In our society, when husband and wife appear before new friends for an evening of sociability, the wife may demonstrate more respectful subordination to the will and opinion of her husband than she may bother to show when alone with him or when with old friends." Further wrote Erving Goffman. "When she assumes a respectful role, he can assume a dominant one; and when each member of the marriage team plays its special role, the conjugal unit, as a unit, can sustain the impression that new audiences expect from it."[15]

As I have asserted elsewhere, "Life is an act: we act in a certain way when we are around certain people in order to make and then sustain a certain impression." I would like to add the following assertion to that: Man is truly himself only when he is alone and is certain that the house or room that he is in is locked; otherwise, he is merely playing "his" character, i.e., he is merely acting as per others' expectations from him.

I was about to qualify my conviction by narrowing it to human beings. However, creatures such as chameleons, caterpillars, walking sticks, and the like, quickly came to mind: creatures that frequently put on an act. Needless to say, some readers will be quick to argue that such creatures use camouflage for nothing but survival; with which they refer to most animals' primary goals: namely, to avoid not having something to eat and to avoid being eaten by something. Well, that is definitely unquestionable. Having said that, I still maintain that at the core of the reason why a man acts in a certain way when he is around certain people hides his desire to survive. For a man's behaviour is, I believe, mostly dictated by his "need" to fit in. (More on that in a few writings' time.)

I would now like to attempt to link my conviction that man is nothing but an actor with the concept of personality.

With the exception of children and people who are insane, we are usually enslaved by the first impression that we have made on others. For once we make a certain impression on others, we are then expected to act as per the expectations that they have from a person of a character or personality such as ours (which they would have assumed from the impression that they would have gotten from how we behaved, spoke, dressed, etc., when they saw us for the first time). In other words, a man who gets divorced merely because he is said to have changed or to no longer be the man that his wife married is a victim of nothing but having acted in a manner that gave his audience (i.e., his wife and possibly other people) an impression that is incompatible with the impression that his audience have already attached to him. "To *be* a given kind of person, then, is not merely to possess the required attributes," Erving Goffman is said to have written, "but also to sustain the standards of conduct and appearance that one's social grouping attaches thereto."[16]

Man's so-called character or personality is by no means the only concept that enslaves him with regard to the kind of behaviour that those who know him expect or even demand from everyone with a character or personality such as his. There is, of course, another enslaving tool called a designation (i.e., a name, description, or title, typically one that is officially bestowed); e.g., priest. Although we all know that priests are unique individuals who have different personalities, there are certain things that we expect from every single person who is titled as such. For example, how such a person is supposed to behave toward and when around others, and the kind of words that are to leave and those that are never to leave their holy mouth. "A status, a position, a social place is not a material thing, to be possessed and then displayed." Further wrote Goffman, "It is a pattern of appropriate conduct, coherent, embellished, and well articulated. Performed with ease or clumsiness, awareness or not, guile or good faith, it is none the less something that must be realized."[17]

Slavery to expectations that are brought about by the title that one is given is almost always witnessed whenever a comedian or an intellectual is interviewed. The former will, with every single sentence that leaves their mouth, try as hard as they can to make the interviewer and the audience laugh. Whereas the latter will, with every single word that leaves their mouth, try as hard as they can to come across as intelligent. Which then means that we are somewhat slaves to every single label or title that we are given. For example, a man who is said to be funny, intelligent, and humble is forced to—if he is to continue reaping the fruits reaped by men so labelled—act and speak in a manner that will at worst sustain and at best polish the impression of being regarded as funny, intelligent, and humble.

In a word, a designation is expectations (from the named, the described, or the titled) compressed into a word or three.

At any rate, Chris Rock once remarked that, "When you meet somebody for the first time, you're not meeting them. You're meeting their representative." Although I concur, I would like to omit "for the first time" to make his remark truer: "When you meet somebody, you're not meeting them. You're meeting their representative." And to that I would like to add an already published aphorism of mine: "We seldom look like the way we look like when people we like are looking."

Anyway, as I have already asserted, man acts as per the expectations of those that he is around. For example, though he is the very "same person" in both instances: how a man behaves when he is around his male friends is seldom the same with how he behaves when he is around his employer or his in-laws. (Finally, let us bring language into this.) Likewise, the aforementioned man's daughter's choice of words is likely to be different whenever she is conversing with him. For example, instead of using "shit!" as an exclamation of disgust as she always does when she is around her friends, she will replace that with interjections such as "ewww!" or "yuck!" or "ugh!"

Speaking of friends, allow me to conclude this writing with another relevant aphorism of mine: "There is no such thing as a shy person. There are just people whom one is comfortable around and those whom one isn't comfortable around."

Clothes Make the Man

In a materialistic society, man is likely to value the opinion of a rich man over that of a poor one, even when it comes to opinions that have absolutely nothing to do with making money.

With that aphorism, I wanted to remind the reader that what a man has or does not have usually determines how he and what he says is regarded. With this writing, I will touch on how and why appearing rich can be and usually is as rewarding as being rich is.

Allow me to cite an extract from the introduction of *The Presentation of Self In Everyday Life*, a book that is said to have been written by Erving Goffman. "When an individual enters the presence of others, they commonly seek to acquire information about him or to bring into play information about him already possessed. They will be interested in his general social-economic status, his conception of self, his attitude towards them, his competence, his trustworthiness, etc. Although some of this information seems to be sought almost as an end in itself, there are usually quite practical reasons for acquiring it. Information about the individual helps to define the situation, enabling others to know in advance what he will expect of them and what they may expect of him. Informed in these ways, the others will know how best to act in order to call forth a desired response from him.

"If unacquainted with the individual, observers can glean clues from his conduct and appearance which allow them to apply their previous experience with individuals roughly similar to the one before them or, more important, to apply untested stereotypes to him. They can also assume from past experience that only individuals of a particular kind are likely to be found in a given social setting. They can rely on what the individual says about himself or on documentary evidence he provides as to who and what he is."

When it comes to profiting from one's appearance, as is the case with profiting from one's religion, the truth is not really a prerequisite. Sounds far-fetched? Perhaps. But luckily, I have four things that should instantly change the minds of those who think so: viz., makeup, fake hair, false teeth, and push-up bras. Anyway, when endeavouring to shape or choose how he comes across to others and what others think of him, in addition to the way in which he behaves and what he says about himself, the civilized man has concrete things such as his clothes, his car, his house, his better half, and the like, at his disposal. Such things, too, can be and are usually used to shape the impression that he will make on his audience, that is, those whom his performance is watched by.

Needless to say, the aforementioned costumes and props are one of the many brushes with which man is able to paint, on some canvas called the minds of his audience, a favourable image of himself.

At any rate, when it comes to a man's endeavour to come across as prosperous, the mere act of wearing an "expensive" suit is a thousand times more vivid, more dramatic, and more believable than verbally claiming to be so. Even though the suit could be a stolen counterfeit that he has borrowed from his friend. What's more, the truth with regard to the claim that is made by the brand name that the suit bears, and the unstated claim that the suit is his, does not really matter. What matters is that those who constitute his audience believe that the suit is his and that the suit is a genuine product by the up-scale brand so-and-so. (By the way, that is what inspired me to assert the following: "If clothes indeed make the man, then being the man can be bought, borrowed, or stolen.")

As may be expected, many a poor man who desires to reap the fruits that are reaped by rich men spends a large chunk of his minuscule paycheck on things that promise to make him appear less poor than he is, if not rich. For appearing rich is a million times quicker and a billion times easier than being rich.

Finally, I find the difference between oral and written claims and what one might call "visual innuendos" or "visual claims" worth mentioning: one cannot reasonably call a poor man whose attire made him appear prosperous a liar. For unlike oral and written claims, he cannot be said to have said that he is or has whatever that his audience assumed him to be or have.

Beliefs Make the Believer

Amongst other things, man used the things, opinions, and beliefs that he has, during the manufacturing process of who and what he is, that is, his personal identity. As may be expected, he will do all in his power not to lose all or any of the aforementioned mental bricks with which he has constructed a mental being called self.

Let us start with his possessions.

Most, if not all, wealthy men's personal identity revolves around their bank balance and their valuable possessions. Hence they will move heaven and earth to at worst preserve and at best multiply their wealth. I mean, what is a wealthy man without wealth?

Let us now bring debates into this. (Needless to say, debates generally revolve around the debaters' opinions and/or beliefs.)

Debates are generally a waste of time, not because debating is incapable of moving those involved forward with regard to the subject of their debate, but because at the core of almost all debates hides, I believe, the debaters' egos, not genuine desires to find facts or to search for the truth.

Let us use the existence of God debate as an example.

Because of nothing but the fact that most, if not all, believers incorporated their belief with regard to the existence of God when constructing their personal identities, most, if not all, believers will do all in their power to either prove nonbelievers wrong or to simply ignore whatever that is said to disprove the claim of there being a God, regardless of how plausible whatever that is said to do so is. Reason? Simple. If I am what I believe and what I believe is proven wrong, who or what will I then be?

At any rate, the only instances where such debates stand a chance of being fruitful is when the debate is between a maximum of two debaters and a maximum of zero spectators. Otherwise, the debaters' egos will, more often than not, be a hindrance to the potential fruitfulness of the debate. To sum up, there are usually two reasons why debates seldom end up with unanimity: (1) many a debater used his opinions and/or his beliefs when constructing his personal identity; and (2) the debate has spectators.

As may be expected, debater1 will do all in his power to defend his belief, even if he is eventually convinced into seeing the truthfulness or the superiority of debater2's belief or argument over his.

Needless to say, although *debate* and *discussion* are usually used interchangeably, they differ with regard to intent. A debate's primary aim is to produce a gold medalist, whereas a successful discussion can end with both parties still being of the very same opposing opinions. Like someone once said, "The purpose of a debate is to find out *who* is wrong; the purpose of a discussion is to find out *what* is wrong."

Anyway, Russell Bertrand is widely quoted as having said that, "Most people would die sooner than think – in fact they do so." Allow me to alter that as per the topic in question. Here goes! "Most people would die sooner than change their beliefs – in fact they do so." Speaking of Russell Bertrand, allow me to share a reply of his that I find ad rem. After being asked if he would be prepared to die for what he believed in, he is said to have said: "Of course not, after all, I may be wrong."

(Side Note: Sad to say, such intellectually humble human beings, people who are aware that their belief might in fact not be a fact, are in short supply. As may be expected, such people are intelligent enough not to be ashamed of being proven wrong and eventually having to change their beliefs or opinions. For they know and acknowledge that they are not their beliefs and/or their opinions. So doing so does not mean or lead to mental suicide.)

Man Is Man-made

Man is, with regard to the concept of personal identity, both the inventor and the invention.

While man might not have invented, say, organisms to which we refer with the word *cattle*, he came up with the practice of naming things and words such as *cattle*.

("And Adam gave names to all cattle, and to the fowl of the air, and to every beast of the field." — Genesis 2:20, KJV. Ah, I finally found a biblical verse that substantiates my assertion.) To that, one could, of course, add concepts and personal attributes such as selflessness, reliableness, thoughtfulness, faithfulness, et cetera.

I would now like to, before I bring our exploration of the concept of personal identity to an end, touch on the concept of individualism.

Believe it or not, there was actually a time where "individuals" as we know them did not exist. That is to say, there was a time where man did not really regard himself as an entity that is separate from the environment and other human beings. "Medieval society did not deprive the individual of his freedom because the 'individual' did not yet exist; man was still related to the world by primary ties." Erich Fromm is said to have written. "He did not yet conceive of himself as an individual except through the medium of his social (which then was also his natural) role. He did not conceive of any other persons as 'individuals' either. ... Awareness of one's individual self, of others, and of the world as separate entities, had not yet fully developed.

"The lack of self-awareness of the individual in medieval society has found classical expression in Jacob

Burckhardt's description of medieval culture: 'In the Middle Ages both sides of human consciousness—that which was turned within as that which was turned without—lay dreaming or half awake beneath a common veil. The veil was woven of faith, illusion, and childish prepossession, through which the world and history were seen clad in strange hues. Man was conscious of himself only as a member of a race, people, party, family, or corporation—only through some general category.'"[18]

In a nutshell, although we have been, mentally speaking, individuals from the very beginning of our species' existence, our being individuals mentally is made easier, if not possible, by concepts and theories such as individualism.

Culture and the Fools It Fools

(I would now like to borrow two ad rem writings that I have already published. Apart from touching on culture and nationality, they, like the writing that follows them, allude to the concept of personal identity.)

Do Afrikaners own Afrikaans, *potjiekos*, and khaki shorts?

Do Japanese own sushi, karate, and meditation?

Do Zulus own *phuthu*, arrogance, and topless women?

Would a Frenchman be a fool should he prefer conversing in Sepedi over his mother tongue?

Would a Chinese man be seen as Africanized or disloyal should he prefer *pap* and *mogodu* over a bowl of noodles?

(Side Note: Granted, some things are associated with some people. Having said that, nobody owns anything. In other words, while Asians are usually the very first race that comes to mind when most people think of karate, Asians do not "own" hands, fists, feet, knees, elbows, foreheads, et cetera, or even karate.)

Fooled by Patriotism

Perhaps the most common delusion that we share as human beings is the conviction that: (1) what we know is the best there is to know; (2) who we "have" is the best there is to have; (3) what we do is the best there is to do; and (4) who or what we believe in is the best there is to believe in.

At any rate, if given the opportunity, many, if not

most, people would readily bet with their lives that their country is the best country in the world, even those who have never made use of a passport.

Anyway, unless you have died before, it would be ignorant and arrogant of you to assert that life is better than death.

Finally, allow me to share an ad rem remark that is said to have been said by George Bernard Shaw. "Patriotism is, fundamentally, a conviction that a particular country is the best in the world because you were born in it."

Bushmen and Prawns

As random as it was, the continent or country or region in which a child was born will nine times out of ten be one of the factors, if not the only factor, that mold or molds "his" or "her" taste.

Because of that, one can usually tell where a man was brought up, from nothing but what he asserts to be the most delicious meal or dish in the world. Obviously, the probability of correctly guessing where the man was raised will be high in cases where what he asserts to be the most delicious meal or dish in the world is associated with a particular culture or country or region, e.g., *phuthu* and *potjiekos*, whereas the probability will be low in cases where the meal or dish is not associated with or exclusive to a particular culture or country or region, e.g., hamburgers and hot dogs.

Anyway, as we all know, children eat whatever it is that they are fed, and as may be expected, they usually end up liking a particular meal or meals that they are regularly fed. Eventually, many, if not most, blindly label one or two meals as the most delicious meal or meals in the world; despite the fact that they have never tasted even one meal that isn't on their culture, country, or region's finite menu.

That is, of course, normally how one's taste is tattooed on one's tongue.

At any rate, as is usually the case with other people's beliefs, we are almost always exposed to other cultures' cuisines only when we are too old for us to taste and then judge them without our tongue and as a result our judgment being contaminated by the fact that we generally prefer cuisines that we were frequently fed when we were growing up over those that we have tasted only after we have grown to love some of those that we were frequently fed when we were growing up.

The f.Law of the First

Would *Titanic* have been less of a box-office success, should the character of Jack Dawson have been portrayed by Tony Kgoroge or some random blue-eyed white young man?

It is, of course, near impossible to imagine the aforementioned role being played by someone else. And that includes actors whom one believes to actually be better actors than Leonardo DiCaprio. What's more, although there were other great pianists when it was recorded, it is hard to imagine *Finding Oneself* or *Darkness Pass* having been brought to being by anyone other than Moses Molelekwa. In the very same way that it is near impossible to imagine the role of Sarafina having been played by anyone other than Leleti Khumalo.

At any rate, as subjective as it is, chances are that Michael Jackson's execution of "Man in the Mirror" is not the best that there could have been. Despite that, it is near impossible to imagine another artist performing the song better than him, even those whom one regards as better performers than "the King of Pop."

Needless to say, in those examples' case, as is the case with branding—the business of the management of perceptions—being the first is usually as profitable as being the best is. As it happens, the first are usually perceived as the best. What's more, as is the case when it comes to profiting from believing the claim of there being a God, the truth does not really matter. What matters is that consumers believe that brand so-and-so is the best.

Prophets, Untruths, and Profits

Our lives do not revolve around or depend on truths as much as we believe to be the case. To substantiate that, I will simply remind the reader that more than two in every three human beings are said to be religious. And as I have attempted to demonstrate in the previous chapter, religion's fruitfulness is by no means dependent on whether or not its fundamental claim, namely, the claim that God exists, is truthful.

To add to that, I would like to share an ad rem aphorism with which I attempted to sum up man's general attitude towards many a fact of life. "Man is more likely to believe a lie that he wanted to hear over a fact that he wishes was a lie."

At any rate, motivational speakers, like liquor stores owners, drug lords, fortune-tellers, preachers, and the like, would be the last to starve should things not go well. As a matter of fact, the harder life gets for the so-called civilized man, the more profitable their products or services become. Owing to the fact that they are one way or another in the business of exploiting hopelessness by manufacturing and then selling hope.

As I once aphorized, "To avoid starvation, a preacher exploits his congregations' hopelessness; a beggar exploits his spectators' pity."

Needless to say, motivational speakers' products and services are based on two comforting but not always truthful claims: namely, "You can do it!" and "Everything is going to be okay!" Here, too, to get by, many a man profits from believing that whatever claim that he is told and sold is truthful. Whether or not it is does not really matter. What's more, as we all know, in many a case such a claim turns out to be nothing but a white lie.

At any rate, as depressing as it might be, if truth be told, although preachers and motivational speakers' livelihood depend on convincing the civilized man otherwise, what many a troubled man calls a rough patch is quite a smooth patch when compared with what life has in store for him. For the rest of his life is left with nothing but rougher rough patches.

Anyway, as I have argued in the previous chapter,

many a civilized man does not have the intellectual stamina required to face life for what it "is," that is, reality without the myths that he is continuously fed and/or intoxicants that he continuously consumes. To substantiate that, I will simply remind the learned reader that there exist a tendency to which we refer with the word *escapism*, i.e., the civilized man's tendency to seek distraction and relief from unpleasant realities, especially by seeking entertainment or engaging in fantasy. That is, of course, by no means limited to religion and alcohol.

As we all know, most, if not all, homeless glue sniffers sniff glue to achieve the very same thing that many a man who reads the Bible and all those who drown their sorrows do so for: namely, to either escape an unpleasant present for a few hours or to make reality appear less unpleasant than it actually is—which usually gives them the mental stamina needed to carry themselves from an unpleasant today into a hopefully less unpleasant tomorrow.

To wit, sniffing glue is a homeless nonbeliever's prayer.

Perhaps that is the reason why churches, drugs, entertainment, alcohol, motivational speakers, and the like are so popular, and why social critics seldom win popularity contests. Reason? Simple. Social critics always tell us that things are not okay, whereas motivational speakers always tell us that things will be okay. As George Lichtenberg is said to have said, "You can make a better living in the world as a soothsayer than as a truthsayer."

Alcoholic Doctors and Smoking Nurses

While many, if not most, readers are likely to disagree with me with regard to some, if not most, claims that I have asserted thus far, one can, with reason, presume that not a single reader will disagree with me when I say that no human being is completely rational, or rather, no human being is rational at all times.

We all know countless rational men who smoke: people who are without doubt aware of the dangers of smoking. If such people were rational at all times, then the mere placement of the "cigarettes cause cancer" warning that is found on most, if not all, cigarette packages would have resulted in a sharp decline of the number of people who smoke. That obviously gets more interesting when one brings, into that, the fact that we, like other organisms, are born with an innate desire to live until hell freezes over. Hence one would necessarily expect that desire to be strong enough to make us prioritize our health over everything, particularly things that threaten to shorten our lifespan.

At any rate, in some facets of our lives, we habitually suspend logic. In the very same way that we intentionally suspend disbelief when we are in front of a switched on TV or an open novel in order for us to quadruple the odds of us being entertained and/or escaping reality for an hour or twenty-four. Owing to the fact that, as I have argued when concluding the previous chapter, without the audience's suspension of disbelief, no work of fiction would work. To that, I would like to add an ad rem remark that is said to have been said by Sigmund Freud. "Satisfaction is obtained through illusions, which are recognized as such, without the discrepancy between them and reality being allowed to interfere with the pleasure they give."[19]

Needless to say, man is nothing but a bundle of contradictions. At times, he willingly deceives himself. It is not uncommon to find a man sweating blood to convince himself that he does not miss his ex-lover whom he misses terribly. Or a woman who managed to convince herself that she is not in love with a man whom she is extremely in love with; merely because unlike her, the poor man does not believe in Allah. Or a gold digger that has successfully convinced herself into sincerely believing that she is in love with a man whose bank balance is the only thing that she loves about him. Like Nassim Nicholas Taleb is said to have said, "When a young woman partners with an otherwise uninteresting rich man, she can sincerely believe that she is attracted to some very specific body part (say, his nose, neck, or knee)."[20] And as I once aphorized, "Money cannot buy you love. But it sure can buy you things that some people will 'love' you for having."

Anyway, my assertion that man is by no means a creature that is rational at all times can be substantiated by the mere act of bringing, to the reader's mind, the phenomenon to which *doublethink*—a term that George Orwell is said to have coined in his novel *Nineteen Eighty-Four*—refers, i.e., "the acceptance of or mental capacity to accept contrary opinions or beliefs at the same time, especially as a result of political indoctrination."[21] Perhaps that is the reason why there exists many a man who is appropriately labelled as a "religious scientist," and countless women who, for hygienic reasons, are reluctant to shake hands, particularly with strangers; yet they readily suck the penis of a man whom they met an hour or six before doing so.

Finally, allow me to share an ad rem anecdote.

My former neighbour is a Christian chemistry student. To excuse herself from the tug of war between religion and science (theism and atheism, to be precise), she alternates between being a theist and being an atheist. She says that when she is in a laboratory, she rejects the theory of there being a God. However, she rejects the theory of there not being a God, as soon as she leaves campus.

Last but not least, allow me to cite a portion of the introduction of *The Image*, a book that Daniel J. Boorstin is said to have written. (Boorstin wrote, in the aforesaid book's foreword, "It [the book] is about our arts of self-deception, how we hide reality from ourselves.") Here goes!

"In this book I describe the world of our making, how we have used our wealth, our literacy, our technology, and our progress, to create the thicket of unreality which stands between us and the facts of life. ... We want and we believe these illusions because we suffer from extravagant expectations. We expect too much of the world. ... When we pick up our newspaper at breakfast, we expect—we even demand—that it bring us momentous events since the night before. We turn on the car radio as we drive to work and expect 'news' to have

occurred since the morning newspaper went to press. ...
We expect new heroes every season, a literary master-
piece every month, a dramatic spectacular every week,
a rare sensation every night. ... We expect everybody to
believe deeply in his religion, yet not to think less of others for not believing. ... We expect anything and everything. We expect the contradictory and the impossible.
We expect compact cars which are spacious; luxurious
cars which are economical. We expect to be rich and
charitable, powerful and merciful, active and reflective,
kind and competitive. ... Never have people been more
the masters of their environment. Yet never has a people felt more deceived and disappointed. For never has
a people expected so much more than the world could
offer."[22]

In conclusion, I would like to share an ad rem remark
that is said to have been said by Sinclair Lewis. As the
sharp-witted reader is likely to notice, apart from it being relevant to the aforementioned tug of war between
man's heart and his brain, the following remark touches
on patriotism. Here goes! "Intellectually I know that
America is no better than any other country; emotionally I know she is better than every other country."

Why Do Sane Men Imitate Each Other?

Let us first get the most obvious out of the way: Belonging to a society is one way or another beneficial to the individual. What's more, civilization as we know it would not have been possible without cooperation or teamwork. For civilization is a stage that was and is reached as an end result of the collaboration between a handful of men's minds and multitudes of men's hands. "One important element is the fact that men cannot live without some sort of co-operation with others." Erich Fromm is said to have written. "In any conceivable kind of culture man needs to co-operate with others if he wants to survive, whether for the purpose of defending himself against enemies or dangers of nature, or in order that he may be able to work and [re]produce. Even Robinson Crusoe was accompanied by his man Friday; without him he would probably not only have become insane but would actually have died."[23] (The "[re]" in "[re]produce" is mine, not Fromm's.)

As we all know, a community cannot really be without some form of conformity. Two senses of *New Oxford American Dictionary's* definition of *conformity* are ad rem: (1) compliance with standards, rules, or laws; and

(2) behaviour in accordance with socially accepted conventions or standards.

Needless to say, communication is impossible without some form of conformity. For there needs to be at least two people who comply with standards or rules of the use of words in a structured and conventional way for that particular use of words to count as a language. Anyway, that is not the form of conformity that I would like to touch on. I am more interested in exploring the reasons why, for example, some God-fearing Hutus—people whom one can, with reason, expect to abide by the "Thou shalt not kill" commandment—readily joined some of their fellow Hutus when they were slaughtering some Tutsis. What did they have to gain from following the crowd? What would they have lost should they have decided not to join their fellow Hutus when they were slaughtering some Tutsis? (Well, in the latter question's case, they would have each been seen as a double-crosser or a Judas, which would have probably led to the loss of their "ethnic membership." In the former's case, they not only avoided being ostracized, but they also strengthened their ties with their fellow Hutus.)

At any rate, belonging to a community gives man an opportunity to evade something that he fears almost as much as he fears death: isolation. "Religion and nationalism, as well as any custom and any belief however absurd and degrading, if it only connects the individual with others, are refuges from what man most dreads: isolation." Erich Fromm is said to have written. "Unless he belonged somewhere, unless his life had some meaning and direction, he would feel like a particle of dust and be overcome by his individual insignificance. He would not be able to relate himself to any system which would give meaning and direction to his life, he would be filled with doubt, and this doubt eventually would paralyze his ability to act—that is, to live."[24]

What's more, a community has what man needs to quadruple the odds of his gene seeing yet another generation: namely, a potential mate. That being so, no man in his right mind will intentionally do something that will lead to him being ostracized from the *primary community* that he belongs to. ("Primary community" could be as narrow as the group of people with whom one inhabits a particular area or place, or as broad as one's society, which could, of course, be referring to one's countrymen, people with whom one shares a continent, or even the human race as a whole.) Without acceptance into a primary community, man is unlikely to be able to ensure the continuity of his gene through reproduction. However, he would still be able to do that if he were to be ostracized from a *secondary community*, with which I refer to a group of people with whom he is united by an interest, a profession, an illness, or a stigma. For example, a man's loss of his cherished membership to the Lawyers Who Meet Once A Year To Show Off Their New Cars Club is unlikely to reduce the odds of him being seen as worth reproducing with by potential mates in his primary community.

Let us, as another example, bring religion back into this.

Some believers do not agree with some rules of behaviour that are preached at the pulpit. Be that as it may, they still abide by them lest they be ostracized—which will, of course, lead to the loss of the two most sought-after things that religion provides or will provide the religious with: namely, a sense of belonging and a one-way ticket to heaven.

At any rate, the civilized man's need to belong can be and is usually used by other men to keep a tight rein on him. Although he is usually too busy working or being entertained to think that far, the civilized man's sex life, too, is governed by social systems that his thoughts and actions are governed by. Sounds far-fetched? Perhaps. But I am almost certain that the reader will agree with me when I say that: To most employees, having sex between 9 a.m. and 5 p.m. during the week is out of the question. (It goes without saying that that applies to every single day of man's life, in cases of they who work Monday to Monday.) Anyway, as usual, I will not let an opportunity to say something "silly" go to waste. Here goes: If working hours were natural, employed men would be impotent between 9 a.m. and 5 p.m. (during the week). As we all know, employed people generally have sex after work—i.e., between 5:01 p.m. and 8:59 a.m.—on weekdays. After civilization has squeezed as much energy out of them as it possibly can.

Let us now bring the exploitation of man's need to sustain his life, his need to belong, and his desire to reproduce, back into this.

It is near impossible for the civilized man to sustain his life without taking part in the complex process with which humanity chases some fleeting stage called civilization. As a result, the civilized man cannot really feed himself without first feeding some beast called civilization: a beast with an insatiable appetite. For civilization has transformed man from a food gatherer into a gatherer of pieces of paper (diplomas, employment contracts, money, etc.).

At any rate, being normal, or at least being regarded as normal, is, in many a case, a prerequisite for being accepted as a member of a group. Hence those who are and those who are regarded as abnormal seldom reap the fruits that those who are labelled as normal are reaping. By the way, that is how a society encourages conformity. Anyway, as may be expected, man will do all in his power to say or do whatever it is that needs to be said or done for him to be labelled as normal or to avoid being labelled as abnormal. (Needless to say, being normal is, with regard to one's behaviour, generally relative. For it is usually dependent on a group or a society's laws, standards, or expectations. Naturally, society$_1$'s normal is sometimes society$_{2, 3, 4, 5, etc.}$'s abnormal.)

To sum up, the civilized man's behaviour and deeds or lack thereof are almost always controlled by others' exploitation of his desire to become and then remain a member of some primary community, seldom by reason or will.

Finally, allow me to share two already published aphorisms of mine with which I attempted to compress the gist of this writing: (1) A wedding is a ceremony men fund with money they know they do not have to prove the love they think they have; and (2) A salary is to a man's employer what a vagina is to his woman: a tool that is used to reward and to control him.

Real Men Do Rape

Spending Billions on Telling Hobos That Life is a Bitch

Although many a reader will strongly disagree with the assertion that this writing's title is made up of (readers who grasped the gist of the chapter on language will suspended judgment until they find out what I mean by "real men"), I strongly believe that most, if not all, readers will agree with the following assertion: Most, if not all, sane rapists knew, before raping, that rape is illegal.

If that is indeed so, then aren't we wasting time and money on trying to put an end to something that isn't really brought about by a lack of awareness by telling those whom our message will reach—particularly those who did, do, or might do—that forcing another person to have sexual intercourse with one without their consent and against their will is a crime? To put it more bluntly, aren't we fooling ourselves by relying on "Stop Rape", "No Means No", and "Real Men Don't Rape" campaigns, which seldom tell us something that we did not know, in our desperate attempt to put an end to rape?

Well, even though I, too, like most concerned people, do not know which is the right one, I think that we are barking up the wrong tree.

Anyway, if my second assertion is anything to go by, then one can, with reason, assert that at the core of "Stop Rape", "No Means No", and "Real Men Don't Rape" campaigns hides the misconception that rapists' ignorance with regard to the unlawfulness of forcing someone to have sexual intercourse with them without their consent and against their will is the root cause of rape. But isn't that analogous to attributing a starving man's act of stealing a loaf of bread to his ignorance with regard to the unlawfulness of doing so instead of hunger, his country's unequal distribution of its wealth, his fear of starvation (which is, of course, brought about by man's innate desire to protect himself from harm and death), and the like?

To sum up, allow me to restate my second assertion through an analogy.

Most, if not all, criminals who are in prison for, say, armed robbery, knew very well, before robbing, that robbery is illegal. What's more, I doubt that there are would-have-been criminals who were saved, a few seconds before they were about to commit a crime, by the mere act of recalling the claim that your average anti-crime campaign feeds us, namely, "Crime does not pay," which is, of course, not truthful in countless instances. For, as I once aphorized, "Crime does not pay ... if you get caught."

Repetition Is a Double-Edged Sword

Repetition sure has its advantages. For some people need to be told the very same thing more than once before they do or stop doing whatever it is that they are doing or not doing. Needless to say, repetition is so powerful that we sometimes find ourselves humming the tune or lyrics of a song that we actually hate.

Having said that, repetition can also leave us, as could be the case with the campaigns in question, no longer worrying about an issue or issues that we should be worrying about. Owing to the fact that, although the chances of us taking action or, as is usually the case, telling those who care to listen that "enough is enough" (something which we unfortunately equate with taking action) increase everytime we read about or hear of yet another rape incident, after some point, the more we read about or hear of yet another rape incident the more powerless we feel and the more passive and the less likely to act we become.

To sum up, the downside of repetition is its likelihood to make those who are told the very same thing a million times less sensitive to whatever it is that they were told a million times. For example, a man's decision to move, from once a month to once a day, the frequency of instances were he tells a woman whom he met a few months ago that he loves her is likely to increase the odds of her believing him with regard to the sincerity of that claim, whereas moving the frequency of doing so from once a day to once every minute is likely to decrease the odds of her continuing to believe that claim.

Using False Teeth to Prevent Loss of Teeth

Because of our misbelief that people commit crime only because they are evil, we spend most of our resources on endeavouring to get rid of men and women who commit or committed crime instead of endeavouring to get rid of whatever it is that induce or induced them to do so.

An example, which substantiates that assertion, is in order. For that I will use our use of the so-called "correctional facilities" as an attempt to eradicate crime. (By the way, I am of the conviction that in many a case imprisonment is nothing but an attempt to mold man's behaviour as per the wants of civilization instead of molding civilization as per the needs of man.) In their attempt to put an end to crime, or to at least appear like they are doing something about it, the powers that be cage the so-called criminals instead of trying to eradicate the things or conditions that have succeeded in persuading or bullying them into stealing, killing, or raping.

Needless to say, many, if not most, crimes have been with us since the day that we invented law. And because of that, one can, with reason, assert that caging people, that is, imprisoning the so-called criminals, will never eradicate crime. For, as I have joked elsewhere, "Prisons were not really invented to put an end to crime; they were invented merely to console those whom someone stole from, assaulted, or killed someone close to them."

Haven't we given prisons enough centuries to prove or disprove their effectiveness? Or is our continuing to cage others merely the price that they pay for our misbelief that doing an ineffective deed is more effective than not doing anything at all?

Anyway, my seemingly idealistic take on the correctional facilities in question is by no means a plea for us to stop punishing wrongdoers. With what I have just asserted, my humble attempt was to show or remind the reader that imprisonment does not always stop people from raping or killing again. Well, that is if the undeniable fact that there are countless rapists who served a jail sentence between their raping victim₁ and their raping victim₂ and countless murderers who served a jail sentence between their killing victim₄ and their killing victim₅, is anything to go by.

In a nutshell, imprisoning criminals does not increase the chances of us eradicating crime. Doing so merely decreases the chances of an imprisoned killer or rapist killing or raping again. As I have argued earlier, laws do not prevent unlawfulness; they merely encourage lawfulness.

Sanity Is Temporary: When Turned On, We're All Insane

Like most sane men, 94% of the foolish things that I have done or promised to do are attributable to either or both my being in love or sexually excited.

Let us start with emotions.

Although we are well aware that being rational over being emotional is almost always worthwhile, when torn between being emotional and being rational, our emotions usually carry the day. To substantiate that, I will simply remind the reader that there are countless heavily indebted women who readily buy an expensive handbag or pair of shoes that just stole their heart on credit to add to their collection of more than twenty handbags or pair of shoes.

Needless to say, emotions, like looks, can be deceiving. For example, anger easily makes an undersized man whose wife he has just found in bed with some oversized man believe that his wife's other man will be the one whose face is rearranged after he is done expressing his anger with his fists. Similarly, a wife's love for her abusive husband usually works in favour of her husband by also functioning as a psychological chain that prevents her from leaving him.

With that, I hope to have demonstrated that it is easy for emotions to have a detrimental effect on an emotional man's appearance.

Let us now bring sex hormones into this.

Sex hormones, like emotions, easily overpower reason. To further substantiate my conviction that ignorance isn't the major cause of social ills such as rape or theft, allow me to share another conviction: Not every HIV-positive person who got infected through unprotected sex found out that unprotected sex could leave them infected with HIV after they were infected with HIV. Sometimes some people have sex without a condom, not because they have never heard of such an invention or because they do not have or afford one, but merely because when we are sexually excited, the part of our brain that makes it possible for us to be rational goes on leave. Or so it seems.

Finally, I would now like to attempt to show the reader how easy it is for sex hormones to have a detrimental effect on a sexually excited man's body.

Every now and then, hormones get the best of man. I do not really need to enumerate the irrational things that we usually do in the name of love or, more relevant to the topic in question, in the name of an orgasm or two. I will, instead of doing that, share an anecdote that substantiates my seemingly far-fetched convictions. Here goes: Some medical doctor, someone who, on an average day, sees the horrible effects of sexually transmitted diseases, had sex with a former neighbour of mine, whom he met a few hours before their one-night stand, without a condom. The end.

Masturbation: To Unstigmatize or Not to Unstigmatize

As is the case with some religious laws (which are, I believe, nothing but a holy attempt to subjugate civilized men's thoughts and behaviour), there are innumerable religious people who are of the conviction that the Bible prohibits masturbation, while countless people, believers and nonbelievers, are of an opposing conviction. Be that as it may, I strongly believe that, regardless of who is right with regard to the Bible's stance on masturbation, in most, if not all, cases, an anti-masturbation person's attitude towards masturbation was molded by nothing but religious teachings of the religion that they are an adherent of.

Needless to say, most, if not all, of those who are against masturbation regard it as unnatural. Even though children as young as two years old are reported, by their parents, to have been caught masturbating.[25] What's more, as the learned reader knows, some animals also masturbate[26] (perhaps that is because such children and such animals do not have a religious rule or law to consider before they unashamedly submit to their natural urge to be sexually pleased) and, perhaps more interesting than that, there are countless religious girls and women who are still virgins, even though they have orgasmed gazillions of times. The most interesting thing about that is that in some cases such girls and women's compliance with their religion's "No sex before marriage" law or rule would not have been possible should they have not disobeyed their religion's unstated "Thou shalt not play with thyself" commandment.

At any rate, although it would be unfair of one to attribute all rape incidents to the condemnation of masturbation alone, maybe, just maybe, there is a correlation between the average number of rape incidents that take place within a society every single year and that society's general attitude towards masturbation.

Like I said, maybe.

Anyway, I believe that one can, with reason, presume that some rape incidents would not have occurred should we have not stigmatized masturbation—something that gazillions of people who publicly declare as "dirty" and "unnatural" do behind closed doors. Granted, unstigmatizing masturbation alone will not eradicate rape. Be that as it may, I strongly believe that doing so is likely to keep many would-have-been rapists as non-rapists.

Finally, I would now like to, in my attempt to justify such a seemingly implausible conviction, bring our sex hormones' habit of overpowering the part of our brain that makes it possible for us to be rational back into this discussion.

In a word, the one thing that most honest men will attest to is the fact that their hormones give in to whatever part of their brain that makes it possible for them to be rational as soon as they are done ejaculating. By the way, that is usually the stage where a man thinks to himself that spending the amount of money that he has just spent, in order that he is given the permission to have sex with the woman with whom he just had sex, was not worth it. Or that having sex with his sister-in-law was a foolish thing to do. Or that he should have at least used a condom.

Women Who Do Not Play Hard to Get Are Hard to Get

We have, as a society, conditioned women who are and those who would like to come across as "righteous" to initially act as if they are not interested in a man whom they are interested in merely because they have just met him lest they come across as promiscuous or easy or immoral.

Because of nothing but my being more rational than emotional, I find courtship irritating. As may be expected, whenever I am expected to run after a woman who is playing hard to get, I simply excuse myself from the list of men who are pursuing her. Anyway, the purpose of this part of this writing isn't to bore the reader with my impatience with regard to courtship rituals. With it,

I would like to attempt to substantiate, by means of an anecdote, my conviction that women's habit of playing hard to get has unwittingly led to some rape incidents.

Like some men, I have had a handful of instances where a woman towards whom I initiated what would have been our first sexual intercourse responded by playing hard to get. As I once quipped, "88% of women love making their first love making incident with a man seem like an accident." Anyway, instead of doing what men usually do and are usually expected to do in such circumstances, namely, beg, promise the woman the moon or forever, kiss the woman's ass (figuratively, that is), et cetera, I simply stopped. However, I was later told by the women in question that they also wanted us to have sex and that they were playing hard to get merely because they did not want to come across as promiscuous or easy or immoral.

To make a long story short, at the risk of coming across as if I am defending date rapists, which I am not: It is understandable, to me at least, why many a date rapist truly believed that the woman whom he ended up raping was merely playing hard to get lest she come across as promiscuous or easy or immoral when she responded to his initiation of their first sexual intercourse in an aloof or uninterested manner, if and only if he once had an instance where a woman whose aloof or un-interested response to his initiation of what would have been their first sexual intercourse prevented them from having sex later told him that she also wanted them to have sex and that she played hard to get merely because she did not want to come across as promiscuous or easy or immoral.

Believers' Eggs and Nonbelievers' Sperms

(I have herein attempted, with a few aphorisms, to remind the reader that social constructs are unnatural. I will, with this writing, attempt to show the reader how Mother Nature always proves to us that, although most of us blindly worship them, social constructs are unnatural.)

As we all know, many, if not most, people prefer to date and to marry within their race, their culture, their religion, their country, their social class, their ethnicity, their clique, et cetera. (That, of course, substantiates my conviction that there is no such thing as unconditional love.)

Needless to say, children whose parents belong to a

group or a class that is or is merely regarded as superior to others are usually sold the superiority of their "kind" from an early age. As may be expected, $child_1$ is usually discouraged, implicitly or explicitly, from being friends with $child_2$ merely because: (1) $child_2$'s parents—unlike $child_1$'s—do not believe in God; (2) $child_2$ was born into a family that belongs to a different ethnic group; (3) $child_1$ and $child_2$ were born on opposite sides of a border; (4) $child_2$'s parents earn fifteen times less than $child_1$'s; (5) $child_2$ is "black" whereas $child_1$ is "white"; (6) although both are Christians, $child_2$'s parents are members of the Zion Christian Church whereas $child_1$'s parents are Lutherans.

At any rate, limiting the "kind" of people with whom one socializes to, say, one's culture or one's religion, protects one from having to negotiate. As we all know, cultural and religious laws and dos and don'ts free man from the demanding task of thinking for himself. For example, as we have already discussed, some Christians believe that eating pork is prohibited, whereas some believe that it isn't. Because of that, something as simple and as innocent as buying groceries can easily turn into a debate between a Christian man and his wife who has an opposing conviction with regard to the Bible's stance on eating pork. (The chances of that happening are, of course, usually decreased to zero by women's custom of espousing their spouse's cultural and religious beliefs and practices as soon as they are "made one" by a priest, marriage vows, and two circular pieces of metal.)

In other words, the primary, if not the only, reasons why a tribe subtly encourages its members to reproduce amongst themselves is to: (1) first and foremost, protect its customs and its beliefs from perishing or being diluted; and (2) prevent its members' genes from mixing with those of members of other tribes, particularly tribes whose members they regard as inferior to them. That is, of course, usually achieved through endogamy, i.e., the custom of marrying only within the limits of a local community, clan, or tribe.

Exclusively socializing or mating with people with whom one shares the same beliefs or worldview protects one's beliefs or worldview from being questioned or challenged. For example, a theist who socializes only with other theists is unlikely to be asked, by those with whom he socializes, to prove God's existence. Likewise, a wife is unlikely to question the logic behind or the usefulness of rituals that she is expected or demanded to partake in, in cases where a husband was prophetic enough to marry within his church or his ethnic group.

Needless to say, Mother Nature always reminds us

that dividing ourselves by race, nationality, language, religion, age, social class, et cetera, is artificial whenever: (1) a woman whose mother tongue is "French" is impregnated by a man whose mother tongue is "Swahili"; (2) a "white" woman is impregnated by a "kaffir" or a "nigger"; (3) a "South African" is impregnated by a "Nigerian"; (4) the daughter of an extremely "rich" man is impregnated by the son of an extremely "poor" man; (5) a "Jewish" is impregnated by a "gentile"; (6) a "thirty-year-old" woman is impregnated by a "fifteen-year-old" boy; (7) an "educated" woman is impregnated by an "uneducated" man; and (8) a "theist" is impregnated by an "atheist."

In a nutshell, if Mother Nature saw theists and atheists as naturally incompatible, then theist women's eggs would religiously reject atheist men's sperm.

(Side Note: With this writing, I hope to have brought, to the learned reader's mind, a phrase that is relevant to the gist of this book, namely, *distinction without a difference*, which refers to, an artificially created distinction where no real difference exists.)

Why Are All Parents Tyrants?

Most are not. All that most parents want is the best for their children with regard to things like what to study, what kind of people to be friends with, where to study, what kind of a person to fall in love with, whether or not to believe in God, which God to believe in, the number of times that their child or children should go to church in a month, et cetera.

Having said that, as well-meaning as most parents are whenever they seem to be imposing their taste, their beliefs, their lifestyle, and the like on their child or children, sometimes what they force their child or children to do or not do is not good for their child or children's happiness, talents, health, dreams, future, et cetera. What's more, some of the beliefs that they subtly force or forced their child or children to believe are not facts. Needless to say, most parents do not do so because they are tyrants, they do so merely because they sincerely believe that what they have forced or are forcing their child or children to believe or do or not do is or will someday be good for them. And they do not do so because they are liars, but merely because they sincerely believe that the myths and beliefs that they have subtly forced or are subtly forcing their child or children to accept are facts.

Naturally, such parents' children are expected and at times forced to believe in whoever or whatever it is that their parents believe in, because their parents—like most people—used things like "their" beliefs when constructing their personal identities. I mean, who or what is a Mokhonoana without his or her forefathers' beliefs?

(Side Note: Speaking of beliefs, allow me to share *New Oxford American Dictionary's* ad rem differentiation between a *belief* and an *opinion*, "a *belief* differs from an *opinion* or a *view* in that it is not necessarily the creation of the person who holds it; the emphasis here is on the mental acceptance of an idea, a proposition, or a doctrine and on the assurance of its truth.")

The Cycle of Indoctrination

We are mainly indoctrinated by our teachers and by our parents with regard to subjective things like what success is, the minimum number of dollars that "our" ideal lover ought to earn every month if they are to date someone with our surname, things that human beings cannot do, who or what to call God, et cetera.

At any rate, there was a time when teachers were students and a time when parents were kids, which then means that (some of the) students whom teachers are indoctrinating today will indoctrinate tomorrow's students. Likewise, kids who are being indoctrinated today will indoctrinate tomorrow's kids.

In a nutshell, society is made up of kids: kids and former kids.

In Defense of Annoying Jehovah's Witnesses

If your child or friend were taking illegal drugs, which you sincerely believe to be or will someday be harmful to them, wouldn't you work relentlessly to try to get them to stop doing so, even if that were at the risk of annoying them?

Doing so is, of course, less likely to be frowned upon because most, if not all, of us sincerely believe that illegal drugs are harmful. For an instance that is more likely to be frowned upon, let us replace illegal drugs with beliefs: Suppose you sincerely believe that what someone whom you care deeply about sincerely believes to be a fact is in fact not a fact, wouldn't you work relentlessly to try to disprove their belief, even though that would be at the risk of annoying them?

At any rate, believe it or not, most, if not all, believers

and nonbelievers actually mean well whenever they try to either convert nonbelievers into believers or believers into nonbelievers. For the former sincerely believe that God exists, while the latter sincerely believe that He doesn't.

Anyway, perhaps we can all agree that it would be unappreciative of a drug addict to hate their parent or friend for having annoyed them during their relentless endeavour to get them to stop taking illegal drugs because they sincerely believe that illegal drugs are not good for them.

Now the question is, aren't we being unappreciative whenever we respond in a rude or insulting manner when a well-meaning theist who sincerely believes that God exists tries to convince us to start believing in God, or when a well-meaning atheist who sincerely believes that God does not exist tries to convince us to stop believing in God?

Perpetrators Are Victims

We were born as blank canvases mentally with regard to what we regard as immoral, what we believe, what we know, what we regard as good, who or what we call

God, et cetera. Some, if not most, of "our" beliefs, "our" hatred, "our" opinions, "our" prejudices, "our" aspirations, et cetera, are nothing but colourless brushstrokes that were subtly painted by some faceless artist called society.

The things that we think we know and the things that we know we think were mainly fed to us by our society, that is, our parents, our friends, our neighbours, our teachers, et cetera. What's more, although we would like to believe otherwise, "our" dreams too are almost always fed to us; some were tattooed on our minds from such an early age that we ended up believing them to be our own. For example, many a kid wanted to be a boss as soon as he understood what a boss is, not because he realized the good that he could do through owning a company, but merely because he has bought his materialistic society's claim that he who is a boss is a billion times more of a man than he who has a boss.

Needless to say, we readily direct all our sympathy towards the victim, when a man who was successfully indoctrinated by his father into believing that believers are superior to nonbelievers and that the world would be a better place if all nonbelievers were killed kills another because of nothing but their disbelief in God. But isn't the killer in a way a victim of indoctrination?

In other words, isn't an insane man whose insanity seduced him into killing his own mother a victim of insanity? Isn't a greedy man whose greed seduced him into enslaving other men a victim of greed? Isn't an insecure man whose insecurity seduced him into killing his wife a victim of insecurity? Isn't a starving religious man whose hunger forced him to violate the "Thou shalt not steal" commandment by successfully seducing him into stealing a loaf of bread a victim of hunger or his natural desire to protect himself from harm or death? Isn't a man whose unusually high sex drive seduced him into cheating on his wife who then divorced him because of that a victim of an unusually high sex drive or a victim of being a dog if he has cheated merely because he is a dog? Isn't an HIV-infected man whose misbelief that having sex with a virgin cures HIV seduced him into raping a 5-year-old girl a victim of the virgin cleansing myth? Or is attributing our deeds to things like our upbringing, our hunger, our education, our beliefs, our passion, et cetera, limited to "good" deeds?

As we all know, we readily attribute an educated man's sensible deeds to his education. However, we are reluctant to attribute an ignorant man's foolish deeds to his ignorance. In the same way that we readily attribute our successes to our looks, experience, talent, the number of hours that we have slaved, et cetera, whereas we are reluctant to attribute our failures to the aforementioned factors.

At any rate, in most instances, our decision to act or not act, and how to act if we decide to do so, is dictated by our way of thinking, what we know, what we believe, et cetera. Our way of thinking, what we know, what we believe, et cetera, are usually end products or byproducts of our educational, cultural, religious, or social conditioning, not an end product of our own thinking. That is to say, most people did not think to think the way they think; they were merely sold a particular way of thinking by those that they think are thinkers.

(Side Note: This writing is by no means a plea for us to free man from his responsibilities as a member of a society. With it, I was merely attempting to remind the reader that there are countless men who were, while still boys, successfully sold the belief that being a gangster is more honorable than being a puppeteer. In other words, their pulling triggers while the latter are pulling strings is an end result of their social condition or social conditioning, not their genuine desire or an end result of their own thinking.

As I have implied with the first paragraph, morals do not come standard; they are sold to us.)

Social Constructs and a False Sense of Unity

The sight of a united group of people is beautiful. Having said that, there is usually an ugly side to that. For the only true unity with regard to human beings is that of the human race as a whole. Anything other than that is at the expense of at least one category or group or type of human beings. Which then means that although some or even most human beings are united by something, that thing has divided the human race; irrespective of whether it is mental (e.g., religion) or physical (e.g., a border), or natural (e.g., an ocean) or man-made (e.g., race or ethnicity).

At any rate, a group of men who are seemingly united by a social construct, say, a country, are subdivided by another social construct, say, social class, into subgroups that are also subdivided by another social construct, say, religion.

For example, (1) Borders divide Africans in order to "unite" South Africans; (2) South Africans are subdivided by the monetary system into rich South Africans and poor South Africans; (3) Poor South Africans are subdivided by religion into poor South African nonbelievers and poor South African believers; (4) Poor South African believers are subdivided by Islam, Hinduism, Judaism,

Christianity, et cetera, into poor South African Muslims, poor South African Hindus, poor South African Jews, poor South African Christians, et cetera; (5) Poor South African Christians are subdivided into Roman Catholics, Anglicans, Baptists, Seventh-Day Adventists, Mormons, Pentecostals, Methodists, Protestants, Lutherans, Unitarians, Presbyterians, Jehovah's Witnesses, et cetera; (6) Poor South African Jehovah's Witnesses are subdivided by race into poor white South African Jehovah's Witnesses, poor Indian South African Jehovah's Witnesses, poor black South African Jehovah's Witnesses, et cetera; (7) Poor black South African Jehovah's Witnesses are subdivided by ethnicity into amaZulu, amaXhosa, Vhavenda, Basotho, Bapedi, Matabele, et cetera.

(Side Note: Speaking of Christian denominations, it is worth noting that some, if not all, denominations of Christianity were probably brought about by nothing but different and at times opposing interpretations of the very same holy book.)

One's Own Flesh and Blood

Last but not least, a book that is nothing but an attempt to explore the inventions that have divided the human race would be incomplete without touching on the seemingly natural invention that unites human beings, namely, the family, particularly the so-called nuclear family, that is, a couple and their dependent children, regarded as a basic social unit.

It goes without saying that the aforementioned invention has its usefulness. Having said that, grouping people by means of a family is at the expense of every single human being except that family's members. As I once quipped, "Sport unites people by dividing them. Religion divides people by uniting them." And as Voltaire is said to have said, "It is lamentable, that to be a good patriot one must become the enemy of the rest of mankind."

Like the concept of childhood, and that of monogamy, the family is our own invention, not Mother Nature's. "Unlike infancy, childhood is a social artifact, not a biological category." Neil Postman is said to have written. "Our genes contain no clear instructions about who is and who is not a child, and the laws of survival do not require that a distinction be made between the world of an adult and the world of a child."[27] To add to that, I would like to cite a few ad rem passages from, *The Origin of the Family, Private Property and the State*, a book that is said to have been written by Friedrich Engels. I trust that the sharp-witted reader will readily link the following passages with the gist of this writing.

"What does the term 'unrestricted sexual intercourse' mean? Simply, that the restrictions in force now were not observed formerly. We have already seen the barrier of jealousy falling. If anything is certain, it is that jealousy is developed at a comparatively late stage. The same is true of incest. Not only brother and sister were originally man and wife, but also the sexual intercourse between parents and children is permitted to this day among many nations. ... Before incest was invented (and it is an invention, a really valuable one indeed), sexual intercourse between parents and children could not be any more repulsive than between other persons belonging to different generations, which takes place even in our day among the most narrow-minded nations without causing any horror. ... Eliminating from the primeval forms of the family known to us those conceptions of incest—conceptions totally different from ours and often enough in direct contradiction with them—we arrive at a form of sexual intercourse that can only be designated as unrestricted. Unrestricted in the sense that the barriers drawn later on by custom did not yet exist. ... Monogamy was the first form of the family not founded on natural, but on economic conditions, viz.: the victory of private property over primitive and natural collectivism. Supremacy of the man in the family and generation of children that could be his offspring alone and were destined to be the heirs of his wealth—these were openly avowed by the Greeks to be the sole objects of monogamy. For the rest it was a burden to them, a duty to the gods, the state and their own ancestors, a duty to be fulfilled and no more. ... Monogamy, then, does by no means enter history as a reconciliation of man and wife and still less as the highest form of marriage. On the contrary, it enters as the subjugation of one sex by the other, as the proclamation of an antagonism between the sexes unknown in all preceding history."

With those extracts, I hope to have substantiated the following convictions: (1) the family was brought about by the needs, if not wants, of civilization, not Mother Nature. As I once aphorized, "Dating isn't a natural need; it is a social want"; and (2) what is regarded as normal in some societies is usually regarded as abnormal and/or disgusting in others. To add to that, I would like to restate a conviction of mine that many a man who has a loving family does not want to hear: namely, being a member of the family whose members one is related to by blood is nothing but an end result of chance. As is the case with our country, our family did not choose us. And that includes the so-called planned children. That is to say, while your parents might have been "lucky" not to have had you by mistake, they did not choose you from a catalogue that was made up of thousands or millions of fetuses.

Needless to say, many a man would do almost anything for his family. Many a man slaves to ensure that his siblings do not starve. Many a man has abandoned his own dream merely to quadruple the odds of his children realizing theirs. Many a man readily went so far as to donate a portion of his liver in his attempt to save the life of his child, sibling, or parent. There is, of course, absolutely nothing wrong with that. With that, I hope to have quadrupled the odds of what I am about to propound sounding plausible. Anyway, in addition to doing that, my aim was to bring, to the reader's mind, the honorable sacrifices that many a man readily makes for his family members; because of nothing but the love that he has for them: a seemingly natural and unconditional emotion or state of mind that was brought about by an invention of man, not Mother Nature.

If truth be told, most, if not all, of us would not have chosen most, if not all, of our family members, should we have had the privilege of choosing family members. Many a man would not have chosen the disabled son that his wife's womb produced, should he have had the privilege of choosing a son from a catalogue that had at least one abled boy. Many a man would not have chosen his "ugly" daughter, should he have had the privilege of choosing a daughter from a catalogue that had at least one beautiful girl. As a matter of fact, many a man would not have chosen a daughter, should he have had the privilege of choosing a child from a catalogue that had at least one boy. Many a man would not have chosen his poor father, should he have had the privilege of choosing a father from a catalogue that had at least one man whose pockets are deeper than his father's. Many a man would not have chosen his obese mother, should he have had the privilege of choosing a mother from a catalogue that had at least one woman whose waist is smaller than his mother's. Many a man would not have chosen his insane brother, should he have had the privilege of choosing a brother from a catalogue that had at least one sane male. Many a man would not have chosen his promiscuous daughter, should he have had the privilege of choosing a daughter from a catalogue that had at least one "righteous" girl. Many a man would not have chosen his one-bedroom-shack-occupying family, should he have had the privilege of choosing a family from a catalogue that had at least one family that has a house that has more rooms than the shack that the family into which he was born resides in.

Now the question is, if the invention of the thing, or rather, social arrangement, to which we refer with the *word* family is capable of making us concern ourselves with the well-being of people who we did not choose, aren't we then capable of conditioning ourselves into concerning ourselves with the well-being of every single human being, irrespective of their race, their nationality, their culture, their mother tongue, their ethnicity, their bank balance, their belief or disbelief in God, and, more importantly, their "imperfections"? Bearing in mind that, as I have just argued, most, if not all, of us would not have chosen most, if not all, of our family members—people whose well-being we would readily die for, should we have had the privilege of choosing family members.

Finally, Pablo Casals is said to have asked, "The love of one's country is a splendid thing. But why should love stop at the border?" Although that is obviously relevant to the chapter on countries, I would like to alter Pablo's words to make them relevant to this writing. Here goes! "The love of one's family is a splendid thing. But why should love stop at the gate?"

The End Is Here

In addition to countless other things, I hope to have reminded the reader that: (1) a word is meaningless in itself; (2) words that we use to refer to things that exist nowhere except in our minds usually mean different things to different people; (3) to be offended is the choice of the offended; (4) social constructs are merely means to ends; (5) our perception is usually contaminated by our beliefs, our background, our religious conditioning, our knowledge, our cultural conditioning, our expectations, our ignorance, et cetera; (6) some generalizations and stereotypes are deadly; (7) money has never done anything; (8) our lives do not depend on or revolve around truths as much as we believe; (9) a wrong or false belief is usually as potent as a fact; (10) man needs to conform in order to quadruple the odds of him seeing yet another day and the odds of his gene seeing yet another generation; (11) a human being is relatively easy to indoctrinate; (12) what is regarded as normal in some societies is usually regarded as abnormal and/or disgusting in others; (13) man is not always rational or as rational as we think: as I once quipped, "If man were a rational creature: his last suspect—namely, his mouth—was going to be his first, whenever he thinks that someone or something is smelly"; (14) we act in a certain way when we are around certain people in order to make and then sustain a certain impression; (15) perpetrators are victims; (16) a man who steals a loaf of bread from the reader could actually be a "good" person who was unfortunately overpowered by our biologically imposed need to eat; (17) xenophobia is manufactured; (18) we seldom look like we look like when people we like are looking; (19) the rich would be poor without the poor's acknowledgement of money; and (20) Nigerians are man-made.

But more important than that, I hope to have left the reader a billion times more understanding with regard to this complex process called man, especially those whose beliefs, behaviour, opinions, and worldview differ from or even conflict with the reader's, and those who sincerely believe that their mother tongue, their country of birth, their culture, their bank balance, their ethnicity, their race, their belief or disbelief in God, et cetera, make them superior to the reader.

In a word, I hope that instead of telling a boy that he is a boy, the reader will simply act like a man. For, as Mahatma Gandhi is said to have said, "An eye for an eye only ends up making the whole world blind."

One Love :)

Other published writings

To browse other books and essays by Mokokoma, visit *www.mokokoma.com* (each book or essay is listed with links to <u>some</u> retailers from whom you can buy it).

Be one of the first to know

For the most convenient and less noisy way to follow Mokokoma's work, simply subscribe to his newsletter at *www.bit.ly/mokokoma*. Other than an occasional link to his new book, essay, cartoon, or design, his newsletters are made up of nothing but his new aphorisms, which, if you subscribe, you will receive *a week or two before he shares them anywhere.* Your email address will never be shared with anyone, and you can unsubscribe at any time. The maximum number of newsletters you will receive in a month is 4; the minimum is zero.

Liked a few things in this book?

If you found this book worthy of your time, please consider leaving a review, even if it is only a-sentence-or-two long. That seemingly insignificant gesture will immensely help Mokokoma and, more importantly, some, many, or even most of the people who your review will have convinced to read this book.

REFERENCES

PROLOGUE

1. Rahula, Walpola, 1959, *What the Buddha Taught*. Oxford: Oneworld Publications.

LANGUAGE

1. Chase, Stuart, 1966, *The Tyranny of Words*. San Diego / New York / London: Harcourt Brace Jovanovich.
2. Postman, Neil, 1993, *Technopoly: The Surrender of Culture to Technology*. New York: Vintage Books, A Division of Random House, Inc.

CULTURE

1. http://en.wikipedia.org/wiki/Dog_meat

THE MONETARY SYSTEM

1. Chapman, Tracy, 2000, "Paper and Ink" (Telling Stories), Elektra Records.
2. Mumford, Lewis, 1934, *Technics and Civilization*. Chicago & London: The University of Chicago Press.
3. Boorstin, Daniel J., 1992, *The Image: A Guide to Pseudo-Events in America*. New York: Vintage Books, A Division of Random House, Inc.

COUNTRIES

1. http://en.wikipedia.org/wiki/Xenophobia_in_South_Africa

RELIGION

1. Postman, Neil, 1993, *Technopoly: The Surrender of Culture to Technology.* New York: Vintage Books, A Division of Random House, Inc.
2. http://freakonomics.com/2011/04/25/does-more-education-lead-to-less-religion/
3. http://freethinker.co.uk/2012/05/26/atheists-are-more-intelligent-than-religious-people/
4. Postman, Neil, 1993, *Technopoly: The Surrender of Culture to Technology.* New York: Vintage Books, A Division of Random House, Inc.
5. Mumford, Lewis, 1934, *Technics and Civilization.* Chicago & London: The University of Chicago Press.
6. Postman, Neil, 1994, *The Disappearance of Childhood.* New York: Vintage Books, A Division of Random House, Inc.
7. Chase, Stuart, 1966, *The Tyranny of Words.* San Diego / New York / London: Harcourt Brace Jovanovich.
8. http://en.wikipedia.org/wiki/Christianity_and_homosexuality
9. Postman, Neil, 1993, *Technopoly: The Surrender of Culture to Technology.* New York: Vintage Books, A Division of Random House, Inc.

10. Fromm, Erich, 1997, *To Have or to Be.* London / New York: Continuum.
11. Fromm, Erich, 1997, *To Have or to Be.* London / New York: Continuum.
12. http://www.livescience.com/4017-churchgoers-live-longer.html
13. http://www.merriam-webster.com/dictionary/holywater
14. Postman, Neil, 2006, *Amusing Ourselves to Death: Public Discourse in the Age of Show Business.* Penguin Books.
15. http://en.wikipedia.org/wiki/Suspension_of_disbelief

EPILOGUE

1. Taleb, Nassim Nicholas, 2004, *Fooled by Randomness: The Hidden Role of Chance in Life and in the Markets.* New York: Penguin Books.
2. http://en.wikipedia.org/wiki/Curtis_Mayfield
3. http://en.wikipedia.org/wiki/UEFA_Champions_League
4. Stockdale, Steve, "Korzybski's Structural Differential and Hayakawa's Abstraction Ladder".
5. Stockdale, Steve, 2009, *Here's Something About GENERAL SEMANTICS: A Primer for Making Sense of Your World.*
6. Chase, Stuart, 1966, *The Tyranny of Words.* San Diego / New York / London: Harcourt Brace Jovanovich.
7. Boorstin, Daniel J., 1992, *The Image: A Guide to Pseudo-Events in America.* New York: Vintage Books, A Division of Random House, Inc.

8. Boorstin, Daniel J., 1992, *The Image: A Guide to Pseudo-Events in America*. New York: Vintage Books, A Division of Random House, Inc.

9. Hogben, Lancelot, 1983, *Mathematics for the Million: How to Master the Magic of Numbers*. New York / London: W W Norton & Company.

10. Goffman, Erving, 1990, *The Presentation of Self in Everyday Life*. Penguin Books.

11. http://en.wikipedia.org/wiki/Sometimes_in_April

12. http://www.imdb.com/title/tt0400063/

13. Clark, Michael, 2007, *Paradoxes From A to Z (Second Edition)*. London / New York: Routledge.

14. Postman, Neil, 2006, *Amusing Ourselves to Death: Public Discourse in the Age of Show Business*. Penguin Books.

15. Goffman, Erving, 1990, *The Presentation of Self in Everyday Life*. Penguin Books.

16. Goffman, Erving, 1990, *The Presentation of Self in Everyday Life*. Penguin Books.

17. Goffman, Erving, 1990, *The Presentation of Self in Everyday Life*. Penguin Books.

18. Fromm, Erich, 1969, *Escape from Freedom*. New York: Henry Holt and Company.

19. Freud, Sigmund, 2010, *Civilization & Its Discontents*. Martino Publishing.

20. Taleb, Nassim Nicholas, 2010, *The Bed of Procrustes*. Allen Lane.

21. *New Oxford American Dictionary*

22. Boorstin, Daniel J., 1992, *The Image: A Guide to Pseudo-*

Events in America. New York: Vintage Books, A Division of Random House, Inc.

23. Fromm, Erich, 1969, *Escape from Freedom.* New York: Henry Holt and Company.

24. Fromm, Erich, 1969, *Escape from Freedom.* New York: Henry Holt and Company.

25. (1) http://www.med.umich.edu/yourchild/topics/masturb.htm (2) http://www.soc.ucsb.edu/sexinfo/article/childhood-sexuality (3) http://www.city-data.com/forum/parenting/851538-caught-son-experimenting-how-react.html (4) http://www.babycenter.com/400_my-daughter-7-years-old-is-masturbating-since-1-year-ago_7541737_365.bc

26. https://www.youtube.com/playlist?list=PL540322C914A242F8 (Playlist made up of videos of animals masturbating)

27. Postman, Neil, 1994, *The Disappearance of Childhood.* New York: Vintage Books, A Division of Random House, Inc.

Printed in Great Britain
by Amazon

18531854R00195

KISS THE

RYAN QUINN FLANAGAN

ROADSIDE PRESS

COPYRIGHT

Contents

Tippi Hedren Called

Tippi Hedren called,
I said.
She wants her birds back.

The woman I was with tried to shush
me with a finger to my mouth.

The pet shop kept the lizards beside the birds.
In these tiny little cages like loneliness
under a hot light.

Some toothy sales kid on commission
walked up and asked if he could be of any assistance.

It that any way to treat the lizard people?
I shouted.

Sorry sir, I don't understand.

Your superiors, the lizard people.
Locked away like common muggers.

They seem happy,
he said.

Please ignore him,
I heard a voice from behind me.

Do you have any sharks?
I asked.
Besides the ones that work on commission,
am I right?

I work on commission,
the toothy kid admitted.

Not enough junior,
I smiled.

She was ignoring us both now.
Had moved onto the puppies and kittens
in the back.

That passive-aggressive sign that always
asks you not to knock
on the glass.

If she returned to the pet shop
or the mall,
she never did it with me.

She got a dog, I know that much.
Some pure breed
that would make Leni Riefenstahl
blush.

Superior slobber
and all that shit.

No idea what happened to Captain Commission.
Probably started his own line of pet recliners
and made a bundle.

Getting in on the ground floor
just like the elevator in my building
always does.

All Our Bombs Are Custom Made

Terrorists don't hang signs
in shop windows
to drum up business,
but if they did,
the sign would probably
read something like:
All Our Bombs Are Custom Made:
Get Yours Today While Supplies Last!
and business would be booming
because everyone has enemies
so that you'd start to see:
Bomb Makers Needed!
Sales Experience a Plus
in the want ads
to help supply
keep up with demand,
and perhaps you'd even
apply yourself,
trying to land some of those
paid holidays and flexible hours
you have been hearing
so much about.

Staying in the Room Where Her Ex-Husband Used to Beat Her for $49/Night

She seems to know I don't have it in me,
staying in the room where her ex-husband used
to beat her for $49/night,
the nice couple that own the place
imploring us to pet their dying cone-headed dog
as they hand us the key,
reassured that such matters are just a precaution,
that he kept itching where he should not itch
which sits just fine with a man who has been itching
the short and scragglies for almost a half century
of higher gas and lower expectations
and she moves right in as though she never left
which makes me feel bad because this is a family place
and family should give you better although
it never really does.

A Bar Mitzvah Made to Look like a Suicide

Rabbi Rosen can be a stickler when it comes
to reciting the Torah and stammering Lenny Horowitz
is really slogging through the theological jungle;
it is painful to watch, friends and family gathered,
a Bar Mitzvah made to look like a suicide
and you get the feeling little Lenny doesn't want to enter manhood
at all and who could blame him: *wise boy!*
And I can feel his face on fire, each new acne breakout
establishing its own city limits.
That terrified cracking voice you can barely hear,
even at the front of the church –
poor little Lenny, he was such a nice boy;
helped his mother with the groceries
on the long walk back from Ziemann's.

Poem for a Man Who Thinks He's An Elevator

His moods are up and down all day, so that I sit to write this poem
for a man who thinks he's an elevator. Each mood a different floor,
I wait for him to make that little beeping noise to announce a new arrival.
His lips parting like those mirrored sliding doors.
Little people inside him pushing the buttons, getting off on different floors.
A maintenance team constantly dispatched to make sure he is running
in optimal form. Not like some health nut at all, but like the elevator
he is and should always be.

Zeke Thinks His Spit is Carbonated

You can tell a man anything and he will hear something else,
walking past all the clearance sale signs that have been up for years
and Zeke thinks his spit is carbonated, fingers around in the bubbles
of a fresh pooling on the table, the restaurant owner coming over
to warn against spitting on the tables, but Zeke needs to see
all that carbonation so that we have to leave and not come back
which is just fine with Zeke who imagines that soft drink pop
of the cap each time he opens his mouth to speak; usually to me,
but I hardly hold a monopoly on anything and later this kid
with a big bass guitar rushes by on his way to a gig no one
can remember booking: agents, promoters, club owners…
everyone at a loss.

My Linoleum Will Floor You!

A pun can be intended just as blunt force trauma
can and you should know right off that
my linoleum will floor you! Astound you, really,
like some browbeater Prometheus sticking his head inside
the mouth of a cowering circus tiger in cages
large enough to house half a dozen men on their
way to lethal injection without a note from a doctor
which is how ditches become culverts and the Pollyannas
pretty up everything including these spanking
new floors you can't help but walk over
with that dominatrix friend with a cricket paddle
and fine British accent full of safe words
and a few of the other kind.

The Devil's Coffee in a Cold Styrofoam Cup

Pulling up that brown 70s cigarette burn comforter
at $79/night,
I sit and listen to the main strip traffic splash
through the flooded drainage system
for a few hours,
play with a rounded switch on the bedside
lamp that went out when Hirohito
poisonous blowfish bit it under a carless knee-jerk sky
that had moved on to other things,
that hyena pack deck of cards missing the one-eyed jack
in the Gideon's preachy side table;
another cold water 5 am shower
and I am back on the road –
the devil's coffee in a cold styrofoam cup
in my lap and dawn's motionless deer
still littering the long gutted highway
with eyes wide as watermelons.

"You were once the mighty Roman Empire, what happened?"

I was having a few beers
with this Italian buddy of mine
who could never keep a woman
for more than a few months.

His life was always in complete disarray.
When he cracked his beer it foamed
all down his hand.

He stood there defeated.
As though Caesar salad never crossed the crouton.

"You were once the mighty Roman Empire, what happened?"
I asked.

He threw his arms in the air like some
failed brown machismo.

I pointed to his car.
*"Any man who has tinted windows after the age of forty
is trying to hide something,"*
I said.
*"It looks like you're driving around in a pair
of sunglasses."*

Then I told him I was out of work again
which seemed to cheer him up.

He tried to give me a beer he had shaken up
so mine would foam as well.

"*Nice try jabroni!*"
I laughed.
Pulling a fresh one out
of my pocket.

He was still sucking the foam off his knuckles
like some second-rate hooker
forever working the stroll.

Finder's Fee

The gravy and meatloaf
had driven over 12 hours
that day.

To this rest stop
along the side of the freeway
that stayed open 24 hrs.

And standing over the urinal,
he looked at this latest missing person
poster tacked up to the wall.

The $10, 000 finder's fee
for any information.

He looked at the poster again,
but had not seen that face.

Zipping up disappointed
and returning to that awful
belly buster coffee.

And some waitress
with a nametag that said: Stacy
even though she looked much more
like a Corina or Julie
or someone else who could
really use that $10, 000
that wall of the Men's crapper
was promising.

Bride Come Groom

Seems as natural as following
the slaughterhouse right to hungry
dinner table conclusion –
it's bride come groom, that cheering crowd
of game show prizes, the priest from the Greek
Orthodox down the street full of more olives than scripture
which makes for a salty ceremony indeed;
Lot's wife just some horny bridesmaid on the cheap
while ZuZu Bailey leaves her wonderful life
to remind us that every time a stoolie sings,
a hitman earns his wings.

Spilling the Beans

My parents tried to kill me,
threw me down a flight of stairs
when I was eight months old.

I had to be airlifted with a brain hemorrhage,
was given a less than 10% chance of living
by the doctors.

And when I survived,
my mother waited until I was
old enough to understand language
to tell me:
"I hate you and wish you were never born"
on many occasions.

Then she started in on my little sister.
Pulling on her hair as she combed it out
each morning, yelling at her to stop crying
like a little baby and calling her "a little bitch."

And when I tried to protect my little sister,
my father stepped in and always
protected my mother.

Until he cheated on her
with this waitress he met at one
of his favourite restaurants.

Finally building up his asshole courage
to leave my mother and move in
with the waitress of his dreams.

The Eagle Has Landed

The buildings were closed at night
so the janitorial team could come in and clean.

Blocks of buildings done in rotation.
By the same three man team.

Dunceler was the lead.
Sussman had been there a couple years
and Walthan was the new guy.

Each in charge of separate floors
as they went from one building to the next.

Dunceler had recently introduced a new walkie-talkie system
to make sure everyone was awake and doing their job.

You there Sussman?

No answer.

Sussman, quit playing with yourself!
You there?
asked Dunceler again.

Then a voice came back over the walkie-talkie.
The eagle has landed.

Then another different voice:
The hawk has dropped another egg.

Quit fucking around you idiots!
said Dunceler.

*Don't you realize we have four buildings
to do tonight?*

The wiener has been tugged,
came Sussman's voice.

The eagle has been dusted,
Walthan's scratchy voice
chimed in.

Dunceler wanted to laugh,
but there wasn't time.

Four buildings were a heavy night.
Each building with many rooms and floors.

The Walthan has dropped a deuce,
came Sussman's voice again.

Just laughter from Walthan.

Dunceler began to think this new walkie-talkie
system may not have been a good idea.

That they would all be out of the job.

The Dunceler has been oiled,
came Sussman's voice.

Dunceler said nothing.
Emptying all the garbages in the room
before turning out the light and
moving on.

Gymnasium

That knot
in your stomach
is the end
of a gymnasium rope,
for you are
a gymnasium
and not a Being
with a stomach
at all.

The Sleeping Bags on the Subway Grate Are Not a Sleepover

Another extreme cold advisory from those never left out in it,
frostbite in moments according to the public health officials
who look good on television after hair and makeup
and I can see my breath as I walk down by Dundas Square,
bundled up like some fine knitted yeti under all those bright
advertisements flashing from every corner;
the sleeping bags on the subway grate are not a sleepover,
shifting every so often so you know that someone is still
alive under there, no one really even taking a notice anymore
of something that is always there; that birthmark on your thigh
or that used bookstore full of musty dog ears –
I never see their faces, but the shame is to be shared
even if the cold is not.

If You Are Going to Hemorrhage Anything, It May as Well be Blood

If you are going to hemorrhage anything, it may as well be blood;
I am all for authenticity in the emergency room,
those calipers for eyes that cannot stop measuring grief –
yesterday, during an especially short walk,
I realized I have been breathing someone else's air
my whole life, whether by injury or insult,
pieces of my scalp tumbling away like falling rocks,
my fraudulent lungs filling with bad cheques
and forged signatures;
a snapping tree in the distance,
one crisp split so that I turn to find
a sky of birds panicked back
into reluctant flight.

20 bucks says you chicken out.

Make it 50 and you got a deal!

David and Evelyn shook on it
and waited for the phone to ring.

Castor & Polyps

Grab your spears and horses,
another demonstrable game of follow the Leda,
some castor for those polyps, that growth that is
said to be desirable in some boom boom big picture sense –
electrical tape does not make you an electrician,
that has to be said sure as Sunday,
mythological creatures jumping through
toothpaste oral traditions under the big top,
a grant for Ulysses, no way to tell how the spigot
will sputter; painting this town some atrocious
robin's egg blue, paving over the roads with
the heavy brush of baseless accusation:
no one beyond fighting age, all these gallantry
statues in public parks to remind you.

The Junkie in the Bathroom

James Bond was invented in the faraway Caribbean
so that there are no heroes in real time
and I stumble over the junkie in the bathroom
drooling across a sickly institutional green
tiled floor that has not been cleaned since
mental health went looking for answers up the nose;
half a dropper's blood still sticking
out of some bruised patchwork arm
that probably knew it had a hot shot coming;
the sound of the hair dryers still going
so that I know I am not the first
to such discoveries,
but perhaps the first to care.

Care Package

It is climbing freshly out of the mouth of October.
Just when I had started to think that no one cared,
I received this care package through the mail.

One of those sickly tartan tins
that sound like a bank vault being robbed
by the oils from your hands.

All sorts of goodies under a single thrown back
sash of wax parchment:

7 sharpened no. 2 pencils

2 conflicting treasure map napkins

a tape measure with long yellow tongue

3 packages of unopened tissues

a single lock of hair purporting to be Anastasia's last known growth
spurt

6 blue thumbtacks

2 bottles of cough syrup

an instruction manual to an old boat motor

and some of those shaped cookies with a fine dusting
of granulated sugar across the top.

*

The three packages of tissues were gone in under three hours.
There was no return address, so the care package could
have come from anyone.

Morocco Jane or the ghost of Federico Fellini.
It was cookies and cough syrup for dinner.

You're Not An Actor, Just Another Waiter with Headshots

When you sit around counting sycophants
on your one good hand, and the drinks that come
are watered down, bumping sharks instead of uglies –
two forks caught together like warring buffalo
from the plains right to your plate:
"you're not an actor, just another waiter with headshots,"
and now haughty-go-lightly won't bring a single thing
to the table; his truth meant to be snide and mine
more truthfully hurtful so that we seem to have reached
some kind of understanding about the very public
impossibility of one another; my date eyeing the exits
like sizing up other men on the fly.

The Only Crushes that Last Are Trash Compactors

Come off the hunt, that lingering dum-dum safari!
Don't need another school of piranhas moonlighting
as "educators" of the late night tv preacher ilk.
The pictures on the wall all with faces you could
drink with if the Spanish siesta ever made it over
to far rockier shores.

No one would want to make it if they knew the sour
lemon rind truth of the made. Plucked eyebrows
like a personal skyline. Hipster records never played
backwards for tapas bar Satan. Get off your own
sprawling high, those niggling glass shards that never
come back from broken.

The only crushes that last are trash compactors,
all those lease-to-own doomsday kisses in the dark.
And your hand over my leg, some college radio heavy
doing deadlifts for the human ear. A used couch
on the repurpose like second-hand destinies.
Our clothes hanging off the bed like faded denim
sherpas balled up around another slurring
midnight encampment.

Never Beat a Phone Book with Another Phone Book

What is this, amateur hour?
That's the first thing you learn from the torture experts,
the finger nail pullers brought in from Iran
to beautify the current torture scene.
And they put it right there in print on the instructional manual:
never beat a phone book with another phone book,
all you get are personal bruises to explain away
as this guy with horrible hair plugs looks to the tip
jar by the cash for emotional support
and a tarmac full of Bond villain jets sits fueled
at the private airport three miles away
while I flip through the yellow pages looking for
reputable cowards at unreasonable hours
at the foot of a rod iron chair that looks as if
this fine evening will finally impale itself.

My Attic Has Space, Just Not Outer Space

He said there was plenty to explore.
Had I not seen those cave paintings from France?

I told him French finger painting wasn't really my thing.

He suddenly face washed me as though we were old retired
hockey players that were much closer than we were.

I told him his scented cream hands were so soft
I might try to fuck them later.

Then he started talking about all these boxes
he had stored up in his attic.

My attic has space, just not outer space.
I definitely remember him saying that.

That he would totally get with aliens.
I suddenly wondered just how much
we had drunk.

Did you know one of Jupiter's moons is full of water?
he leaned in close.

I can't wait for its water to break,
I said.

*Astronomers think there's a tenth planet
hidden away in our solar system,*
no shit!

Good thing there is no shit,

I said.
That would be unsanitary.

Just then,
his youngest kid walked out
and bear-hugged him.

Knocked him right in the nuts.

I showed the kid that trick
where you pretend to pull off
your thumb.

He seemed amazed
even if I was not.

Ran back inside to get his sister.
Screaming bloody murder
about the miracle he had just
witnessed.

You're good with kids!
he smiled.

You're good for nothing,
I shot back.

He punched me on the shoulder
most affectionately
as though one or both of us
may be into that.

Another thoughtless
Jell-O mold sun
wasting away.

A New Pair of Gloves

My dead grandfather came to me
in a dream last night.

Told me I needed a new pair of gloves,
so I'd imagine something is going to happen
to my hands soon.

Might want to be a little more
careful in this house of knives.

The dead
don't come all the way back
to the living for nothing.

The Machines Can't Take Over

The machines can't take over,
they've worked in all the same sorry joints
I have, at least I collected a wage,
though it wasn't much,
at least I had bathroom breaks,
the machines forced to work even in the lunch room,
reheating some god awful cup of nothing;
even the punch clock by the door a machine,
they seem to have things even worse
which is always possible and most important
to remember.

Who's On Point?

The commanding officers had all been clipped
off in firefights and now they were on their own.

You're on point Nate,
said Hightower.

Fuck that man,
I was on point when Sgt. ate it!
You really want me being your eyes?

You are a useless motherfucker!
laughed Ridley.

Nate flipped him off.
Why don't you come up here
and show us how it's done Big Time.

I'm a short timer, got less than 3 weeks left in country.
You think I'm sticking my neck out for Uncle Sam?
Get Baker to do it.

I have a whole company named after me,
the point is beneath me.

Not that shit again!
said Nate.
You're just a grunt like the rest of us,
regardless of some bullshit name.

You calling my name bullshit?
Baker tapped his helmet with a fresh mag
and loaded.

Probably isn't even your real name,
said Nate.
Doesn't Baker look much more like a
Pennywhistle or a Humperdinck?

Ridley laughed
as Hightower stepped in to break
the other two up.

I guess we draw straws,
said Baker.

Where the fuck you gonna get straws?
laughed Nate.
You carrying straws on you or do we just
hit the next Denny's we see and ask them?

I'm not drawing straws,
said Ridley.
Short timers don't do point.

Nobody is drawing straws
because we're in the middle of a fucking
warzone and not sharing a coke at some
malt shop in butt fuck Idaho.

Rock, paper, scissors then?
offered Hightower.

What are we six years old?
mocked Nate.

The enemy had torn through the lines.

The Howlers

Many of the clubs downtown are connected,
even if some of the girls
are not.

That overwhelming flood of lights.
The promise of cheap drinks.

And all the howlers out front
trying to bring in the foot traffic
with the promise of "WALL
TO WALL PUSSY!"

Handing out all those bogus free drink cards
to get you inside.

The muscle always close by
so that the howlers feel emboldened.

Jump right in your 90 proof face.
Across from that under the table tattoo place
where all the dirty girls get their coochies pierced.

And the girl with the purple hair offers
a free blowjob with every Prince Albert
off the clock.

Lobbing Old Ideas Over New Walls

She tells me she is thinking of leaving her job
and I tell her she really shouldn't tell her kids
and husband of umpteen years that

and she slaps me on the arm
like storming walls of hulking gooseflesh
with that trebuchet of careless charm lobbing
old ideas over new walls

and it's siege warfare with car payments,
it's dried lipstick over all the glasses

while I listen to her talk down her supervisor
and complain about the taxes,
forgetting to refill the ice tray
in spite of constant cries for attention
from the cheap seats.

Flustered Custard

A little gravitas if you please,
no one likes a flustered custard –
secure the damn bridgehead and then
we can talk numbers like some pimply
math department integers thrown into
a honking buzz saw of migrating geese;
banging sex shop wind chimes spoofing
their bubbles and snuffing those rangy
particular silences that stand between a
man and his only working tweezers:
how many questions until you become
a questionnaire?
how many flowers before she demands
a waiting watered garden?
it is crucial that you hold the line,
that sparkling water geometry gullet
throwing back warm brewskies on
the foaming solemnity paramount…
no flora way to enter fauna heaven;
just these ashes, this book-slim
puncher's chance.

She Says Her Cat is in Love with Javier Bardem

She tells me she sat up late watching
Being the Ricardos.

That it is better than you would think
which is what everyone says about everything
but the apocalypse.

Throwing one of those scrunchies up in her hair
like trying to contain the mess.

A trick of beauty that she still turns heads.
Says her cat is in love with Javier Bardem.

Woke up out of a dead sleep on the couch
to watch him most attentively.

When she sleeps, she's out!
she says.
She doesn't do that for anyone.

I've taken to calling her cat Mrs. Bardem
the last few days.

The cat seems to get embarrassed
if cat embarrassment away from the litter box
is such a thing.

Throws litter all over the place.
She never did that before.

Take it easy compadre,
said Hackett.
We got a long way to go
and I'd hate for us to go it
without you.

Bironas grinned as a rat trap went off.
The fry cook did not seem to understand.

Aren't you worried that the guy behind you
with the knife may get a little stabby?

Hackett laughed,
grabbed the mop in the corner
and started to dance with it.

Bironas was about to cut in
when the taskmaster came back:

I'm not paying you delinquents
to jack each other off!

You're hardly paying us at all,
muttered Hackett.

What's that? You want me to send you back
to the big house?

Hackett said nothing
and went back to the dishes.

One accusation from me about you stealing
and you're out of service just like that.

My word against yours, who are they going to
believe, genius?

Bironas put his head down and went back to work.

That's what I thought!
said the taskmaster.

The fryer cook let out a laugh
under his breath
and turned the radio off.

A pungent grease over all the walls.
The clock on the wall at a standstill.

If this was hell,
there were sure a lot of plates
to go around.

Sitting in a Dark Bathroom Waiting for the Poop to Come

I do not wonder how I got here, this is not "lost time"
or some philosophical tract stuck on the cyclical fly paper
Peloponnese; those Hellenics all with great beards
so that you know they would look amazing in some 1970s
swingers club with pink bubble gum lettering
and nowhere decent to park, and here I am a half-century
moon pie after those red red Russkies of Little Odessa
started playing roulette in a whole new way;
my blood-pumping heart through the flap of my ear,
sitting in a dark bathroom waiting for the poop to come,
seeing familiar shapes in the tiles of a floor the soles
of my shoes cannot help but stick to; that faint sound
of early Bowie through these walls these walls...
grout lines like taking a grainy failing train
of the mind.

Kiss the Heathens

The tower is alive, still unbeaten,
grass-fed along some country road
where spent goldenrod forgets to live.
Arguments in cars that sit in stone driveways
steaming up the windows.
That clumsy truck stop way Sloppy Joe beliefs
stay behind to kiss the heathens.
Stand over flooded urinals of
endangered elephant ivory.
One for the road to El Dorado, instances of smoker's cough,
an adulterer's blanket through crinkled toes,
that pavement burn that never quite
heals like you want it to.
That thing they call a burn,
another French kiss mouth
with more tongue than sense.
So many stairs to climb
in the dark that our painted
caffeine Pharaoh just back
from coffee bar Egypt
never tries.

The 13 Year Old Girl with the 14 Year Old Back

What if my ear is just a beehive producing wax instead of honey,
what then? What of the Spanish dancers at Trafalgar?
The dry county taking on water? And I begin to tear all the newspaper
off a dense cocoon of windows, think of the 13 year old girl
with the 14 year old back, that long coil of spine like crossing
wires with freckled gooseflesh; the small of the back like
a distant fjord with some unpronounceable name.
It is often said that we all have our demons –
yes, yes, but what of our angels?
So much is made of our demons and not our angels.

Do You Dream of People in Masks Now?

We were almost two years into some blurry day drinking
pandemic that had failed everyone
when she asked me that question.

Do you dream of people in masks now?
she asked.

I had never thought of it,
but told her I dreamt of them the old way.

I could see the surprise on her face.
I could tell that she did not.
Not anymore.

It was probably another six months before
I had my first masked dream.

Then I started to see them everywhere.
Jumping out of the popcorn ceiling overhead.

When I told her I finally saw them,
she seemed to feel a little better.

Not that I was seeing what see was seeing,
but that she was not alone.

All that wine.
The way you start to clank
when you walk.

Sardonic Colonics

No one wants to be a cynic when they
sit down to Brussels sprouts for the first time,
watch those screeching Kubrick long shots
descend into an ocean of salty blood.

But the heaving heart can only take so much.
It's bottled betrayals and sardonic colonics
the whole way.

That long hose trying to suck all the spoils
out of your smelly brown treasury.

And if you outlive your present misfortunes,
there is a Farmers' Market of indignities
waiting for you.

Where they sell those very same Brussels sprouts
that got this whole bloody thing started.

Which is why I can't be bothered to be bothered
as this enough is enough goes along.

This bathtub taking on water.
Someone's dying wish fortune cookie
dropped like government defoliants
on a failing garden.

Plug & Play

The working man
should have a place in the world:
simple, salt of the earth;
that hardly seems revolutionary,
provide for family, give loved ones
a better life than came before;
I would go to prison before I went to war,
no telling when the patriotism
left me, syphoned off like a tank of gas
you can barely afford;
I just never seemed to care about
what everyone else was hot on,
not the haughty grade school girls
demanding a tasteful dance
or the plug and play line worker
like failed trimesters –
no way I continue, there is a sickness
that was never mine and only a small part
of you, see you grunting hopelessly
around a muddy microwavable pen;
the titans just gods in waiting so that history
is nothing but upper management
laying out spreadsheets instead of randy
gin-soaked lovers that leave the light on
when they fuck which is as honest
as anyone can be.

Hitting the Road

There was no telling what drug he was on
or if there was not some deeper mental thing,
but there he was crouched out in his tighty whities
hitting the road with the fleshy bottoms
of balled up fists.

Looks like another Kerouac is hitting the road,
I said.

My girlfriend at the time did not find that funny.
Someone called the cops.
It was after 2 in the morning.
There were tended gardens to think of.
Children had school in the morning.

I could already feel a hangover coming on.
The next day would be absolute hell.
And not just because another Kerouac
had been led away in cuffs.

I knew that would be me if I stayed where I was.
Around people that puzzled about their fridge magnets
far too much. Worried about their onion bulbs
each summer as though they were a knife
to your only living breathing throat.

Woman with a Blue Drink

She sits three tables over
petulant as pigeon swoon,
a sun hat so large and intrusive
that it bangs against the backs
of other patrons

and my lazing hammock eyes
sit people watching,
an open patio to bring in foot traffic
from the big wide world

but the woman with the blue drink
can't stop running into scissors
in a social sense

and I get the feeling one or two other patrons
may be planning her murder
in the budding chestnut of their heads

while the waiter with the clip-on tie
comes running out with a tray
loaded down with dishes

for the table full of hip huggers
just into town,
their boxy sequined luggage
tucked under the table
amongst an army of freshly
painted toes.

Mercy Hospital Keeps Trying to Resuscitate the Dead

I am all for irony as a writer of the written word
and Mercy Hospital keeps trying to resuscitate the dead,
on that gurney wheeled in and out of theatres
like some box office poison oak that has you itching
the small of your back for weeks, areas unseen
and all those dipping sauce baptisms finding marbles
under the bed as Bazooka Joe blows a gasket and Our Lady
of Perpetual Hunger scarfs down three boxes of egg rolls
in a single sitting.

Dotting Father

Papa Legba hemorrhoids for Papa Hemingway
haters littering the streets with flatulent tin can opinions
and his last letter from butt sweat central
claimed he was "a dotting father" which made me
think he was drawing dots on the foreheads of his children
or that he had become some Seurat pointillist
centuries after the fact which sat with me just fine,
sometimes for many hours, over a can of Hereford
corned beef mixed in a bed of mustard so that everything
looked yellow, even the medal of honor.

This Lipstick Across my Face like a Treasure Map to Nowhere

Champagne to the room
and I start to think what that suite
may be like;
it is good to have something to celebrate,
that is the only redeeming factor of invading armies,
and this lipstick across my face like a treasure map
to nowhere and the rains in the street, all wet
and no purification which makes sprinters
out of loafers; designer handbags huddled under
popular awning that may as well be one of those
overly polite bomb shelters that hands out mints
for the lazy bunk bed end times.

Nowhere to Park That is Not a Marriage

You've been buttressed around the score.
Picking meat hooks out of thieve-thick shoulders.

Leap year jumpers and library late fees
that stay with you forever like limp
spaghetti strap pork butt lifers.

Short of breath and short on rent.
Nowhere to park that is not a marriage.

The overflow from the cart return
wheeling itself back to dirty shave water
conveniences.

All that cologne
so straight to DVD cellophane
recommends can go
into hiding.

Fly the flag, sink into a long miles
to the gallon depression.

The windows replaced
so someone can overcharge
and someone else can pay.

That smell of fresh asphalt
over everything.

It is never a personal rebuilding.
You have always been on you own.

Octopus

I bet you I can change colour
like an octopus: purple, red,
eventually blue –
just watch.

Starting right in.
Never naming his terms.

How he held his breath
right there in that dingy
cigarette burn motel room
with that firing squad showerhead
always pointed down at you.

And there was the octopus:
turning purple, then red in the face
as he struggled a little
by the bed.

The blue came later
with death
just as he promised.

This octopus
of the not so deep.

I didn't even dare him.
That is important
to remember.

All you calamari queens
stuck on Squid Games
and never the octopus.

Those rangy pipe cleaner arms.
A faded band shirt from some
local outfit I had never
heard of.

The Angels of Our Better Nature All Off Bleaching their Puckered Assholes into Complete Nonsense

She tells me to use sacrosanct in a sentence
and I tell her to use Life in a sentence,
but she doesn't seem to understand.

The angels of our better nature
all off bleaching their puckered assholes
into complete nonsense.

That sorry animal in captivity look
a vacuum cleaner salesman always has
after going door-to-door.

That gravel pit of a singing voice
sitting in dark bars over a warm beer
with the label peeled off.

Getting Loose

Does the tiger lament its enclosure?
You bet your stripes it does,
but I've been getting loose for hours,
this bottle here beside me like a tart purple warrior
who couldn't give two samurais what you think
about swinging dicks in the field or anything else,
the most obnoxious music the ears could find;
you can keep your bloody date nights
and company gas card, I can feel the great unwind:
no filters, no fees...
just this Joan Jett cherry bomb getting off
as off as off!

while the other two robbed all the other
businesses in town.

Just enough to not be readily noticed.

Then we hit the bank.
It wasn't long before we had more money.
Then we fronted the money back to the businesses
and offered protection from the thieves
for a small fee.

By now, people knew there were robbers about.
We promised to find them.

The businesses signed a contract I had made up.
When they could no longer pay the protection money,
we took their business.
They could still manage it, but we owned it.

Then we hit the bank again.
I hid the money under a wall of chairs
and only kept some float money on the books
for our own business.

Then we got greedy and hit the bank a third time.
One of the tellers caught us in the act and complained
to the god people.

It wasn't long before they found out we had been extorting
all the other businesses as well and had contracts that claimed
we owned all the businesses in town.

The bank was nearly broke
and so was everyone else.

One of our co-conspirators ratted to save
his own skin and they recovered
all the money.

Everyone was ushered back downstairs.
Career Day was over.
We were kept upstairs until our parents
came to pick us up.

What had transpired was inevitably explained
to our parents,
but they never said a word about it.

Even back then,
I didn't want to be a working sucker
like my father.

Maybe he didn't want to be that either.
Maybe he was secretly proud,
I don't know.

There were no more Career Days after that.
We all went back to being kids.

I learned that I had to work alone
if I didn't want to get caught.

Fashioned machine guns out of Lego,
started a gang war and supplied both sides.

Shoichi Yokoi Comes Out of the Jungle

It took 28 years
for some local farmers
to find him hiding away
in the jungles of Guam
after the war,

but Shoichi Yokoi came out,
only to be told the war had been over
for almost three decades now

which I can only imagine
the Japanese Sgt. did not take
so well.

A Fresh Shave to Back the Sink Up with a Forgotten Prickle Bush of Hair

The outside world begins to mean a little less
all the time.

It's turtle nest trappings
for a rigged shell game with spotters
that can't wait to take your money.

Which is why I choose to hibernate when I can.
Wrapped in that very 1970s blanket
my grandmother sewed just after my grandfather
had died.

Mustard yellow and mud yard brown
with periodic instances of white.

The yarn so thick you could stay warm
through a long Canadian winter.

And when the blanket was no longer enough,
the bottle tipped down eager gullet
warmed the belly.

Just as my grandfather had always done.

A fresh shave to back the sink up with a forgotten prickle bush of hair.
Some sorry motel television always
on the egg scramble.

Four floors up
and the only elevator on the fritz.

Drunken stairwells always an adventure.

The Leaner

For someone
so out of the loop,
she's all over everything,
leaning against walls,
upon razor-talon elbows
pressure pointing
tables of spent acupuncture,
leaning on people most of all,
for a crutch and sometimes
for love though she'll never
admit it, this resting head upon
tired shoulders that have
swept century home chimneys
of kaleidoscope spiders
for far too long.

Irish Bartenders are Bad for Business

We are driving back home.
Through the last thoughtless dregs
of some wrinkled hamper full
of tired winter laundry.

That cold toe tag way everything is dead
or hibernating except your latest asbestos-heavy
visit to kitschy gift shop apprehensions.

And leave it to the government mint to coin the phrase.
A limo service of tinted windows riding the brake
back in time.

But we are still making the payments.
In some blacked out truck with silver palm
tree tramp stamp.

Enduring some god awful radio offering
where the singer sounds computerized
with this horrible unbelievable rhyming scheme
about how he took this girl to Majorca.

That guy has never been to Majorca,
probably couldn't point it out on a map,
I say.
Never met a woman there
and he couldn't afford her even if he did.
Majorca is expensive!

I'm sure he just needed something
that rhymed,
she laughs.

Weaponizing His Smiles

He started going with this one
he met at a bar
which never ends well.

Not even for the bar
or barmaid who stood over
happy hour introductions.

And his car is rusted with scurvy.
And she told him to stop weaponizing
his smiles.

He doesn't even know
what that means.

I told him to chop up
a bunch of hotdogs and stuff them
protruding from his mouth.

To tell her they are missiles
pointed right at her drunk dial face.

He laughs
and says he is impressed I know
what a drunk dial is.

Thanks me for my advice,
but says he'll take a pass.

Drives off in that gangrenous chop shop mess
with four doors like some sputtering
junk in the trunk Rushmore.

Personal Lies for Separate Truths

Not so fresh rain
and I'm poaching old tiger print
out of cigar pipe Magrittes
coughing up fiery downed Hindenburgs
into the throaty python slow
strangle absurd

&&
Cocteau bombed
out of fleeting
mind—glib
Paris

&
powerlines across the face
like Bolivian gold stretch marks
of the blinding El Diablo
Etcheverry

&&&
drooping short on gas cul-de-sacs
with nowhere to go...

forgetful cords from whitewashed walls;
personal lies for separate truths,
the gov'nor on a stay
like a pause a pause
a pause.

Leaving for Croatia

He writes
to tell me he is
leaving for Croatia
in a week

and I ask him
what the hell he thinks
is in Croatia
that is not here

and he answers:
Croatians
as though he is
being smart

so I tell him
to have a good time
in Latvia

where goldfish
dance the jitterbug
and all the buildings
are repeat felons.

Don't Put a Lemon on Our NASA Space Rocket

maybe
you thought it was funny,
but we didn't

and two days later,
after your impromptu
press conference

you died in that mysterious
electrical fire

with two others
who couldn't seem to
tow the line

that everything
was top notch

and then we found some
astronauts to
play ball

not named
Gus Grissom.

Tag Lines & Talking Points

One mouth begins the process,
followed by all the others.

The exact same words
in the exact same order.

On all the major media outlets.
So you know these are the tag lines
& talking points.

What you will hear regurgitated verbatim
in lunchrooms across the country.

Sold as news instead of common deflection.
The same way children point fingers.

The cookie jar is not going to incriminate itself.
So the circus goes on.

All clowns and makeup under
the big top.

Dan the Besmircher

He always had
something to say
and it was never good,
behind those
deep dark aviator shades
that would cut
a man's parachute
right out from over him
the whole way down;
that was
Dan the Besmircher,
a demolition site
in human form,
but never of himself
which is how
a man keeps going
year after year
like some greasy
fat turbine engine
on the take.

All These Hours of Well-Cushioned Static

Peek under the hood, the door;
that shadow sees six more weeks of stairwells as protected
is my witness –
turn off the Max Headroom and come
to signal hijacked bed, Carlos the Jackal antiperspirant
working for the highest skyscraper cleaning windows
in the Kimchi-soaked stratosphere,
all these hours of well-cushioned static:
old change & radio signals back to college,
foul-mouthed DJs with herpes-catchy names
playing back all the tears of yesteryear;
the blessed know belief before they ever know
the lord, think locusts in the porridge with wings
that get a little leathery like that sixth inning chewing tobacco
way some hot shot just out of the minors
with 1 out and 2 on tries to get himself out of a jam
before the manager ever comes
to the mound.

Ending the Strike

It happened in that backyard on Bernick Drive.
With that babysitter who took our parent's money
and starved us.

And one day my cousin came by.
Saw me playing with the Tonka trucks
in the sandbox.

He grabbed the trucks
and made them all sit still.

Unresponsive Tonkas!
he said.

When I tried to move them,
he shook his head no.

I guess his company was on strike.
Why he was able to drop by in the middle of the day.
I think he wanted me to learn something.

I usually liked my cousin,
but I wanted the trucks to move.

Waiting until he left
before I ended the strike.

At the tender age of five.

That tired old sandbox
suddenly a hub of activity
once again.

Potluck

If anyone tries to sell you drugs,
just say no, and sell them drugs of a far superior quality;
make a cornucopia out of paper funnels and squander
all the papercuts in a fit of potluck and blood –
I always had the worst of attention spans in case
you can't tell your rodeo clowns from melty cheese-stuck spatulas
and the chemicals made things worse (or better),
built up the mulch until I had some flee-foot to stand upon;
some graceless cockatoo scream so the megaphone lobby
would not have to go it alone.

You Set 'Em Up, I'll Knock 'Em Back

You set 'em up, I'll knock 'em back,
I say like nobody's badass
as the bowling alley with the smelly shoes
replaces all the pins
and I throw a gutter ball
down the alley
before another for
good measure,
while the perfect game
four lanes down really woots it up
like he just stuck his fingers
in the hole and lost his virginity
instead of his car keys.

Generating Interest

He went on television
and did this interview
where he made nothing
but random sounds.

Are you crazy?
his agent asked.
You just killed your career!

He smiled and reassured her
he knew what he was doing,
that he was just generating an interest
that was not there.

Then he was booked for another interview
because everyone loves to
see a meltdown.

But he talked for this interview.
Was eloquent even, in his own way.

First,
people tuned in
to see what the sound guy
would do.

Then word of mouth got around
that the sound guy had talked
and everyone had to hear what he
sounded like.

The ratings were higher than
the networks had ever seen.

What would the sound guy do next?
There was great speculation.
Betting lines with possibilities.
Everyone needed to know.

The Sky and the No Sky Spilling Stars like Parlour Room Gossip

Had this dream where they lined those powdered doughnut horses up for general inspection. Whipped a few of the more willful into snorting sidestep position. Then I stepped away and found myself on some old train tarmac looking for my luggage. The conductor with a whistle all the dogs could hear seemed eager to leave. The sky threatening to rain while distant muggers threatened everything else, I was sure of it. My luggage lost as I was. The neighing man beside me pretending to be some horse in evening dress. That way I stared would have made anyone else most uncomfortable. Fingering that punched ticket hole in my pocket. The sky and the no sky spilling stars like parlour room gossip. Some coal in the stocking woman running for a one puff train eternally in the black and looking to make its well-teased bustier run for the hills.

If This Be Mismanagement

If this be mismanagement,
I would ask what living breathing life
was ever in charge.

Shave-less week long stubble
so that the scratch can return
to the itch.

Some failing second-hand
record player forever
in hock.

Let me see the books.
Dismount gymnasts
from careful firm-foot
beams.

One last way to see each other
back from the brink.

One last bed
that is not betrayal.

Dressing Room

First, the room puts on a pair of wool socks,
followed closely by some red boxer shorts
with little yellow pineapples on them,
then comes the pants that button up in the front
and finally a long sleeve shirt that has been
purposely faded which is much the trend
these days.

Lip-locked

She said they were lip-locked
when she walked in on them
and I told her
at least they weren't landlocked

and she demanded to know
how landlocked was worse
than lip-locked

and all I could say
was that the people that lived
near the water always told
the landlocked people that
it was bad and that the
landlocked people seemed
to believe them

and she moved away
and never came back to me
for advice again

so best I can figure it,
she took my advice and moved
to the water.

His Brother Came Through

Drinkwater's older brother had bought the booze.
They waited for dark to head into the woods
to play pass the bottle.

Your brother overcharges,
said Parsons.

That again!
scoffed Jax.
*Where the hell else are we supposed to get
booze in this lousy cow town?*

Amen!
said Drinkwater taking a long swig.

Now you're religious?
asked Parsons.

Drinkwater gleeked all over Parson's pant leg.

Parson's fell back into a tree.
Swatting at his pant leg as though it were on fire.

*Why do we have to hide out in the woods
like wild animals?*
asked Gregg.

Because we are wild animals,
said Jax.
Well, some of us anyways.

Parsons let out a howl.

The others followed suit.

I want my own bottle,
said Jax.
Some of you pricks have Aids.

I get my own,
said Drinkwater.
If it wasn't for my brother,
you'd all be dry counties.

No one said anything.
It was true.

Drinkwater's older brother had come through again.
Sure he overcharged, but they had what they needed.

Then Gregg said he was leaving.
I'm not just going to stand around in
the woods all night like some idiot Bigfoot.

The others mocked him,
but soon followed.
Each with their own bottle on the go.

Walking back up out of the woods
across to the Allandale Heights Rec. Centre
where they climbed up on the rooftop.

Kicking the stones around at each other
as a light rain began.

Why the hell does Drinkwater get a bottle at all?
said Parsons.

Measure for Measure

This ruling class of rulers,
I can't think a worse storm out of
its sullen bramble bush of rain;
measure for measure, it's monsoon Mary
taking you for a fallout shelter again,
a prison break of black mascara runs
making for the gate –
I used to have charisma in a past life,
now it's nothing but bad skin and bills to pay;
pen cap work orders while the nine-brained octopus
of the sprawling ocean deep makes a mockery
of this old school wine & cheese
in-house lobotomy crowd.

Drug Trials

The bailiffs lead a tiny round pill into the courtroom.
Set it down in the defendant's seat.

Stubby stenographer fingers at the ready.
Then the judge entered and everyone stood.

The defense lawyer picked the pill up in his hand.
Held it out for the judge to see.

Then everyone sat back down.
12 more pills listening to the facts
of the case from the jury box.

A jury of its peers.

As the prosecution laid out its case.
A blister-packed courtroom sitting on
every accusatory word.

Not Even Pilots Wing It

Not even pilots wing it,
so what of putty in shortened
lifeline hands.

Voodoo queens with beaded doors
the dead claim to walk through
on their way back to sun
without the shine.

Those voices the dark tear
right out of the sweaty living.

Those Tommy gun lymph nodes underarm
so the printers without paper
can perspire.

An evening of dry mouth
at some familiar crotch rot bar.

Competitive foosball tables
tipping poorly as some strung out
gangplank informant giving $5 handies
in the back parking lot
after a fresh rain.

Working the Graveyard and Never Once Thinking of Death

If you're looking for a way out,
a path seasoned trackers will give up on
in spite of high motivation and toilet training
in the extreme –
I've worked long enough
that I never want to bend to the faltering hours again,
not in the factories, not along the line,
muling my back out for decades
like something meant to fail,
working the graveyard and never once thinking of Death;
that timecard in your hand
like there's a nearby punch clock
to swipe in case of troubles,
with your laminated name on it
like all the others that
came before.

Get the Jab

Someone pulls a blade.
Complete strangers in a sketchy smeared
hock shop sense.
Drives it deep into the gut.

Get the jab.
Away from prying eyes.

Bleeding out behind another coup d' état dumpster.
Pissy juice jar bums rifling through
saturated pockets.

Ole Bessie, shitting herself
like a human volcano.

The pockets pulled out.
All the good stuff taken.

A blue surgical down around
that double chin.

No one sees anything
in a world of the blind.

Sirens in the distance
making a production of some
other play.

Farmacia

Blanco was a ghost.
Because of his shockingly light skin.

Miguel was older.
Both Blanco and Ernesto looked up
to him.

All sporting black bandanas
as they broke the front glass panes
of the Farmacia and took what they could carry.

Spray painting the cameras
and running back to Miguel's place
with their haul.

Most of the bottles had long names
that no one could pronounce.

I think these ones are dick pills,
said Ernesto.

Blanco grabbed the bottle
and looked at the label.

These are for blood pressure, esai.
Dick pills aren't gonna help you grow a dick anyways,
Blanco joked.

Miguel laughed,
took a hit off the joint and passed it
to Blanco.

Never to his face.
My father was in charge of payroll.

He thought that made him better than them.
It didn't.

Page Turner

I pull some careful dust jacket thing
off her bookshelf and start reading.

Flip to a page
that came before everyone else,
so that the glue of the spine
has to work a little.

Something about Byronic love.
Must be one of her mother's clumsy
English undergrad page
turners.

Then I leave for work.
In my parent's car.

Some used car lot lemon
always on the sour.

Lining up to punch in again.
Mule out my back for a solid eight.

Heidi from HR
always lost in the cause
as to why I keep getting shorted
on that hazard pay
even though the dead
always have it
coming.

Two days later,
we are leaving the No Frills parking lot
and we see them both walking into the grocery
store together.

I guess she promised him again,
my wife says.
And he's such a weenie that he keeps
coming back.

I guess she's not moving,
I joke.
At least Fozzie Bear Cat will be happy.

My wife agrees
pulls out into traffic
and accelerates.

The snow has stopped coming down.
These tiny reprieves we all get
from the waiting storm
ahead.

Fantasy + Opportunity

No one rich in the language of the land.
Fantasy + opportunity, why anything happens
at all: that flightless ostrich egg Hope,
the gurgling backwash sea…
It could be enough if it were never enough,
snakeskin wallets on the death rattle,
not a single baguette in the French Quarter,
I call bullshit, I call my grandmother who has been
dead almost twenty years –
you'd think every personal speakeasy this side
of the wretched vomitorium would not find
noise metal so hard on wax poetic ears,
flying banners standing in for the buzzing
insect world; why this mind on cosmic loan
has stolen all the covers
and become its own fertile dark
jailbreak bed.

"They're going to find her murdered in a closet"

Sitting around on the general pacify
watching reruns of *Mediterranean Life*
with my rocking brown Barcalounger wife.

About this bubbly fairy floss Argentine
who claims to be from everywhere
but Argentina.

Her best friend along for the ride.
Some sloppy joe facelift so that you think
of water treatment plants full of shit.

And she loves the big dining room table.
Threatens to invite everyone over,
even strangers.

"They're going to find her murdered in a closet,"
my wife says.

I tell her I did not agree at the start,
but I do now.
"They really are,"
I say.

Her friend with the runaway Dali painting facelift
seems to be into everything,
even gangbangs on the moon.

I get tired just watching them.
Throw a yawn out like an errant Frisbee.

" You're going to bed, aren't you?"
my wife laughs.

I tell her it's late

"It's a quarter to eight,"
she laughs.

"Never too early to get started,"
I say.

Backyard composts filling up
with all those wasteful
watching hours.

Pouting chap stick mouths
more fish than famine.

Recessed lighting
for the bully boy that never left
the school yard.

Stolen car windows
knocked in like the faces
of battered women
that never see it coming.

Boot Scootin' Snow Forts

I'll see you when I'm kerosene –
everyone eating the flu so we know
it isn't a knife, the flightless bird of baggage
handlers never once thinking of themselves
as ostrich egg psychiatrists, great healers
in the human sweat lodge sense;
boot scootin' snow forts not named Sumter,
Lauderdale or Knox…
if it weren't for my more thorny of proclivities
you could nest in my arms, my scrumptious egghead mind,
but the boot that wanders has no time for marigolds;
kicking down the door
as though it does not belong
there.

On This Day…

Julius Caesar
crossed the Rubicon
according to this
silly little calendar
I picked up

that tells me
about important things
in history
that happened
each day

and I'd ask for
my money back,
Man is never worth
the price of
admission,

slogging away
in the trenches again
on this cold January 10th

thinking monks
back into the bad beer:

that thrusting armoured pikeman
of black rod iron
that seems to impale the dying sky
a little more all the time.

Kayak

Its water over water
in the ancient Inuit sense,
everything back to the land
except the value

and I throw out my arms
like willful spasmatic paddles
against the fluttering
eyelid rapids;

name a lake
after this latest spurting whitehead
putting the bait back
into each johnny football
high school tackle,

each word
almost gift-wrapped
so that you are destined
to fall in love.

If You Eat Enough Woodchips, You Become the Deck

I could care less about the hive mind at Carpenter Bee Central,
all those scandal rag buzzings that trap their own honey.
But the advisory is still in place for a reason;
if you eat enough woodchips, you become the deck,
my words through some patchy megaphone mouth
screaming broken tibias back into the sprite bobby sock annals
of standing water and all the best tyrants are off giving hair advice,
nothing but scotch tape and retired sumo wrestlers to hold
down the fort. Can you believe the heat we are having?
I didn't even know some of those places could sweat.
The hottest summer on record since Led Zeppelin 4.
Monkees pretending to be Beatles pretending to be the son
of an appliance salesman from Hibbing, Minnesota.
My less than goodness gracious. All this wood
and not a decent lasting chubby for miles.

Toast to Toast

I raise up my glass
like Lazarus three days late,
a toast to toast,
even those burnt bits
like cadaver dogs sifting through
the wreckage after a fire:
if they don't turn up soon,
I'm guessing they never will!
I hear some manicured mouthpiece say,
which gets me to thinking
how women with feather bags look like
stilt-tall ostriches by other means,
free radicals through the body
just tiny saboteurs from the inside
and that crunch of the crust,
how it can hurt teeth that have been
neglected, but we take another bite:
we love our toast, that ever-careless
smear of melty butter.

A Big Fan of Natural Light

She walks around in all the finest fashions.
Cheating the sweaty white knuckle Calvinists
out of easy street.

Jokingly complaining that she is "Gucci poor."
On a budget from her ex who can only pay
for so many trollops with a sea view.

And there she is with some self-proclaimed real estate guru
always showing over budget.

And then comes queenies latest proclamation:
"as you know, I'm a big fan of natural light,"
as though everyone would not
be a fan of that.

Some government cheque mother
with a needle in her arm.

Juice jar flophouse piss jars
with the lid removed.

Egg Salad Chlamydia

She's just out of school,
shoulders so tall you can hear
a personal Rushmore in her voice,
good with people instead of numbers
which means you better buy into that sappy
group hug currently going around
like egg salad Chlamydia,
that fruity hipster IPA summer patio crowd
manning the buns, the rare vinyl
like half the endangered species list
at cost.

I Guess It's Not a Silent Movie

We are sitting down to dinner and a movie.
A warning comes on at the start.

I guess it's not a silent movie,
I say to my wife.
Apparently, there is language throughout.

I think they mean bad language,
she laughs.

Never heard of it,
I say.

That Concierge with Banana Bread Arms

Why would I begrudge you expired air filters
taxing the lungs out at 30% mark up?
Congeniality swishing water like a conscripted porcupine.
All the windows blown out and replaced with
sketchy dental records from the thriving
root canal underground.
That concierge with banana bread arms
keeping tabs on crushed soda cans,
not for the Comintern or self-discovery I am assured.
A suitcase of granulated sugar trading hands.
A sweet deal any way you look at it.

Wussy

Balderson
knew he was a wussy
even though he was
his best friend

all the way back
to that first backyard
birthday cake
with less candles
than virtues

which said just as much
about that wuss Balderson

who was enrolling
in a computer programing tract
in the Fall

so he could move away
from all the beatings
they had both grown
so accustomed

to
taking.

Ammo Dumps Just Adrenalin Dumps on a Group Level

The hair on my arms
could have come from anywhere.

Some camera shy Sasquatch
or a pickling jar of tart picking
season excuses.

Appetizers in the animal kingdom
just as a motorcycle club has nothing to do
with motorcycles.

It's pickup lines at the pumps.
Grocery store carts on three wheels
so the VA hospital can get its greens
from the checkout girl drawing on her
eyebrows like some flirty dark
shift work Picasso.

Which leads me to blow across my arms,
causing a personal jamboree.

Post-colonial literature
always seemed a little late to the party
if you ask me.

Like asking what everyone is drinking
while all the pool furniture is being
tossed into a thriving chlorine abyss.

If I remain behind anything,
it is myself. Checking on faulty
scoliosis posture.

Ammo dumps
just adrenalin dumps
on a group level.

A man at the door
so large you start to think
of hydroelectric dams
and all that water.

Plausible deniability
under an army of sunblock
on some jagged rock beach
of failed geology.

The banshees
and the bagels
making the rounds.

Baseboard heaters
like a poor man's hell.

Nothing but Lyme disease
on the uptick.

I couldn't be more fluent
if I was your throbbing wet tongue
of language.

Purloining, the Saxophonist Smiles

Why must we steal from everyone else,
even love from torn shower curtain hostel bathrooms
that came in on some speeding body lice train
passing through tunnels dark as lousy signals
to nowhere; the saxophonist with those supple
negro lips and ebullient sideshow fingers
and all that jazz so that some zombie just back
from the bathroom rolls his eyes up into the
back of his head like searching out some forgotten
attic for those old as dirt pictures that never
once smile back at you even though they must
have been happy, even if just for an instant.
Life knows life. Surely, they must have
been happy.

Holly Don't Go Lightly into that Good Night with a Red Wheelbarrow Full of Tintern Abbey

I remember that early bean counter way
you sat on your father's clumsily lacquered fence on weekends
counting freckles you planned to steal back from the
aging bully boy sun and how the strays that came by were always
cats until you got a little older –
Holly don't go lightly into that good night with a red wheelbarrow
full of Tintern Abbey, square jawed roofie rude boy bartenders
always talking up themselves and never the drinks
you toss back over music played so loud you imagine
your next period will enter the thriving bloodlust charts,
tie back hair that is just dead sash with a purpose:
make an offer, make a baby from scratch;
there is a recipe to follow for those stuck to the plan –
I think I can't, I think I can.

Vacuum Boots

The money is on the table
which says everything
we both need to know.

Watching her dress
from the bed.

Those less than careful
pimples on her ass.

New villages
from the old city
all the time.

Messy Poe Tame Ea

I recently watched this movie based on The Tell Tale Heart
and didn't have the slightest idea. That is what Messy Poe Tame Ea
does to everything nailed down to treated crucifixion wood. As
though the Appian Way is the only way while King Tubercular dies
in the streets of Baltimore in another man's pants and no one sees
anything strange with that or Mata Hari's sparkly tit tassels doing
patriotic firework skies from the mouths of demure once beautiful
circus lions beaten tame as winding tendrils in the Chairman's
cultural arboretum.
Snake charmers presuppose the devil, don't they? All the cheats
running a hustle hoping you buy in with a money and a time you
don't have.
Bring me meals on wheels roadkill, bring me that black gut-busting
coffee that demands a name tag and a tip. Those liquidation sale
everything must go eyes just back from the bedrooms of this messy
black raven's perch land.

A Gong Who Thought It Was the Sun

It is easy
to confuse all that light
bouncing off you

a gong
who thought
it was the
sun

that shimmering
golden glint

until
put away
in storage

and now
the universe
is dark.

My Wife Wants Hollywood Teeth

She keeps making all these dental appointments
we can't afford.

Having the new Russian dentist in town
put her under every few weeks
and then the bill comes.

My wife wants "Hollywood Teeth."
She has told me as much.

But what about all that coffee you drink each morning?
I ask.
Doesn't that stain your teeth again?

She is adamant that she needs coffee
in the morning.

Asks me if her teeth look different after
$2000 and gets angry when I can't tell.

I guess my wife is not going to Hollywood,
which is good.

I am not going near that place.
Even if she wants her teeth to be there.

Smiling at all the pretty little waiters with headshots.
Charming some sorry rabbit out of it's
last limping keychain foot.

Transatlantic Truth

Scorpion kiss, forget romance,
dirty towel tired of just hanging around;
spider web spun, the record goes round,
city after city, town after town –
that midshipman's scurvy scratch of the head,
taking on water, taking on kids from a previous
previous adds up, it does…
the grind is right in the coffee,
each morning we try to cloud sail off
in other directions;
not a peach to pit, hardly a word,
something dirty and screaming
from the next room.

I hate to say it but...

No you don't.
You're happier than a flag
in the wind.
You couldn't wait to say it!
I shout.

She is playing dumb again.
But now she has said it.

With that dull tofu face
of all kinds of stupid.

Corpus delecti

Flab replaces flesh,
it's corpus delecti above the 49th parallel;
a legal term for some, but a personal
one for me, there are many ways for a man
to fail before his time,
think speedway Tutankhamun failing
to ever get out of the first turn,
that first decade becoming a body of work
like finger paints for rhinoplasty,
that parking garage way everyone finds
it so tough to ever get started –
marble countertops standing in for
a lost renaissance,
the 40 year old pizza boy
hardly transcendental…
that minimum payment I had a dream
of modern psychiatry –
all that stubble you catch in the
briny motion sickness fishing
trawler of your face.

Moe's Cigarettes

aren't what
they used
to be

which is why
everyone has become
a free agent

from Flophouse Fred
to those peek show Pyrenees
always on the dismount;

you got to see what's out there
if you don't want to end up
on the inside

like some grease monkey
mechanic forever
under the hood

which is why crooked trees
branch out over cemeteries
of boxed inaction

while old Moe
has been losing ground
since the late 90s

which may as well be
friction to fire
when everything starts
happening so fast.

Goodbye window dress

Goodbye window dress,
the mannequin is a science class stopper
on a beaker that never once
thought of you.

Another litmus test fail
with the squirts
after that Indian joint
with an earthquake of curry
for belly dancers.

The urinals backed up like
personal sewers.

Your meaty hung manhood
right there with popular
storefront awning.

A regalia in the harbour
so the monied can show off
their old world riches.

No more Chagall,
only a patchwork of carefully
driven narratives.

That reek of dirty fast food fryers
and b/o public transit
talking to themselves.

The homeless
all with dogs like sharing
your misfortune.

That last song you heard
falling back into the waiting
pinch me sea.

Goodbye to you.
Goodbye to me.

The King of Diamonds will Always Find a Market

I have nowhere
left to go
that is not a sanctioned guise
or trap

which is why a shut in
fresh out of the dark
turns back away from
the singing stoolie
sun

lining some whiskey sour yap
yap with a thick gob
of plausible deniability

like rebuilding
the entire skyline
of himself

using nothing
but paid witnesses
and a jury so stacked
they could be a deck
of cards.

Camera Bag

She leaves her camera bag sitting on this
black swivel chair in the corner that cannot stop peeling
under a less than handsome light
which is why she has the Pentax out,
she must enjoy or abhor the view
and wish to capture some of that;
grain fields through the hands by the southbound
interstate whooshing by so that jiggled room keys
can imagine black egret umbrellas snagging
distant fish in the shadows;
invited in to offer a perspective,
not that the county coroner has ever been anything
but a nature photographer with credentials.

John le Carré's Wife

must have always
had questions,

all that espionage
creeps back into a marriage
like some spider on the dark,
dank reverse

spinning webs
in forgotten crawlspaces
so wriggling silverfish cold
with absence

which may explain that quick
second matrimonial
turnaround,

then never
again.

Broth Slurper

The thermometer lies naked.
All those bronchitis swearing campfire oaths.

Everybody wants inside your hellion soup.
Monoclonal time capsules unearthed.

Ghoulish talkies giving lip.
Everybody climbs inside the captain's
steaming soup.

Some domestic across the hall,
so the boys in blue park right beside
the curb like they really mean it.

Butterfly Knife

Butterfly knife
through a sudden
deep plunge sky,
Hammurabi codes
and caterpillar pressure
over the wound;
I like your sass,
your ladies free before
eleven rat bastard
dumpster dive
way of bleeding out
over everything
like some hock shop
guitar playing hero
in the screaming
nylon honey trap
badlands.

The Key to the Bathroom Just the Key to the City by Other Means

Deforestation
has everything to do with standing naked
in front of someone else's failing mirrors,
judgements from the court coming back like
filling back alley dumpsters with screams
no one ever intends to hear
so that a petting zoo becomes a slaughterhouse
of the forgotten; what Joyce could have meant from
The Dead as though he was still writing about the living,
all those fledgling foamy smiles popular
coffeehouse presumable, faded denim legs
counting pre-planned tears –
the key to the bathroom just the key to the city
by other means; some bad dye job barista
handing out her number on brown paper napkins
as though she has an entirely different job altogether
which demands the drumming up of business.

No One Quits This Band

You walk down the hallway with morning dry mouth,
must be nice to have a runway for takeoff –
I pick at the pimples on my forehead like greasy
little volcanoes that weep as any widow
holding the ashes of big tobacco
and someone else has the bomb, you know the one;
I guess this is what they mean by joining the band –
no one quits this band, it's a pretty little outfit
of fear & deterrence, good company if you are in it…
Art has never saved anyone, not even the artist;
the gallery is ready to take a certain loss,
but the ego seldom is – and money?
What a ludicrous notion set down from those
that have it which is why I stand under the shower
for all these centuries that have always been a flood
of banknotes never mine.

Chop Shops like Art School Scissors from the Streets

Drafting board moonlighting
prison stripe zebras,
rebuild some screaming gas guzzler
back from engine zero;
chop shops like art school scissors
from the streets:
new plates and registration,
a fresh paint job like a blow job
so you leave that sassy red
mouth brand spanking
new.

The Music is Never Over

The music is never over.
I hear it more and more all the time.

That wagered dumb domino dance.
Those nesting new spring birds
from the wanting jelly-filled
tree squawk.

And Don McLean is off somewhere,
with a rattled Steinway tickled into
catchy crematorium submission.

Jumping through careful hoola hoop
images just longing for a place at the table.

Doggie mutton scraps
like some whiny teenaged
diary abandoned for drugs.

And *The Dead* of the Dubliners
as honest as Joyce could ever be
with the censors.

The burners of books
forever in tow.

Those many sleepless nights
of *degenerate art.*

But the music peels its way
through old wallpaper.

Reinventing this whole
house of cards all the time.

Wantling back from Korea
and looking to score a little good guy
this time.

Patchen like a bounding
slipstream deer.

And *toot tout* that horn.
All those fluttering wet tongues
of CunniMingus.

Heroin jazz
drumming strange wandering fills
back into long shoed feet
on the painted piggy to market
hustle.

No way forward
that is not some captivity giraffe with
three overly affectionate necks
at once.

Steve McQueen
planning another Great Escape
from some flax seed bagel monger
in the Bronx.

Which gets me to the
get me...

Nine-brained octopus sex
right in the faltering property
value feels.

Captain Ahab!
First Classless Sgt. Splatter
on manoeuvers!

Laying down the tracks
for professional trackers.

And the industry men
thrown into a tizzy.

And mincemeat
flavoured upside
down.

That little King Richard
boogie woogie that has been in
your high sodium head
all day long.

The hair on your arms
standing up at attention.

Not a military thing at all.
Just a simple inescapable
groove.

Pear Down

That chugalug bamboozle bass
and I know,
that bruised produce clerk pear down
rolling across floors that would lick
themselves if fetishes wore aprons
for tongues;
goodbye taste, no one can afford you –
bye bye waste, that constant flush
of public bathrooms…
hold my head so the thoughts
can scramble themselves,
wheeling around this well painted
carpark of empty shelves:
give us a smile, a coupon, a rebate;
the runt of the litter has
to eat too.

Hyperbole Derby

Goodbye Harpo, no room for Marx.
Baby names in the heather, a hyperbole derby
selling wolf tickets by the fang.

The worthless count their worth, empty shopping carts.
And that is what they do – damage control.

Hello Jackson, in statuesque.
No more east with your mind in the west.

Bone cold scars in a stairwell of flies.
Hardly a bang, usually a whimper.

Empires/people end – that is what they do.
Droopy in the eye of an apple truck bruise.

Leaflets drop from barracuda sky.
Goodbye Buddha, no love for pest.

Walnut Grove

My cracking bones get older with each step,
the words and the mind more unsteadied:
unmoored, less entrenched, increasingly unsuited
to protracted war by the day;
nothing but orange construction cone off ramps
closed off like cynics and strangers,
posture experts with mighty ramparts for arms –
these heavy wheezing lungs through Walnut Grove;
things that used to be so easy, once so fun.

Fucking Her Pussy into Oblivion

We never grew up together like two trees sharing a forest
and now she says she wants me to fuck her pussy into oblivion.

I tell her I can try, but that oblivion is a big ask.
Dropping my pants and climbing on top.

Wondering why she wants her pussy
to be gone so badly.

The Failed Magician Has Arm Hair Up His Sleeve

These are just words, no trick! And rabbits run free as open road cars.
The failed magician has arm hair up his sleeve, what did you expect?
I no longer think of screaming ladies when someone cuts into
a birthday cake.
The veil has been lifted like a momentary fog.
It's kaput for my dorky coin collectible mind. A rummage sale of old
thoughts dusted off for the great unwind. When you see me in the street,
assume my gait is that of a dancing leopard,
a salty breaker wall back to shore.

Maybe

Maybe you put out feelers mistaken for some hippy dippy communal
Maybe the bucket seat is just a bucket and I am some of Conrad's Polish fire water
Maybe the people of Hungary have always been starving for something
Maybe personal grooming is left over from the dog days, lead to collar
Maybe Mrs. Dalloway was much more well written than well read
Maybe travelling on a budget is as easy as turning on the sink
and thinking of waterfalls
Maybe fossil fuels were how the dinosaurs had all that energy
Maybe you never learned how to make love which explains
all these hours of pretend
Maybe this cut on my hand will bleed no more
Maybe the Pearl Harbor Russkies could make K129 look like China
Maybe it was March 1968
Maybe a saxophone sounds like brass loneliness
Maybe I don't have any money because I don't have a job
Maybe spunk is a rare earth mineral
Maybe three stooges was contractual because four stooges seemed excessive
Maybe the convenience store is trying to inconvenience you
Maybe you can't stomach all those dark paintings because
the Dutch masters ate their turpentine
Maybe the reaper is just a misunderstood farmer from distant fields
Maybe someone put sand in the gas tank of your car and
maybe I know who that was
Maybe just maybe if you wish and hope and slow play things long enough
Maybe if I were the last man on Earth
Maybe my tonsils could play poker if I held the cards and all bets were blind
Maybe the trim around your windows is just worldly eyelashes
Maybe you can get behind me like a back taillight knocked out for the night
Maybe nothing is as hard as rebar steel makes it look.

Timber Road Lumber Truck

We drive past
this army of felled stumps.

That Timber Road lumber truck
on its way to the Espanola pulp
and paper mill.

I wonder why they call it Timber Road?
I joke.

Well, that's a lot less timber now!
my wife says
turning up the radio.

As we speed down out of the North.
In our blacked out truck with palm trees
on the back licence plate.

After this longest of winters
up in the woods
which are getting a little bit thinner
all the time.

Tocayo

Confusion is to be expected,
the megaphone aiming for reach
and never clarity –
Queen Isabella wrapped in a gold leaf donair
and that Tocayo who went down for you
just last week; identities there to be mistaken,
it's doppelganger pie with a common phone book name,
instances of shame coming back from funeral flowers,
cigarettes for sex and that bright orange ancillary;
the quiet bones of your body like an afterhours museum,
thick jungle canopy for a head of hair,
that silence of busy elevators on their way
to tilted ghost ship floors –
Asbestos in all the stairwells,
in failing big tobacco lungs…
a gelding of dirty bathwater blowing bubbles
large as the angry backstretch world.

ARCADE

Garcia liked that the arcade was down in the basement.
That it had switched owners at least three times,
but never had a name.

Just "ARCADE" in that sickly purple
neon lettering outside.

Before that long descent down those narrow
creaky stairs that always reeked of piss
and only allowed for one person
at a time.

If someone was coming out,
one of you had to give way.

Which led to many problems.
Everyone a winning army in their own mind.
Hopped up on high scores, refusing to
surrender ground.

And it was worse once you were down in the bowels.
Every degenerate you could imagine.

Garcia knew he could find Fowler there.
Even during off hours.

Your mother giving it away again?
Garcia tapped Fowler on the shoulder.

Don't know,
Fowler responded without looking up.
He was working on getting all the top ten

high scores on this shoot 'em up game where
you could be the cops or the robbers.

Fowler was never the cops.
A smile beaming across his face each time
he wasted another badge.

It was as though he was killing his father
and his mother and society all at once,
most satisfying.

His father had bailed before he was born.
Now his mother sold herself out of their Tamarack Woods
townhouse across the street.

Look at these bunch of losers!
shouted Will.

He had just climbed out of the cockpit
of his favourite race car game.

You crash and burn?
asked Garcia.

Can't win 'em all,
said Will.

Speak for yourself,
said Fowler while loosening his grip
on the trigger.

Will waved him off and bumped fists with Garcia.

Will's father had bailed before he was born as well.

His mother worked a couple biker bars out along
the highway.

Haven't seen you down here in days,
smiled Will.

My father just got out,
admitted Garcia.
*It was supposed to be this whole big
family thing.*

How are your sisters?
asked Will throwing up his arms.

Nah, that's cool man!
said Will
*They are staying with my grandparents
until my father goes away again.*

So you're finally going away!
a voice bellowed from behind them.

Stebbelton walked up with a fresh roll of quarters

Not yet,
joked Garcia.

Stebbelton was a wildcard.
Just back from the shitter and still full of shit.
He played a little bit of everything.
Badly.

But he had these fake quarters that worked
on all the machines which made him

quite popular in spite of himself.

Fowler grabbed a roll of quarters
and slammed it down on top of the machine.

Replenishing the stocks, eh Fowls?
said Stebbleton.
Just like your mamma.

Will hit Stebbleton across the face.

What?
smirked Stebbleton.

Why do you always have to be such a schmuck?
asked Garcia.

Just then
a fight broke out on
the stairs.

Some new kid
and this older guy named Clint
who robbed cigarette trucks
and sold by the carton.

As the proprietor went to break up the fight,
everyone raided the quarter stocks
behind the desk.

The fight was probably a set-up.
This is what happened periodically
when everyone was low on change.

But it could have been a real fight.
The new kid not faring so well.

When anyone new showed up,
everyone assumed them a narc.

There were patterns of behaviour
old as time
that everyone fell into.
A sudden new arrival always
caused upset.

That kid is totally a narc!
said Will.

Leave him to Fowler
and he'll be filled with holes,
joked Garcia.

Stebbelton was scouring his pants
for extra rolls of fake quarters.

If you're looking for your dick,
you won't find one!
Will joked.

Stebbelton pulled out three more rolls
of fake quarters and held them up.
Enough dicks to slam the entire whorehouse
out of its last bushy charms,
Stebbleton bragged.

Garcia and Will threw a few in the slot
of this Kung-Fu game in a city setting.

Trying to double team their way through
an avalanche of punches and kicks and knifings
that never came from the real world for once,
which was nice.

RYAN QUINN FLANAGAN is a Canadian-born author who lives in Elliot Lake, Ontario, Canada with his wife and many bears that rifle through his garbage. His work has been published both in print and online in such places as: *The New York Quarterly, Rusty Truck, Evergreen Review, Red Fez, Horror Sleaze Trash* and *The Blue Collar Review.* He enjoys listening to the blues and cruising down the TransCanada in his big blacked out truck.

MORE ROADSIDE PRESS TITLES:

By Plane, Train or Coincidence
Michele McDannold

Prying
Jack Micheline, Charles Bukowski and Catfish McDaris

Wolf Whistles Behind the Dumpster
Dan Provost

Busking Blues: Recollections of a Chicago Street Musician and Squatter
Westley Heine

Unknowable Things
Kerry Trautman

How to Play House
Heather Dorn